PRACTICING PUBLIC MANAGEMENT:
A CASEBOOK

PRACTICING
PUBLIC
MANAGEMENT:
A CASEBOOK

C. Kenneth Meyer
University of Oklahoma

Charles H. Brown
Pennsylvania State University

Mitchel J. Beville, Jr.
University of South Dakota

Walter F. Scheffer
University of Oklahoma

Randall L. Preheim
University of South Dakota

St. Martin's Press • New York

Library of Congress Catalog Card Number: 82–60473
Copyright © 1983 by St. Martin's Press, Inc.
All Rights Reserved.
Manufactured in the United States of America.
76543
fedcba
For information, write St. Martin's Press, Inc.,
175 Fifth Avenue, New York, N.Y. 10010

cover design: James M. Wall

book design: Bernard Klein

cloth ISBN: 0-312-63548-6
paper ISBN: 0-312-63549-4

CONTENTS

INDEX OF TOPICS

The text gives major emphasis to topics in cases marked by asterisks.

PREFACE

The aim of *Practicing Public Management: A Casebook* is to acquaint students with the complexities of contemporary public administration and provide them with practice in decision making that will be immediately useful in their careers.

The fifty-one case studies included here reflect real-life situations. These cases, selected from among a much larger number that we have tested in both undergraduate and graduate classes, are the ones that were found to be most stimulating to students. In the classroom they proved to be highly effective in developing students' abilities to analyze problems and find appropriate courses of action.

Unlike most public administration casebooks, which devote a disproportionate number of cases to the federal government, this book presents a balanced discussion of issues in state and local as well as federal government. During the last ten years, state- and local-government agencies have accounted for the greatest increase in employment opportunities for public administration students. Today about ninety-five out of every one hundred new public-service jobs are created at the state and local levels. Most students will obtain their first public-service jobs in county, city, and state government. Therefore, our casebook aims to acquaint these students with issues that are most relevant to the jobs they are likely to find.

In making selections, we also sought to illustrate a broad spectrum of administrative problems and situations. Those chosen range from minor difficulties encountered almost daily in management to high-level perplexities involving principle and policy. As in actual problems in government, most of the cases present not just one dilemma or difficulty but several. Guides to the subject areas covered in each case are given after the table of contents and in the appendix. Thus the cases need not be considered in the sequence in which they appear. The instructor may skip about at will to select cases for consideration that pertain to lecture presentations or that fit the plan of a main textbook. Each case is accompanied by a set of questions and instructions to stimulate thinking about and discussion of the problems presented and a bibliography to direct students in investigating relevant administrative theories, concepts, and practices.

This casebook is adaptable to all levels of instruction—from the two-year college to the graduate school. It is designed primarily to supplement instruction by textbook and lectures. The book can also be used as the core of a course devoted specifically to the case-study approach, a graduate seminar or colloquium, or an in-service training program in government.

Students in public administration, perhaps more than in most other classes, tend to want to share in the planning and conduct of their classes. They expect to be managers and leaders, and they naturally assert themselves in class. Accordingly, in Part I of this book we offer suggestions for use of the case studies that will enable students to participate actively in the classroom.

We are grateful to the following students and practicing administrators, who contributed ideas, information, and material used in the incidents, problems, and situations incorporated in the cases: Harry Allison, Richard Alexander, Gary Anderson, Terry C. Anderson, Stan Anker, Michael J. Baker, Frank A. Bettman, Vicki Brooks, Alan Conroy, Elaine T. Davis, Alexander Dolega, Ann M. Elkjer, Steven Feimer, Mary J. Frasier, Vern Guericke, William Hartman, Terry Huffman, Sandra Jorgensen, Deborah Louison, Jim Julin, Suzanne Julin, Steven L. Mayer, Kim Weber Mulinix, Daniel Murphy, Jeffrey Pederson, Duane Petzoldt, Gail H. Poe, Gregory Protsch, Regina Pryce, Daniel P. Richter, Patricia Riepel, Cathie Rodman, James Schmidt, Timothy F. Smith, Gregory Sogaard, S. R. H. Spicer, Mildred Juanita States, Kent W. Sudman, Marina Sukop, Marvin L. Wagner, and Mark Williams.

Special thanks and appreciation are also given to Donna Epperson and Mary Webster, who most ably coordinated the typing of the final manuscript, and to the other members of the Information Processing Center at the University of Oklahoma, who typed and retyped several earlier versions of the cases: Gerry Pogorelc, Kathy Stowe, Klista Flanagan, Retha Holloway, and Sherry Evans.

C. Kenneth Meyer
Charles H. Brown
Mitchel J. Beville, Jr.
Walter F. Scheffer
Randall L. Preheim

PRACTICING PUBLIC MANAGEMENT:
A CASEBOOK

PART 1

THE CASE-STUDY APPROACH TO TRAINING FOR PUBLIC MANAGEMENT

The Role of Public Administration

In the early years of the United States, jobs in the government depended on the principle of "to the victor belong the spoils." Appointments of middle- and lower-level administrators, to whom the case studies in this book are directed, were made by those who won elections. But as the population grew, as the country became industrialized, as services performed by the government expanded, and as public affairs became more complex with the adoption of controls and regulations considered desirable, the method of filling positions with party supporters was recognized as inadequate.

The continuity needed in public service could not be achieved when there were wholesale turnovers in employees after elections nor could competent ones always be found if job eligibility was based chiefly on allegiance to a political party. Incompetency, inefficiency, and even corruption became so prevalent by the middle of the last century that agitation developed to replace political patronage with a civil-service system. This was finally achieved in the federal government with passage of the Civil Service Act of 1883, but states and cities were slower to effect such reform and indeed the merit system has reached some of them only in the past few years. Public service as a recognized profession requiring academic training is a more recent development, and though university-level instruction in the field began as early as 1911, its greatest growth has occurred in the past fifteen or twenty years.

The need for specialized training to perform the complex role of public administrators is based on significant differences between management in government and management in business and industry. It is sometimes argued that management is the same everywhere because it basically deals with the operational relationships among people, but this notion is an oversimplification. The organizational structure in which government managers work is much more complicated than that of business or industrial managers, even those in the huge multinational corporations that have developed in recent years. Corporation executives are subject to a small board of directors and their competency is measured fairly easily by such items as sales records, production figures, and, finally, the profit or loss registered in the annual report. On the other hand, it is difficult to gauge managerial effectiveness in government because its performance cannot readily be measured by the rules of business and because the goals of public service largely consist of intangibles. The conditions that make the role of public-management administrators more difficult than that of private-sector administrators include the following:

Multiple Direction and Control. The supreme power in a business or industrial concern is vested usually in a small and closely knit board of directors, but in government it is divided broadly into three branches—the legislative, the executive, and the judicial—and it may be further diffused among a host of regulatory agencies, commissions, and authorities. Administrators in the public sector often find themselves subjected to pressures from conflicting centers of power and public opinion.

Impermanence and Change. Top officials in government are elected for specified terms. Policies and goals may shift suddenly with a change in the majority control of Congress, a state legislature, a county commission, or a municipal body or with the election or appointment of a new person to office in the executive branch. Often the work of the bureaucracy goes on only slightly affected by these turnovers, but occasionally aggressive and reforming officials may make demands that are difficult for middle- and lower-level managers to meet.

Legal and Procedural Constraints. The rules and regulations established by lawmaking bodies to insure honesty, protect the rights of employees, and minimize error are numerous and involved and therefore are difficult to understand. Private-sector managers, even in the largest corporations, seldom find themselves so entangled in red tape as those in the public sector.

Measurement of Accomplishment. The most obvious and therefore most frequently mentioned distinction between public and private management is that one is a service enterprise and the other a profit enterprise, but this is an inadequate standard by which to judge their respective effectiveness. The government builds roads and dams, purchases and uses office machines and supplies, provides services for the public, and engages in many other activities that differ little from those of private organizations. Though ultimately there is no profit, such factors as costs, productivity, and efficiency can be determined and compared with those of private enterprise, as they should be. Nevertheless, when public interest is put in the balance it compensates for the occasions when work done by the government seems to be unduly expensive or inefficient. The reason is that private enterprise has left to the government the performance of services for which no profit could be made or that were so vital that the people did not wish to leave them to the vagaries of the marketplace of unaccountable private enterprise.

Expectations of the Public Regarding Government Employees. Higher ethical standards are demanded of government workers than of those in business or industry. Gifts, pay-offs, conflicts of interest, and nepotism commonplace in business are not only condemned as unbecoming to public officials but are also illegal under a number of laws regulating their conduct.

Surveillance of Operation. An important aspect of private enterprise is that it *is* private. It is subject to certain regulations in the public interest, but generally its records are not open to outsiders, its owners and managers ordinarily do not have to divulge their plans and prospects, and there are few restrictions upon who may be hired or fired. The operations of the government, on the contrary, are subject to constant scrutiny—by legislators and city council members, by the news media, by interest groups, and by the public.

The Training of Public Administrators

Although the foregoing discussion of the role of public administrators emphasizes only a few highlights, it is sufficient to indicate that the skills required are exceptional. As a consequence, in recent years there has been a rapidly developing trend of professional training for public-service jobs. This has accompanied the adoption of civil-service and merit systems in state and local governments similar to those established earlier in the federal government and also has paralleled the higher educational requirements demanded for other employment in our technological society. A high-school diploma once signified adequate education for most jobs, but after World War II a bachelor's degree became a more frequent requirement and today master's and doctor's degrees, formerly needed only in academic institutions, are common in business, industry, and government.

Public-administration and public-affairs programs, now firmly established in universities and colleges, are directed toward educating and training students in the professional skills they will need, but this curriculum provides only a part of their required preparation. They must learn also about the political, social, and economic milieus in which government functions; they must be trained in logic and in the statistical and other quantitative skills that individual performance requires; they must be able to communicate orally and in writing; and they must develop the psychological insights needed for understanding and influencing individual and group behavior. Over the years the instructional technique that most successfully combines proficiency and knowledge in these areas with administrative-management practice has been the case study.

The method has long been followed in law schools—indeed has dominated the instruction in them—according to the theory that by examining the precedents established in the settlement of legal suits and actions general principles will develop. With adaptations it was used in the first quarter of this century in business schools with the same idea—that the analysis of actual situations would result in generalizations that could be applied in similar situations. It has since been adopted in such fields as social work, educational administration, financial administration, and public administration.

In a survey of two hundred training directors on the effectiveness of nine different instructional methods for various training objectives, the case-study method had the best overall score. The other eight methods listed in the order of effectiveness were conference discussions, role playing, sensitivity training, business games, programmed instruction, films, television lectures, and lectures with questions. The training objectives rated were knowledge acquisition, changing attitudes, problem solving, interpersonal skills, participant acceptance, and knowledge retention. Case study ranked first in problem solving; second in knowledge acquisition, participant acceptance, and knowledge retention; and fourth in changing attitudes and interpersonal skills.*

In public-administration programs, unlike those of law and perhaps other fields, the case-study method has seldom been the core of the instructional system; more often it has been a supplement. Most collections of case studies are designed to supplement the standard textbooks, assigned outside readings, and lectures traditionally employed in classroom instruction. Its chief aim has not been to arrive at general principles but to enable students to share some of the real-life experiences of management.

In the study of law the cases considered are to be found among those actually introduced into and disposed of in the legal and judicial process, but in other fields they come from the experiences of actual participants who supply the information for accounts describing an illustrative situation or problem. The cases vary in length from a few hundred words to several thousand. Usually they are narratives about the people whose personalities and backgrounds are briefly given and whose thoughts and actions are related as the situation develops in a postulated office or agency of government. All the names used are, of course, fictitious.

Case studies, to be sure, are no substitute for experience, but their simulation of experience can be instructive. In one semester students are

---

*Stephen J. Carroll, Jr., Frank T. Paine, and John M. Ivancevich, "The Relative Effectiveness of Training Methods—Expert Opinion and Research," in William F. Glueck, *Personnel: A Book of Readings,* Dallas, Tex.: Business Publications, 1979, pp. 236–247.

introduced to a variety of experiences that might otherwise take them years to encounter in a job. By identifying with the people in a case history students develop the ability to look at a situation or problem from different points of view, and their broadening empathy is further enhanced by hearing the views of their classmates in the analytical discussions of the policies or perplexities that the cases present. They receive some practice in scientific or systematic thinking by learning to look at problems and situations objectively, by examining the facts available, and by considering a variety of solutions or proposed courses of action for a particular difficulty. They may thus become more flexible in putting abstract rules or administrative procedures and techniques to the test of practical application.

There are some deficiencies and dangers in the case method of which students should be aware. The situational narratives must always be simplifications. All the facts in a situation, conflicts among individuals, and emotional interplay among the participants cannot be set forth in a case history. It is not life but a clouded mirror of life. Solutions that seem so practicable in classroom discussion, courses of recommended conduct that seem so irreproachable, and conclusions that seem so cogent often will not work in everyday affairs. Sometimes they are defeated by the contrariness of organizational members or by the constraints of the system. Thus students who excel in classroom explication should not let themselves be deluded into thinking they have mastered the art or craft of management.

Using Case Histories

The case-study method was developed to approximate the way people derive their information and make decisions in life. Most school instruction by textbook and lecture is prescriptive; it is measured by what the student retains in memory and can transmit on examination. Case study is essentially self-learning through simulated experience. Its goal is not primarily the acquisition of a measurable body of knowledge or information but rather the development of attitudes and training in purposive thinking. Its success depends largely upon the lively interchange of information, ideas, and opinions brought out in classroom discussion. But this discussion must not be just a free-for-all or brainstorming session. It demands preparation by the participants and direction by a leader, either the instructor or an elected or appointed member of the class. To obtain the most out of the examination of cases, therefore, students should observe the following rules:

Come to the class meeting prepared. Read the case history carefully and determine what the main issues are, speculate as to the motivations of the people involved, and seek to define the reasons why the situation or problem arose. Find out what the literature of public management offers on the topics related to the case by reading the works listed in the selected bibliographies appended to each case in this volume.

Be a vocal participant in the class discussion. Since this is a self-learning exercise, letting other class members do the analysis and suggest the various approaches to handling a situation or solving a problem will hinder your development in trying new concepts, expressing new ideas, or looking at new administrative or organizational practices. You should contribute as much as possible and be ready to learn new things not only about administration but also about yourself.

Interact with classmates by criticizing their ideas. Courtesy and civility are important in interactions among people but so is assertiveness. Cross-examine class members on their ideas, ask probing questions about the implications of their proposals, and measure these by the hallmarks of practicality, necessity, ethicality, and legality. Other students and teachers may be so obsessed with attempting to find answers that they fail to ask "What is the question?" By playing the role of Doubting Thomas you can help your class associates clarify the issues.

Consider the discussion an opportunity to achieve self-understanding. Feel free to get thoroughly involved and be open in expressing your own beliefs and feelings. Case analysis, however, is more than the projection of a series of attitudes exemplified in statements beginning with such expressions as "I believe . . . ," "I feel . . . ," or "I am sure . . ." Try to understand the sources of your beliefs, feelings, and convictions and be receptive to those of others before adopting a final stand. Self-understanding may come from asking such questions as these: What does the problem or situation presented in the case mean to me? Is there anything in my own experience that would shed light on the problem or situation? Have I let my emotions or biases dominate my thinking about a problem or situation?

Keep a log or diary of your observations and experiences. If maintained chronologically, this journal on rereading will make possible a comparison of your first thoughts on a topic with those finally held and to trace the changes that occurred, if any. It will enable you to see in retrospect what influences prevailed: your reading in the field, the comments of your instructor, the opinion of fellow students, or whatever may have been a factor in forming your attitudes. Self-questioning will help you follow the honored injunction "Know thyself."*

The procedures that may be followed in studying case histories are numerous, and the instructor and class members will probably wish to use different ones to prevent analysis from becoming routine and to experiment to discover more fruitful approaches. The same method will not do for all histories contained in the casebook. Whatever the approach, students should take extensive notes for their personal log or diary and for reconsideration when they are alone and not affected by the classroom environment. Very often one finds that ideas that seemed at the time to be irresistible will turn out to be irrelevant or trivial.

Sometimes there could be an unrehearsed consideration of a case, which could be announced at the start of a class or group session and followed by discussion after members have had a chance to read it. The spontaneous expression of points of view and suggestions for courses of action to be taken about a situation or problem will result in a lively discussion that will stimulate ideas.

But probably a more effective use of the case histories would be to assign them before classroom discussion so that students may have an opportunity to obtain information bearing on the particular problem or situation to be considered and to organize their thoughts about it. Sometimes they could be asked merely to be prepared to take part in a general discussion. Alternatively, one or more students or a team might be asked to give a presentation analyzing the topic and making recommendations followed by a general class critique. Or the instructor may wish to make a presentation in which a personal analysis and proposed course of action are given. Another method would be for the instructor or an appointed or elected student to lead a discussion in which the

*Dr. Robert B. Denhardt of the University of Missouri-Columbia recommends the keeping of an administrative journal as a means of bridging the gap between theory and practice in public administration. "Through careful use of the Administrative Journal," he says, "you should be able to bring together theories of the individual and the organization on the one hand, and the way you think, feel, and act in administrative situations on the other." He suggests a journal consisting of four main sections and an appendix. The first (Outer Experience) is used to record occurrences relating to public organization; the second is used to record reflections and generalizations about these occurrences; the third (Inner Experience) is a first-person account of how the Outer Experience affected the writer emotionally, physically, and intellectually; the fourth is devoted to reflections and generalizations on the inner experience; and the appendix (Period of Growth) is devoted to a reconsideration of the four sections after an extended period of time to enable the writer to take a long view of his or her personal and professional development. See "The Administrative Journal: Theory and Method," in *Innovations in Teaching Public Affairs and Administration,* Richard Heimovics and Ann-Marie Rizzo, eds., Kansas City–Miami, 1981.

situation or problem is clarified and suggestions for handling it are elicited by conducting a Socratic dialogue.

To avoid making the classroom discussions too academic, the practical or applied point of view may be introduced by occasionally inviting practicing administrators to take part. The guests might participate as members of the class and tell how they would deal with the matter, or they might observe the discussions and conclude the class consideration of a history by evaluating the points brought out by the students and setting forth their own views as to the best course of action. Another way of bringing in a professional viewpoint would be for students to interview public officials—a valuable experience in itself—about a case history to obtain their views and comments for presentation to the class.

Not all the case histories would have to be taken up in class sessions because this is time-consuming. More ground can be covered, if the class and instructor think it desirable, by having members write reports on additional cases to be submitted to the instructor for evaluation and criticism or, if the paper load is too great for the instructor, to assign these cases individually to students for their written criticism.

In the foregoing suggestions on how the case histories might be used, considerable writing is urged. The reason is that it is easier to strip a situation, problem, or perplexity to its essentials; to order one's thoughts; to check on the validity of facts and observations; and to note omissions by using the opportunity for examination and re-examination that putting things on paper affords. The language and construction should conform to the practice of the average educated person in speech and writing. Especially to be avoided is the jargon employed in many official reports and memos known as "government-ese," "gobbledygook," or "bafflegab," which not only retards communication but also interferes with clear thinking.

Analyzing Case Histories

Each of the histories in the casebook presents a problem or difficulty or describes a situation about which action has been taken or is indicated. At the end several questions or instructions are presented as a guide to studying the particular case. These are not intended to be exhaustive, but rather are designed to start a fermentation process leading to other questions and ideas.

For a fuller consideration of a case, and especially for cases arising in actual administration, a systematic method of analysis should be followed that includes (1) assembling facts bearing on the problem, (2) clarifying it by defining the issues, (3) proposing and evaluating suggested solutions or courses of action, and finally (4) determining which one seems best in view of the circumstances. This method is known as problem solving, a classic statement of which was made by the pragmatic philosopher and educator John Dewey in 1910.* As mentioned before, training directors polled on the effectiveness of different instructional methods ranked case study first in developing problem-solving skills. These are important because so much administration consists of making decisions regarding problems, difficulties, and dilemmas large and small that constantly arise.

A great virtue of the problem-solving method is that students learn to view the perplexities arising in day-to-day administration as objectively as possible. Also, they learn to avoid prejudgment and bias and free themselves of emotionalism. A good administrator is not merely a thinking machine. The manager is concerned with human situations and deals with people who behave like people—that is, who sometimes do things that do not make sense, who cannot be persuaded by logic, and who cannot be manipulated like chess pieces on a board.

Mental activity goes on continuously during a person's waking and sleeping hours, but this stream of consciousness hardly constitutes thinking. Only when the images, notions, and impressions arising in the brain are subjected to order does one engage in purposive thought. The problem-solving technique is employed to obtain this consequential sequence.

John Dewey in his description of the problem-solving method distinguished five steps or phases. These are: (1) the recognition of a problem, (2) the definition and clarification of the problem, (3) the rise of possible solutions, (4) the development by reasoning of the implications of the solutions, and (5) further observation and experiment leading to acceptance or rejection of the solutions. Dewey recognized that this process as outlined is an oversimplification. Thinking is too complex to be so well ordered. In what Dewey called "reflective thinking" about a problem or situation the phases do not follow one another in set order and indeed may be so interrelated that they cannot be separated. Nevertheless, the procedure can be helpful in coming to grips with perplexities encountered in the casebook histories and in management.

In developing the first phase of problem solving it is wise to classify at the start the area of management in which the case history belongs. A rough guide can be found in the topical listing in the appendix: accountability, communication, job satisfaction, recruitment, and so on. More than one of these areas may apply to individual cases and students may wish to add others not covered in the listing.

*John Dewey, *How We Think,* Boston: D. C. Heath and Co., 1910. The book was extensively revised in a new edition published in 1933.

Once the basic dilemma or difficulty in a case is defined, it should be submitted to analysis for clarification. Various questions will come to mind in this task: What are the facts in the case? How did the difficulty arise? Who are the people involved? What are their motivations and interests? What are their needs? Was the problem brought about by personality conflicts? If blame can be placed, who is to blame? Are there rules and regulations governing the case? Should the matter be brought to the attention of higher authority? Will the situation finally resolve itself? Is any action called for at all?

If the administrator decides that something must be done, he or she next should consider what possible courses are available and submit them to careful analysis as to which would be best to follow in the circumstances. Again, asking questions will prove helpful in the diagnostic process: What are the likely consequences of the decision? Is the course of action a temporary expedient or a long-term solution? Is the solution feasible? What has to be done to put it into practice? Does it involve the expenditure of money or alteration of existing rules and regulations? Will it be acceptable to the people involved? Will permission to put it into effect have to be obtained from higher authority? Does the decision on what to do conform with regular practice? What group will be best served by the decision—the public, the department, or its employees? Is it in the interest of good government? Is it ethically right? Is it equitable for all those concerned?

In diagnosing a situation or problem and seeking a remedy, the administrator must examine personal motivations. Administrators will frequently be tempted to take the easy way out, to vacillate and delay rather than come to grips with the difficulty immediately. Perhaps administrators will attempt a cover-up or fail to present the matter to superiors for fear of exposing their own inability or weakness. They may resort to merely palliative measures when more fundamental ones are required. They may rule in favor of people they like and against those they dislike. They may put their own personal interests above those of the employees they supervise and the public and government they serve. Difficult though it may be, an attempt to resist these inclinations must be made. In an administrative career, a long-range reputation for probity, square-dealing, and decisiveness will do the manager more good than running for shelter when storms arise in the department.

PART II

CASE HISTORIES
FOR ANALYSIS

1

The Good/Bad
Administrator

Timothy Kingsbury, secretary of the State Department of Natural Resources, considered it a coup when he hired George Krittenbrink as director of the Land and Water Resources Survey. The survey had grown in importance as the environmental consequences of increasing population became more worrisome, yet staff positions had been difficult to fill because the work was highly technical. Krittenbrink was a nationally known figure in his field and Kingsbury thought he could turn the survey over to him and devote his attention to matters that he knew more about.

expert
no check
or
Administrative
ability

For his part, Krittenbrink was glad to take the position, for it gave him an opportunity to ride his hobby horse of long standing: high- and low-altitude photography and remote-sensing pictures obtained by satellites circling the earth. He was a pioneer in applying such information about the earth to better use of land and other natural resources and had contributed authoritative articles to technical journals.

Krittenbrink's interest in this field had begun with aerial photography studies while studying geography in college and he had been excited by the prospects for obtaining more information about the earth's surface from hand-held cameras in the early Gemini and Apollo space flights. Later he familiarized himself with the advances made in 1972 when the National Aeronautics and Space Administration launched the first land-resource survey satellites—Landsat-1, -2, and -3, which provided a wealth of information about the planet.

The Land and Water Resources Survey had done more than most comparable programs in other states in the practical application of elec-

15

tronically recorded and transmitted data via satellite. Krittenbrink determined to make it the foremost program in the nation. When visitors inspected the survey and inquired how its work would help the state, Krittenbrink had a speech prepared for them, as if a guide in a museum. "There are roughly 230 million Americans depending upon approximately 2.3 billion acres of land," he would say. "This means that the per capita land share in 1983 is about 10.8 acres compared to a per capita share of nearly 17 acres in 1940. By the year 2000 the per-capita land share will be $6^2/_3$ acres. We need to use our land resources more effectively as our population grows and the amount of land taken out of production each year by highways, airports, and urbanization increases."

Satellite data, Krittenbrink would continue, would enable planners to identify land-use patterns and changes over time. He envisioned additional applications: monitoring crops for pest infestation and disease, solving hydrological problems, forecasting snow runoff, measuring water characteristics, providing regional indices of water availability, evaluating wildlife habitats, assessing damage in burned-out areas, identifying climatological patterns and trends, mapping thermal pollution, identifying soil characteristics associated with mineral exploration, predicting flood damage, locating new sources of fresh water, forecasting crop yields, conducting soil-conservation studies, detecting archeological sites, and assessing timber-stand vigor.

The day Krittenbrink took over as survey director, he addressed a staff meeting to explain his management policies and goals. He stressed the importance of completing projects expeditiously, of teamwork, and of meticulous attention to detail. The staff quickly learned that he was a strong-willed, nose-to-the-grindstone type of manager who believed that efficiency and organization produced successful results.

The staff of eight scientists and engineers came from diverse regions of the country and represented varied educational backgrounds, including geology; geography; civil, hydrologic, and electrical engineering; computer programming; and planning. Much of their work consisted of preparing and analyzing maps produced from information transmitted from satellites to the Goddard Space Flight Center, where it was placed on computer compatible tapes and readied for use in research and experimentation.

Each time the survey received a request from a city, county, or state agency, Krittenbrink evaluated the work to be done and assigned the project to members of the staff. He expected all projects to be completed on schedule and to meet his stringent quality specifications. When they were not, he was sharply critical and sarcastic in reprimanding the offender.

The most frequent victim of Krittenbrink's criticism was James Cartmill, a young, wisecracking geological engineer who, the survey director thought, lacked the serious purpose and devotion to detail required in scientific pursuits. On one occasion Cartmill failed to meet a deadline. The work had been proceeding according to schedule until the main-frame computer broke down, making Cartmill two days late in completing the assignment. Dismissing Cartmill's explanation that the delay was not his fault because it was caused by a computer malfunction, Krittenbrink angrily replied that he wanted results, not excuses.

The next day Krittenbrink called Cartmill to his office and brought up the matter again. "Cartmill," he said, "you're capable of good work but you've got to change your attitude. Science demands a holy dedication to work. It has no place for fun and games. You waste not only your time but that of others when you chat and joke with them."

Cartmill attempted to explain that the delay in completing the project had nothing to do with his relations with other staff members. A vital computer had malfunctioned, parts had to be flown in from Boca Raton, and a specialist had been called from Atlanta to make repairs, he said. "Cartmill, a man must take responsibility for the circumstances of his life," Krittenbrink replied. "He cannot let outside forces rule him. A man must anticipate external problems and control the exogenous forces in order to succeed." Recognizing that Krittenbrink was not going to accept his side of the story, Cartmill apologized and promised that in the future he would try to be the master of his fate.

Cartmill thought the matter was closed and was shocked when at the next staff meeting Krittenbrink scolded him before his fellow workers for nearly fifteen minutes. That Cartmill had taken lightly the injunction to control outside forces, Krittenbrink said, was clear from a flippant comment on being master of his fate. "Deadlines are a necessity of life," Krittenbrink said. "Without them we would not know what to do or when to do it. This is one characteristic of modern organizations that distinguishes them from the older ones. The professional engineer and technician pays attention to schedule and engages in contingency planning." The staff members returned to their work areas in quiet disbelief.

In the next few weeks Krittenbrink frequently reminded Cartmill of the need for adhering to work programs and once blamed him for the breakdown of a photographic copying machine because he had not followed a careful schedule of preventive maintenance. After a few months on the job, Krittenbrink extended his fault-finding to Donald Fletcher, a young engineer and friend of Cartmill, and three other staff members who all had excellent work histories and records for reliability. Toward the end of Krittenbrink's first year as supervisor, two engineers requested and received transfers to other departments. Cartmill, however, remained in the division, saying that he liked the work and could put up with the fault-finding of his superior.

It was not easy, for Krittenbrink had informed Cartmill that he was recording all work-related problems and transgressions in his personnel file. Cartmill's treatment did not go unnoticed by other staff members, and one morning during a coffee break they decided that, for self-protection, they should keep careful notes on the work they performed, on all problems associated with receiving computer tapes and related data sets, on machinery malfunctions, and on all regulations and project specifications ordered by Krittenbrink.

Joyce Harman, a new employee who had worked three years in the interior department of another state, observed the low morale in the division and the tense atmosphere that made it difficult to meet the exacting standards that the tasks required. Priding herself on being a well-educated and independent woman—she was active in the women's rights movement—Harman was not one to submit to the petty tyrannies of a male supervisor. When Krittenbrink made general criticisms of her work, she demanded specific proof. Krittenbrink, accustomed to the submissiveness of the other employees of the division, usually had no concrete justification and retreated to commenting on the need for expediting projects and for scientific accuracy in the work of the division.

After holding the job for three months, Harman took the initiative in arousing the division staff to protest Krittenbrink's unreasonable demands, selective persecutions, and general denigrations of them as people and professionals. They compiled a list of grievances with documentation that they submitted to Kingsbury, the Natural Resources Department secretary, requesting that Krittenbrink's supervisory behavior be evaluated and a formal hearing be held so that their concerns could be discussed. Kingsbury was surprised to learn about the trouble in the division. He had felt lucky to have as the director so dedicated and knowledgeable a person as Krittenbrink, who was praised by state agencies using the services of the survey. It now appeared to Kingsbury that efficiency and productivity might not be the sum total of good administration.

Questions and Instructions

1. As Kingsbury, what would you do first in taking up the problem? Would you talk first to the staff or to Krittenbrink?
2. Do you think that the differences between Krittenbrink and the staff can be reconciled?

3. Should Kingsbury come to the support of Krittenbrink? Consider both Krittenbrink's ability to get along with his staff and the productivity and quality of the work done by the survey.
4. Is there any justification for transferring Krittenbrink? What implications are associated with transferring the problem employees of an agency?
5. How does one supervise a supervisor? Should problem supervisors be treated similarly to or differently from other problem employees?
6. Is there any way for Krittenbrink to become a more effective administrator? If you were Kingsbury, what suggestions would you offer him in the way of improving his interpersonal relations?
7. Should Krittenbrink be dismissed from all supervisory responsibility? What are the implications of this decision? Elaborate.

Selected Bibliography

Abrahamson, Mark, *The Professional in the Organization,* Chicago: Rand McNally and Co., 1967. Ch. 2, "The Socialization of Future Professionals," pp. 17–57, and Ch. 4, "Professional Norms and Organizational Control," pp. 90–125.

Benveniste, Guy, *The Politics of Expertise,* Berkeley, Calif.: The Glendessary Press, 1972. Ch. 7, "How Experts Acquire Power," pp. 119–35.

Champion, Dean J. *The Sociology of Organizations,* New York: McGraw-Hill, 1975. Ch. 11, "Technological Change in Organizations and Adaptation of Members," pp. 248–80. Also, see "On Informal Communication Patterns: Their Origin, Functions, and Dysfunctions," pp. 181–90.

Drucker, Peter F., *Technology, Management, and Society,* New York: Harper and Row, 1970.

Giglioni, Giovanni B.; Giglioni, Joyce B.; and Bryant, James A., "Performance Appraisal: Here Comes the Judge," *California Management Review* 24 (Winter 1981): 14–23.

Handy, Charles B., *Understanding Organizations,* New York: Penguin Books, 1976. Ch. 2, "On the Motivation to Work," pp. 23–52; Ch. 8, "On Politics and Management of Differences," pp. 212–44; and Ch. 12, "On Being a Manager," pp. 358–79.

Landau, Martin, and Stout, Russell, Jr., "To Manage Is Not to Control: Or the Folly of Type II Errors," *Public Administration Review* 39 (March/April 1979): 148–56.

Leavitt, Harold J., *Managerial Psychology,* 4th ed., Chicago: University of Chicago Press, 1978. Ch. 22, "Developing Managers: Applied Ideas About Influence, Learning and Groups," pp. 244–57; also, Ch. 12, "Authority: One Model for Influence," pp. 136–47, and Ch. 26, "Structure, People, and Information Technology: Some Key Ideas and Where They Come From," pp. 291–304.

Luthans, Fred, *Organizational Behavior,* New York, McGraw-Hill, 1973. Ch. 13, "The Nature and Impact of Technology," pp. 280–305.

Maslow, Abraham H., *Motivation and Personality,* 2nd ed., New York: Harper and Row, 1954. Ch. 5, "A Theory of Human Motivation," pp. 80–106.

O'Reilly, Charles A., III, and Weitz, Barton A., "Managing Marginal Employees: The Use of Warnings and Dismissals," *Administrative Science Quarterly* 25 (September 1980): 467–84.

Perrucci, Robert, "In the Service of Man: Radical Movements in the Professions," in Gerstl, Joel, and Jacobs, Glenn, *Professions for the People,* Cambridge, Mass.: Schenkman Publishing Co., 1976. pp. 215–30.

Stogdill, Ralph M., *Handbook of Leadership: A Survey of Theory and Research,* New York: Free Press, 1974.

Sutton, Harold, and Porter, Lyman, "A Study of the Grapevine in a Governmental Organization," *Personnel Psychology* 21 (Summer 1968): 223–30.

2

Special Privileges for Officials?

Sarah Jefferies had worked in the rehabilitation agency of the State Welfare Department for almost twenty years and had become the administrative secretary to the agency manager, Edward Foster. Jefferies always received superior job-performance ratings from her supervisors and had several letters of commendation for assuming responsibilities beyond those given in her job description. Foster, who had managed the agency for five years, was considered a "good man for the job" and respected for his ability "to get the job done right." The central office frequently depended on him for assistance.

During the past nine months Jefferies had noticed that Foster and other officials often reported to work late in the morning and left the office early in the afternoon. Every agency employee earned ten hours of annual leave a month and could receive payment for the unused portion of accumulated leave at the end of each year. In addition, employees received nine paid holidays a year. Overtime was compensated for by allowing employees to take the equivalent time off. Jefferies was responsible for recording employee hours and leave time and felt that the agency officials were taking more time off than allowed by the state. Her coworkers also noticed this and were becoming upset. At a water-fountain conference Jefferies was selected by the other employees to speak with Foster about the situation.

Jefferies told Foster that some of the employees were disturbed by the agency officials' disregard for the rules governing office hours, leave time, and compensation time. She also informed him that with his approval one official improperly received two weeks' compensation. Foster explained that administrators had more privileges than subordinate staff members. "They are not punching a time clock," he said, "and if they get their work done, that's all that counts."

After her discussion with Foster, Jefferies wondered what she should do.

Questions and Instructions

1. Suggest several courses of action that are open to Jefferies in resolving her dilemma.
2. What are the legal and moral implications of the perceived abuses? Are they too trivial to bother with?
3. Does Jefferies have an obligation to "blow the whistle" about the abuses? If she decides to do so, should she tell Foster of her intention?
4. Should Foster consider more carefully the impact of his behavior on the organization?
5. Would you suggest that the agency policy governing tardiness, absenteeism, and sick leave be applied equally to all employees or differentiated according to administrative rank?
6. Should a flextime approach be recommended in resolving the issues raised in this situation?

Selected Bibliography

Barad, Cary B., "Flexitime Under Scrutiny," *Personnel Administrator* 25 (May 1980): 69–74.

Elbing, Alvar O.; Gadon, Herman; and Gordon, John R. M., "Flexible Working Hours: It's About Time," *Harvard Business Review* 52 (January/February 1974): 18–33.

Graham, George A., "Ethical Guidelines for Public Administrators: Observations on the Rules of the Game," *Public Administration Review* 34 (January/February 1974): 90–92.

Holley, William H., et al., "Employee Reactions to a Flexitime Program: A Longitudinal Study," *Human Resource Management* 15 (Winter 1976): 21–23.

Meier, Kenneth J., *Politics and the Bureaucracy: Policymaking in the Fourth Branch of Government,* North Scituate, Mass.: Duxbury Press, 1979. Ch. 7, "Controlling Bureaucracy: Ethics and Participation," pp. 162–85.

Mosher, Frederick C. *Democracy and the Public Service,* 2nd ed., New

York: Oxford University Press, 1982. Ch. 7, "Merit, Morality, and Democracy," pp. 202–19.

Odiorne, George S., *Personnel Administration by Objectives,* Homewood, Ill.: Richard D. Irwin, 1971. See "Discipline by Objectives," pp. 415–31.

Presthus, Robert, *The Organizational Society,* rev. ed., New York: St. Martin's Press, 1978. Chs. 6, 7, and 8. pp. 143–251.

3

A $5,000 Anonymous
Phone Call?

Jim Johnson began work with the Health Facilities Program in December and after an orientation period became one of five environmental health sanitarians whose responsibility was to survey licensed medical facilities within the state to determine their compliance with licensure, Medicare, and other regulations. He was also responsible for providing part-time consultation to hospitals and nursing homes. Each survey team consisted of a registered nurse and an environmental sanitarian. The nurses were mostly mature, gray-haired women, while the sanitarians, although relatively young, tended to appear straitlaced and serious. Johnson, on the other hand, had curly brown hair that almost touched his shoulders and he wore faded blue jeans and sandals.

Johnson's supervisor was Tom Blake. "I'm a little concerned about Jim's effectiveness as a surveyor-consultant," he said to Frances Maner, his administrative assistant. "I'm afraid many of the people he will be working with will classify him as a worthless bum because of his casual way of dressing."

"But, Tom," countered Maner, "you know he was the most-qualified applicant we interviewed. We both agreed he was intelligent and that there was a great deal of promise hidden under his unorthodox appearance."

"I know," Blake said, "but he doesn't dress professionally!"

Johnson learned quickly and soon showed ample confidence and poise. He was fully capable of performing surveys after he had been on the job three months and showed potential for being a good consultant. Six months after being hired he attended a university for an intense, one-month specialized training course required of all health-facilities personnel conducting surveys under the Medicare and Medicaid programs. When Johnson returned, Blake noticed a marked improvement in his written reports and felt certain his survey activities would also show an improvement. After accompanying Johnson on two surveys, Blake decided he was doing as well as, or better than, any other sanitarian under his supervision.

One morning, while Blake was expressing his satisfaction in Johnson's work to Maner, she reminded him of his earlier reservations. "I know," he confessed, "but Jim has really proven himself, and now he has my full confidence."

"I think Jim will be the best sanitarian on our staff in a few years," Maner agreed. "Just wait and see."

A year after Johnson had been in the hospital and nursing-home program, Blake was called into the program director's office. Larry Dandurand, the program director, and Ralph Andrews, the chief inspector, were there, both looking upset.

"I received an interesting, although anonymous, phone call yesterday that I think deserves our attention," Andrews said. "It concerns one of the staff members, Jim Johnson."

Johnson was stationed in a district office in the eastern part of the state, sharing it with two other Health Department staff members, neither of whom was in the same program. Andrews said that the caller complained of all three persons engaging in horseplay while in the office, although this was not often since they were seldom there between 8 A.M. and 5 P.M. Andrews said that the caller phoned because he thought the central office should know about it.

"I tried to explain that because our staff was involved in survey activities they had to spend quite a bit of time away from the office," Andrews said. "The caller was quite persistent, insisting there was 'more productive work done by the inhabitants of a cemetery than done by the Health Department employees.'" Andrews said the caller ended the conversation with an accusation that Johnson was the worst offender and that he also was associating with undesirable persons, including habitual drug users.

Blake proposed that the episode be ignored since the caller had refused to identify himself, but Dandurand made it clear that he had no intention of letting the matter drop and, since Blake was Johnson's supervisor, it was his responsibility to gather the relevant facts. Andrews suggested that Blake make discreet inquiries to substantiate the information given in the phone call. The idea of going behind Johnson's back to determine the accuracy of the phone call was repugnant to

Blake. "Suppose I talk to Jim and ask him pointblank if what the caller said is true?" Blake asked.

"Fine," said Dandurand, "but let's get this thing cleared up right away."

After returning to his office, Blake tried to clarify the whole situation in his mind. He knew that Johnson did not spend any more time in his office than necessary. In fact, he recalled many unsuccessful attempts to reach him during scheduled office hours. When he had talked to Johnson about his absence from the office, Johnson admitted that he had some "problems" in "disciplining" himself to observe normal office hours. Realizing that he was very young to be placed in a field office without any direct supervision, Blake chalked up the irregular office hours as the price the program had to pay for running a decentralized operation. Besides, Johnson was getting the job done and that was the important thing. But Blake was upset that one of his sanitarians had been criticized by an anonymous phone caller.

The following week Blake visited Johnson at his office and related the whole story to him. "As far as I'm concerned your work is excellent and that anonymous phone call is of no consequence as far as your performance is concerned," Blake explained. He made it clear, however, that the program director was upset over the whole matter and that, as a state employee, Johnson would be closely scrutinized by the public.

Jim was shocked. "Was it really an anonymous phone call, or are you intentionally withholding the caller's name?" he inquired.

"Ralph Andrews took the call and he assured us he tried to get the caller to identify himself—and I believe him," Blake said.

Then Johnson admitted that earlier he had had problems keeping office hours but that in the past two months he had really tried to be in the office when not doing surveys. Blake knew this was true, since he telephoned all of the sanitarians at least once a week and during this period Johnson had always been there. Johnson said also that he did have two cousins who had been convicted of using drugs and that he saw both of them frequently. Johnson declared, "If the state is going to dictate who my friends have to be or the way I have to look, they can take this job and shove it."

"Jim, I assure you nobody in our office is trying to choose your friends," Blake said. "Whom you associate with is none of the state's business. What I really want to do is forget that phone call completely, but I did want you to know about the director's reaction, since it may have a bearing on your advancement potential in the Health Facilities Program." Blake looked Johnson straight in the eye and said, "As far as your personal appearance is concerned, it's a fact of life that external appearance affects the public's opinion about the quality of the work we do. Success is not always measured in terms of hard work and productivity."

At the end of the conference, Blake felt that Johnson had accepted the discussion constructively. But two months later Johnson resigned. Blake telephoned him to find out the specific reasons for this resignation. He learned that Johnson was not leaving state government for a larger salary and, in fact, had no other job lined up.

Johnson explained, "I just wanted to try doing something other than working for the state, and I guess I should make the change now, while I'm still young."

Blake asked him if the anonymous call had anything to do with his resignation, and Johnson said that it had helped him make the decision but was not a primary reason. Blake urged Johnson to change his mind and stay with the program, but after a long discussion he felt that Johnson's mind was made up and the resignation was irrevocable.

After working with Johnson for a year and a half, Blake was certain that the telephone call had far more to do with his resignation than he had admitted. If the phone call could be considered the primary reason Jim resigned, Blake told himself, then it cost the state at least $5,000 in money lost training Jim for the job.

Questions and Instructions

1. Since the phone call was anonymous, should it have been given any consideration at all?
2. How could the substance of the phone call be verified or disqualified by a discreet investigation? If the caller's information could not be substantiated, would it have been necessary to tell Johnson anything at all?
3. Would it have been wise for Blake to transfer Johnson to the central office where he would have had the benefit of direct supervision?
4. Should more emphasis have been placed on the observance of normal working hours when Blake became aware of Johnson's work schedule?
5. If you were Blake and had time to reflect on this incident, what policy recommendation would you suggest to prevent this type of problem from occurring in the future? Should the central office consider having a definite number of hours or specific

times during the day when field personnel should be in the office? What are the implications of this type of policy?

6. Is it possible that Johnson's appearance was beneficial in his employee-client relationship? What should be said or done about an employee's personal dress or appearance?

7. Is a supervisor responsible not only for informing an employee of undesirable attitudes or behavior but also for designing a plan to correct or improve them?

Selected Bibliography

Argyris, Chris, "The Individual and Organization: Some Problems of Mutual Adjustment," *Administrative Science Quarterly* 2 (June 1957): 1–24.

Atherton, Roger M., "Centralization Works Best When Managers' Jobs Are Improved," *Human Resource Management* 16 (Summer 1977): 17–20.

Dawis, Rene V., "Personnel Assessment from the Perspective of the Theory of Work Adjustment," *Public Personnel Management* 9 (No. 4, 1980): 268–73.

Feldman, Daniel C., "A Socialization Process That Helps New Recruits Succeed," *Personnel* 57 (March/April 1980): 11–23.

Flynn, W. Randolph, and Stratton, William E., "Managing Problem Employees," *Human Resource Management* 20 (Summer 1981): 28–32.

Gould, Sam, "Career Planning in the Organization," *Human Resource Management* 15 (Fall 1976): 11–18.

Hall, Richard H., *Organizations: Structure and Process,* 2nd ed., Englewood Cliffs, N.J.: Prentice-Hall, 1977. Ch. 7, "Centralization," pp. 67–100.

House, Robert J., and Mitchell, Terence R., "Path-Goal Theory of Leadership," *Journal of Contemporary Business* 3 (Autumn 1974): 81–97.

Luthans, Fred, and Martinko, Mark, "An Organizational Behavior Modification Analysis of Absenteeism," *Human Resource Management* 15 (Fall 1976): 11–18.

Meier, Kenneth J., *Politics and the Bureaucracy: Policymaking in the Fourth Branch of Government,* North Scituate, Mass.: Duxbury Press, 1979. Ch. 5, "Bureaucracy and the Public's Expectations," pp. 108–29.

Ralph, Pierson M., "Performance Evaluation: One More Try," *Public Personnel Management* 9 (No. 3, 1980): 145–53.

Schleh, Edward C., "Using Central Staff to Boost Line Initiative," *Management Review* 65 (May 1976): 17–23.

Smith, Bruce L. R., and Hague, D. C., eds., *The Dilemma of Accountability in Modern Government: Independence Versus Control,* New York: St. Martin's Press, 1971.

Wright, Moorhead, "Individual Growth: The Basic Principles," *Personnel* 37 (September/October 1960): 8–17.

4

A Moral Dilemma

Upon receiving his bachelor of public administration degree from Central State University, Jerry Grissom felt fortunate when he obtained a job with the State Department of Social Services in the county office near the university. He would be able to gain experience and to earn money while continuing work on his master's degree. Having married as an undergraduate and become a father shortly after entering into the graduate program, he needed the job to support himself and his family as well as to continue his education for a career in government service.

Bright, energetic, and ambitious, Grissom was a young man on the make: he knew where he wanted to go and how to get there. Employment in the county Social Services office was not one of his goals but a means to an end—a stepping stone to a higher administrative post in the state or preferably the federal government.

Although Grissom tended to choose his friends for their usefulness to him and not for the enjoyment of their company, he was well liked, for he almost always was cheerful and entertaining. Quick to grasp a situation and highly articulate and industrious, Grissom had impressed his university professors, who regarded him as a student with the highest potential.

His job with the Social Services Department was not demanding. His main responsibility was inspecting and checking complaints against licensed day-care centers and registered home-care centers in the district. Upon receiving a complaint against a center, he would interview the complainant and then make an inspection to see if any state regulations were being violated. If he found infractions, he would write a report and submit it to the head of the county unit, Adolf Schumann. If Schumann approved it, a notice was sent to the offender warning that if the infractions were not corrected within thirty days his or her license would be lost.

Grissom found Adolf Schumann somewhat forbidding and not so easily charmed by him as most other people he met. Consequently, Grissom was always especially careful in writing up his reports and painstaking in his other work. Although not an outgoing person, Schumann from time to time praised him for his work. Grissom felt sure he would get a good recommendation when he left the county office.

Grissom's rosy prospects were darkened when an unfavorable situation resulted from his following up on a routine complaint made against a registered home-care center operated by Susan Parmenter. His inspection turned up several minor violations—she occasionally accepted more children than she was licensed to care for, trash that might be a fire hazard had been permitted to accumulate, and there was no sink with running water in the area where babies were changed. None of these were serious, but Grissom informed Parmenter that they would have to be corrected. He explained that regulations required that a written notice of the violations be sent to her and she would have thirty days to correct them or run the risk of losing her license.

The report on Parmenter's center was among several similar ones and Grissom had almost forgotten about it when he was called into Schumann's office and found the department head sitting at his desk with the report in his hand.

"This report is utterly uncalled for," Schumann told Grissom. "I can't see anything here that calls for a warning of suspension of the operator's license."

"Well, it's just routine," Grissom replied. "The violations do exist and I was merely following regulations in reporting them."

"I don't want to discuss the matter," Schumann said. "Your petty fault finding amounts to harassment. Mrs. Parmenter is just a woman trying to make a few dollars by taking care of children in her home. She's not operating a professional day-care center. Just tear up the report and let her alone."

Grissom left the office in a mild state of shock. His reports had been questioned on occasion, but this was the first time he had been ordered to withdraw one. The violations he had found at the Parmenter home were so easily corrected that he did not see why Schumann had made a big issue of them. He did learn why a few days later. He had made a few inquiries and discovered that Mrs. Parmenter's brother was Homer Schmidt, a county commissioner and a close friend of Schumann's.

Questions and Instructions

1. If you were involved in a situation similar to Grissom's, would you quietly tear up the report?
2. Is there any substance to Schumann's view that the violations were so minor that sending out a notice to Parmenter hardly seemed worthwhile?
3. What course of action is open to an employee when ordered by a superior to disobey regulations even if over a minor matter?

Selected Bibliography

American Society for Public Administration, *Professional Standards and Ethics,* Washington, D.C.: American Society for Public Administration, 1979.

Appleby, Paul H., *Morality and Administration in Democratic Government,* Baton Rouge, La.: Louisiana State University, 1952.

Barnard, Chester, *The Functions of the Executive,* Cambridge, Mass.: Harvard University Press, 1938.

Berg, Larry L.: Hahn, Harlan; and Schmidhauser, John R., *Corruption in the American Political System,* Morristown, N.J.: General Learning Press, 1976. Ch. 2, "Corruption and the Responsible Citizen," pp. 31–58.

Boyarsky, Bill, and Boyarsky, Nancy, *Backroom Politics,* Los Angeles, Calif.: J. P. Tarcher, 1974. Ch. 1, "Introduction—The People Who Can Make Life Miserable for Us All," pp. 1–17, and Ch. 4, "Corporations above the Law," pp. 71–96.

Caiden, Gerald E., and Caiden, Naomi J., "Administrative Corruption," *Public Administration Review* 37 (May/June 1977): 301–9.

Cobb, Anthony T., "Informal Influence in the Formal Organization: Perceived Sources of Power Among Work Unit Peers," *Academy of Management Journal* 23 (March 1980): 155–61.

Mertins, Herman, Jr., and Hennigan, Patrick J., *Applying Professional Standards and Ethics in the '80s,* Washington, D.C.: American Society for Public Administration, 1982. See "Conflicts of Interest," pp. 17–18, and "Public Disclosure and Confidentiality," pp. 20–21.

Monypenny, P., "A Code of Ethics as a Means of Controlling Administrative Conduct," *Public Administration Review* 13 (Summer 1953): 184–87.

White, Bernard J., and Montgomery, B. Ruth, "Corporate Codes of Conduct," *California Management Review* 23 (Spring 1981): 92–96.

5

A Plethora of Problems

The Graphics and Photography Division of Midstate University provided services for the academic, business, and maintenance divisions of the institution. It was divided into five units: Graphics Production, Printing and Duplicating Services, Photographic Services, Equipment Maintenance and Distribution, and Educational Films Library. The division employed twenty-five staff people full time and from fifteen to twenty students part time.

The division was not happy. The unit supervisors were empire builders of the first order who jealously contended for more funds and more employees. Meetings of unit heads with the division director were marked by bickering and there was little cooperation among the units. Because there was little esprit de corps among the division administrators, there was likewise little among the employees.

The director of the division was Dr. Olaf Johanssen, a likable man who in the fifteen years he had held his position had been generally viewed as a weak administrator. Now sixty-three years old and planning to retire at sixty-five, Johanssen had increasingly relaxed his control over the division, leaving administrative and personnel matters chiefly to Lester Best, the assistant director.

Best, who was thirty years old, had held his position for five years and was extremely eager to get ahead. To his superiors, he had always shown a respect that bordered on servility, but with his coworkers he was thoughtless, tactless, inconsiderate, and arrogant. He had a campus reputation as a womanizer and his relations with women staff members were marked by sexual overtones.

Difficult personnel problems had arisen particularly in the Photographic Services unit, supervised by Jerome Christianson, and in the Equipment and Maintenance unit, supervised by Donald Waterman. The smallest unit of the division, Photographic Services employed three people and usually one or two students. Christianson, age thirty-one, was highly qualified in education and professional experience for his job. He had begun work for the unit six years before as a Photographer I and within a few months had been made supervisor. Because of cuts in appropriations throughout the entire university, a promotion for Christianson was not immediately foreseeable and his pay increases had not kept pace with the cost of living.

Because Christianson's unit was small, he had closer contact with his staff than most supervisors. A principal personnel problem had involved John Bishop, twenty-eight, who had worked as a Photographer I for ten years. He was married and had two children but difficulties in his home life interfered with his work.

Three years before, Bishop's work became so poor because of a family crisis that Christianson attempted to have him dismissed after first discussing the matter with Johanssen. After the termination procedures were well underway, Johanssen told Christianson to halt the proceedings, explaining that he thought Bishop now saw how matters stood and would improve his work. "We shouldn't be too severe with him," Johanssen said. "After all, he has a wife and children to support." Bishop's performance did improve for a time, but it never became entirely satisfactory. Recently it had again become so poor that Christianson had to mention it to him. Upon Christianson's recommendation, Bishop and his wife sought out a marriage counselor, but if his home life improved it did not show up in the quality of his work.

Another personnel problem for Christianson concerned Andrew Polk, age twenty-six, the newest employee in the unit. Christianson and Polk had been good friends for several years. A former newspaper photographer, Polk took a job as a photo lab technician to earn money while doing graduate work in journalism at the university. Polk's work was decidedly superior and he was well liked throughout the division. Early in his employment Polk was called upon by the assistant director, Best—who was acquainted with his work as a newspaper photographer—to take pictures, assignments that were not included in his job description. He received overtime pay for these special assignments.

Toward the end of Polk's six-month probationary period he discussed the possibility with Christianson, the Photographic Services supervisor, of being raised to the Photographer I level. Often called upon to perform Photographer I duties, he felt he should receive overtime pay commensurate with that rank when taking pictures. Christianson agreed and told him: "Best is using your talents as photographer but he isn't paying you the Photographer I scale. I think he should. Why don't you ask him about raising your salary?"

The next day Polk was in the main office picking up his mail when Best approached him about another assignment. Polk replied, "I'd be glad to help you out, Lester, but I feel it's only fair that I get paid overtime on the Photographer I scale rather than the lab-technician scale."

Best, surprised that a person still on probation would make pay demands, protested: "But you forget that during your interview we stated that from time to time you would be asked to perform overtime duties."

"Well, I remember that Johanssen did say I would be asked to on occasion," Polk said, "and I'm willing to do so. However, he made a point that he didn't want me doing the work of a photographer because others might complain I wasn't hired for that type of work. I'm willing to do the work. I'd just like to get paid for it."

"Well, we will just have to see about that," Best said and walked away in a huff.

Next morning Christianson was called to Johanssen's office, where he found the director and Best awaiting him. Johanssen said that Best reported that Polk had been insubordinate and that he should be reprimanded by Christianson.

Christianson returned to his own office and explained to Polk that he was to do whatever was asked of him. "I know it isn't fair," he said, "but that's the way this place works. Maybe after a few months I can get you raised to Photographer I."

During the next four months, Polk performed all tasks requested by Best and Johanssen without complaint. Both he and Christianson kept a record of extra duties performed to use as "ammunition for a promotion" when additional funds became available for another Photographer I position.

Meanwhile, Donald Waterman in the Equipment and Maintenance unit had been having problems. Now sixty years old, Waterman had worked in the division for eighteen years. He planned to take an early retirement "because this damn place will never shape up."

Three weeks before, one of Waterman's technicians resigned because he was "tired of waiting for two years for a promotion from Johanssen." Five days before the effective date of resignation, the division director raised the position from Electronics Technician I to a II. The office rumor was that the promotion was pushed through to make the position more attractive and easier to fill, since the university's salary scale made it difficult to hire technicians.

Hired for the job was Roscoe Flinch, age forty-two, a TV repairman, who in accepting had negotiated a deal by which he would receive a raise after his first month of employment. This speedy raise would give him a salary $1500 higher than that received by Waterman after eighteen years of service. Waterman was furious and exclaimed on first learning about it: "How can I supervise him when he makes more than I do?" He was so nettled that he determined to take it easy during the two years before he retired.

A few weeks later employees were surprised to observe Flinch taking pictures of various activities of the division. Andrew Polk was curious and asked him, "What are you doing? I didn't know you were a photographer."

Flinch grinned and said, "Best wants some pictures for a slide show illustrating the services the division provides and asked me to prepare them."

Polk went to Christianson's office and told him of the project. Angrily Christianson rushed to Johanssen's office and confronted him. "What the hell is Flinch doing with a camera?" he asked. "He's not working in the photography unit."

"Well, he is working on a slide show for us," Johanssen said.

"That's what I hear. Why wasn't I told about the project and why wasn't the photography unit given the job?"

Passing by the open door of the office, Best heard Christianson's protest and quipped: "Maybe he is interested in photography, Jerome."

Christianson realized he was a victim of another of the division's unaccountable administrative procedures and, too overwhelmed to say more, returned to his own office. He had lost another skirmish in the civil war being waged in the Graphics and Photography Division.

Questions and Instructions

1. Evaluate the administrative abilities of Jerome Christianson and Donald Waterman.
2. In view of the attitudes of the director and assistant director, what courses of action might the supervisors have taken to prevent the situation in the division from arising and developing as it did?
3. What does the situation in the division reveal about the overall administration of the university?
4. If you were vice-president of administration at the university and became aware of the discord in the division, how would you deal with it?
5. Most grievance procedures established by institutions apply only to nonadministrative employees. Should there also be a grievance procedure for administrators?

Selected Bibliography

Blau, Peter M., "Strategic Leniency and Authority," in Golembiewski, Robert T.; Gibson, Frank; and Miller, Gerald, *Managerial Behavior and Organization Demands,* Itasca, Ill.: F. E. Peacock Publishers, 1978. pp. 158–61.

Brinks, James T., "The Comparable Worth Issue: A Salary Administration Bombshell," *Personnel Administrator* 26 (November 1981): 37–40.

Filipowicz, Christine A., "The Troubled Employee: Whose Responsibility?" *Personnel Administrator* 24 (June 1979): 17–22.

Freedman, Sara M., and Montanari, John R., "An Integrative Model of Managerial Reward Allocation," *Academy of Management Review* 5 (July 1980): 381–90.

Kramer, Fred A., *Dynamics of Public Bureaucracy—An Introduction to Public Management,* 2nd ed., Cambridge, Mass.: Winthrop Publishers, 1981. Chs. 10, 11, and 12 provide a useful overview of various types of executive, legislative, and judicial controls.

Lau, Alan W.; Newman, Arthur R.; and Broedling, Laurie A., "The Nature of Managerial Work in the Public Sector," *Public Administration Review* 40 (September/October 1980): 513–20.

Lutz, Carl F., "Efficient Maintenance of the Classification Plan," *Public Personnel Management* 2 (July/August 1973): 232–41.

March, James G., and Feldman, Martha S., "Information in Organization as Signal and Symbol," *Administrative Science Quarterly* 26 (June 1981): 171–86.

Porter, Lyman W.; Lawler, Edward E., III; and Hackman, J. Richard, *Behavior in Organizations,* New York: McGraw-Hill, 1975. See "Conflict Resolution," pp. 463–66.

Remick, Helen, "The Comparable Worth Controversy," *Public Personnel Management* 10 (No. 4, 1981): 371–83.

Schulkind, Gilbert, "Monitoring Position Classification—Practical Problems and Possible Solutions," *Public Personnel Management* 4 (January/February 1975): 32–38.

6

Blocking the Super Block

Rivertown, Ohio, a quiet city of 85,000 people along the banks of the Ohio River, grew only slightly in population in the years after World War II and there were few gains or losses in business activity during this period.

To spark the city's development, in the 1960s City Manager James Hill proposed the creation of a Super Block in the downtown area. This Super Block would include a major hotel complex, a civic auditorium, high-rise office buildings, and new facilities for stores. Hill also proposed the construction of an intricate roadway system from the nearby interstate that bypassed the city to the Super Block. A major hotel chain pledged itself to invest in the project and soon several large business firms indicated an interest in locating in the city. Plans were drawn for the transportation systems and highways and the Super Block seemed to be becoming reality.

However, the business community became concerned about the problems that might arise out of the creation of the Super Block and the huge expenses involved. Some businessmen feared they would lose business to incoming firms and others were angered because the construction of the roadway system would force them to move. Some expressed concern over the possibility of downtown traffic and parking problems, an increase in crime, and destruction of old riverside landmarks.

Hill tried to convince members of civic clubs and the Chamber of Commerce that the Super Block would not harm established firms but instead would attract people to the central district and increase the volume of business. Hill also assured them that traffic and parking would be adequately handled with the elaborate above- and below-ground parking lots. "Yes," Hill stated, "some businesses will have to move in order to accommodate the new downtown roadway, but the benefits to be gained of added taxes and more job opportunities for the community will far outweigh the unpleasantness and temporary destruction created by the projects."

Parts of the business community continued their opposition to the Super Block, but Hill stood his ground. Both sides tried to influence the City Council, whose members were divided on the issue. Finally, after the plan had been debated for nearly eighteen months, the hotel chain withdrew its commitment and accepted a similar offer from a city a hundred miles away in Kentucky. This defection caused other businesses to withdraw from the project. It became increasingly obvious that Hill's Rivertown Super Block was not to be realized. He announced his resignation and accepted a job as city manager in Missouri.

Years later Rivertown built a civic center in the area where the Super Block had been planned. Hill was invited to speak at the dedication of the new facility, and the subject of his address was "Dreams vs. Realities."

Questions and Instructions

1. What mistakes did James Hill make in announcing and promoting his plan for a Super Block?
2. Was Hill ahead of the times in proposing his plan for the downtown district? Was the civic center built later possibly the result of Hill's earlier dream?
3. If you were Hill, what are some of the ideas you would set forth in your dedication address for the civic center?
4. Although the idea for the Super Block was Hill's, would he have been wiser to work behind the scene for its fulfillment and let some other person or an organization receive the credit?
5. Is it the role of a city manager to create policy or merely to carry out policy determined by elected city officials?

Selected Bibliography

Aleshire, Frank, and Aleshire, Fran, "The American City Manager: New Style, New Game," *National Civic Review* 66 (May 1977): 235–39.

Catanese, Anthony James, "Information for Planning," in So, Frank S.; Stollman, Israel; Beal, Frank; and Arnold, David S., eds., *The Prac-*

tice of Local Government Planning, Washington, D.C.: International City Management Association, 1979. pp. 90–114.

Friedman, Stephen B., "Economic Development: The Planning Response," in So, Frank S.; Stollman, Israel; Beal, Frank; and Arnold, David S., eds., *The Practice of Local Government Planning,* Washington, D.C.: International City Management Association, 1979. pp. 589–99.

Goldfield, David R., and Brownell, Blaine A., *Urban America: From Downtown to No Town,* Boston: Houghton Mifflin Co., 1979.

Hall, Richard H., *Organizations: Structure and Process,* 2nd ed., Englewood Cliffs, N.J.: Prentice-Hall, 1977. Ch. 3, "Goals and Effectiveness," pp. 67–100.

Harrigan, John J., *Political Change in the Metropolis,* 2nd ed., Boston: Little, Brown, 1981.

Houghton, David G., "The City Manager and Politics: The Cycle Is Completed," *Southern Review of Public Administration* 3 (March 1980): 356–83.

Larson, Calvin J., and Nikkel, Stan R., *Urban Problems: Perspectives on Corporations, Governments and Cities,* Boston: Allyn and Bacon, 1979.

Rapp, Brian W., "You Can't Manage City Hall the Way You Manage General Motors," *Good Government* 92 (Summer 1975): 12–15.

Stipak, Brian, "Local Governments' Use of Citizen Surveys," *Public Administration Review* 40 (September/October 1980): 521–25.

7

Sick Leave in Spring Valley

Slashes in federal aid programs to cities, a decline in revenue from a two-percent sales tax, and higher costs in everything from cleaning supplies to wages had brought hard times to the elected officials of Spring Valley. The combination of these factors made it seem impossible for Robert Donizetti—the city manager—and the budget committee of the City Council to provide a balanced budget for the city.

Situated in a northeastern state, Spring Valley had a population of twelve thousand, a declining one that matched its declining revenue. In casting about for means to finance the small city's operations, Donizetti saw few opportunities for increasing the revenue. In the past year one of its chief employers, the Acme Manufacturing Company, had been forced to close its local factory, and all parts of the local economy had been affected by the national business recession. Hence, Donizetti went carefully over departmental budgets seeking ways to cut costs and eliminate waste.

One area in which Donizetti decided savings could be effected was through changes in policy concerning sick leave. The city's work force consisted of only about 150 full-time employees, and figures in Donizetti's office showed that sick leave in the past six years averaged 7.34 days per year per employee. This was not only costly in dollars in terms of Spring Valley's budget but meant a loss of labor efficiency and productivity. His statistics showed that female and older employees used more sick leave than males and younger workers. Donizetti prepared the following tables of sick-leave averages by age and sex for the budget committee:

Table 1. Sick Leave in Spring Valley by Sex, 1978–83

Year	Male	Female
1978	6.1	7.9
1979	5.9	7.7
1980	6.4	8.4
1981	6.3	8.7
1982	6.5	8.5
1983	6.8	8.9

Table 2. Sick Leave in Spring Valley by Age, 1978–83

Year	Under 30	Over 30
1978	5.1	6.8
1979	5.3	8.4
1980	5.7	8.1
1981	5.5	7.7
1982	5.8	8.3
1983	5.6	8.6

Spring Valley had not had many labor conflicts. Employee relations were handled through the personnel director, William Danforth, and the City Employees' Association, whose president was Joshua Blum. In respect to sick leave, the city had in recent years agreed to include in it family care, doctor appointments, and emergency time off for such events as funerals.

After study of the problem, Donizetti recommended that the City Employees' Association and the personnel department together devise a sick-leave incentive program. It would serve as an incentive to save sick leave, as a deterrent to sick-leave abuse, and as an equitable plan for the different uses of sick leave.

On June 6 the personnel department presented its proposal. Under its plan, employees would be reimbursed on February 1 of each year for 20 percent of the sick-leave credits accumulated during the past year. An employee would have to have built up forty-five sick-leave days in order to draw cash payments, a move intended to reduce turnover in employment in the city.

The City Employees' Association made a counterproposal that included a choice by the employee to consider sick leave as vacation time or else to triple it and add it to retirement service. Unused credits diverted to retirement were to be made at a rate of 100 percent.

The main point of contention at this stage concerned the percentage of sick-leave credit for which an employee might be reimbursed. The city offered no alternative to minimum yearly reimbursement while the employees demanded that some sort of retirement-related incentive be adopted. After several fruitless negotiations, the two parties agreed to present the problem to a fact finder. His or her findings and suggestions for resolution of the issues would be used as a basis for further negotiations. The fact finder chosen, Alfred Cartaret, conducted private hearings with both parties and submitted his report on July 15.

Questions and Instructions

1. Assume that you are the fact finder in the case. Analyze the sick-leave problem in Spring Valley and propose a plan equitable to both parties.
2. If you were the city manager, entrusted with pursuing the best interests of the city, which provisions in the proposal would you accept and which would you attempt to change?
3. Assume that you are the union negotiator. Which provisions would you accept and which would you attempt to change?

Selected Bibliography

Advisory Commission on Intergovernmental Relations, *Recent Trends in Federal and State Aid to Local Governments,* Washington, D.C.: U.S. Government Printing Office, 1980. pp. 3–25.
——, *1980 Changing Public Attitudes on Governments and Taxes,* Washington, D.C.: U.S. Government Printing Office, 1980. pp. 1–7.
Cascio, Wayne F., and Awad, Elias M., *Human Resources Management: An Information Systems Approach,* Reston, Va.: Reston Publishing Company, 1981. pp. 486–528.
Donaldson, William V., "Managing Shrinking Cities: Cincinnati," *Bureaucrat* 10 (Fall 1981): 56–58.
Hunt, J. G., and Hill, J. W., "The New Look in Motivation Theory for Organizational Research," in Golembiewski, Robert T.; Gibson, Frank; and Miller, Gerald, *Managerial Behavior and Organization Demands: Management as a Linking of Levels of Interaction,* 2nd ed., Itasca, Ill.: F. E. Peacock Publishers, 1978. pp. 81–97.
Lawler, Edward E., III, "New Approaches to Pay: Innovations That Work," in Glueck, William F., *Personnel: A Book of Readings,* Dallas: Business Publications, 1979. pp. 279–87.
Lewis, Carol W., and Logalbo, Anthony T., "Cutback Principles and

Practices: A Checklist for Managers,'' *Public Administration Review* 40 (March/April 1980): 184–88.

Nesbitt, Murray B., *Labor Relations in the Federal Government Service,* Washington, D.C.: The Bureau of National Affairs, Inc., 1976. See ''Administrative and Sick Leave,'' pp. 194–96.

Perry, James L., and Hunt, Carder W., ''Evaluating the Union-Management Relationship in Government,'' *Public Administration Review* 38 (September/October 1978): 431–36.

Song, Youngdahl, and Yarbrough, Tinsley E., ''Tax Ethics and Taxpayer Attitudes: A Survey,'' *Public Administration Review* 38 (September/October 1978): 442–52.

''Why Not a Rational Sick Pay Leave Policy?'' *American City and County* 95 (April 1980): 51–53.

8

A Case of Dissatisfaction

Mitchell Floor was thirty-two years old, married, and the father of three children. He attended the state university for two years, majoring in business administration and minoring in sociology. He was one of several new field officers employed by the Department of Human Services Administration. After completing a training program, new employees were assigned to various agencies in the state branches of the Department of Housing, Education, and Welfare.

Floor and others were assigned to a group supervisor named Charles Bass. Floor did a good job and learned quickly, and Bass was impressed with the interest he showed in his clients and their well-being. Bass prepared a first-year evaluation of Floor, finding that he had "performed beyond the normal standards for someone with his level of experience." Floor was promoted along with other field officers of his class at the end of his first year on the job.

The next year the number of cases requiring attention exceeded the capacity of the available field officers at the required salary level for this type of work. To accomplish the work load in a reasonable period of time, Bass assigned some of the cases to lower-salaried personnel who he felt could perform satisfactorily on a temporary basis. Floor, however, claimed that he could continue to handle his share of the work and was confident that any increase would not cause him problems.

For his performance Floor was promoted at the year's end to senior supervisor. His duties included assisting new field officers, answering technical questions, and assisting Bass with his reports. In August, Bass recommended the management-development award for the job Floor had done as senior supervisor. In September, Floor was transferred from the group headed by Bass. Bass told Floor that he greatly appreciated the job he had done and informed him that he had been recommended for an award.

Paul Potts, Floor's new supervisor, had knowledge of his ability and excellent record and used his skills to good advantage. Potts assigned him to a task force in the National Office Training Branch to work with a completely reorganized program for new field officials. The people with whom Floor worked were soon impressed by his skill and ability to focus on the needs of the field officers.

Upon his return from the national office, Floor was again promoted. A few weeks later, however, Potts informed Floor that he would not receive the award for which Bass had recommended him because "the promotion was a sufficient award for good work."

Floor was disappointed, but the rejection did not signal an end to the recognition of his good work. In July, Floor and others working on the programed training material were given a Group Special Award, presented by the director of the national office on behalf of the Housing, Education, and Welfare agency. But Floor did not respond to the award favorably, saying he thought it did not express any real local appreciation for what the participants had done.

In December all the agency offices in the region were reorganized. Some field officials were transferred to new groups and the type of work performed by several groups was changed. New positions were established and a number of the personnel in the region were promoted.

Among those promoted was Floor, who was named group supervisor in charge of ten field officers. He did not receive a salary increase, though other senior supervisors were promoted to higher-grade levels at higher salaries.

In January, before Floor took his new position, he talked to Gregory Marble, director of the agency branch. Floor told Marble that he was not sure he wanted to be a group supervisor and that he could not really support the Housing, Education, and Welfare agency in the capacity of group leader. He offered several explanations for his attitude. One was the rejection of the award that Bass had recommended; another was the promotion of outside senior supervisors to positions above himself. Marble knew of Floor's qualifications and his fine record. He explained why the award was rejected and indicated that he understood how Floor felt. But he could not explain why Floor had not been given a salary increase with his promotion. The conference ended with Floor promising to make a decision and report back. Marble now had reservations about the way Floor was acting and felt that he did not really appreciate the recognition he had received in being appointed to a group-supervisor position. Marble also wondered if Floor was ready to accept the responsibilities of the new position, which required a great deal of fortitude and self-confidence.

By their next meeting, Floor still had not decided. He felt that his career would be jeopardized if he did not accept the assignment but he was still not sure he wanted it. It would mean longer hours and greater responsibility, and, if he was dissatisfied with the job and did badly, it would mean trouble for him in the future. Any failure on his part would make it difficult to obtain a job outside government, especially in management, a move he had been considering for some time. At the meeting Marble told Floor he believed he should take the position and continue to do his usual good job. The meeting ended with Floor reluctantly deciding to take the job.

One week later Marble was stunned to receive a letter of resignation from Floor stating: "Much unfairness has caused me to become very unhappy with my work at the Department of Housing, Education, and Welfare. I am no longer able to be enthusiastic about my job. My last assignment, with no increase in compensation, was the last straw. I can tolerate no more!"

Questions and Instructions

1. Do you believe that Floor made the right decision to resign. Why?
2. Should Marble try to persuade Floor to remain with the department?
3. Identify some of the reasons for employee job dissatisfaction. Are the reasons most likely to be associated with work content or work context? Explain.
4. How important are expressions of appreciation and merit citations in contributing to job satisfaction?

Selected Bibliography

Adams, J. Stacy, "Toward an Understanding of Inequity," *Journal of Abnormal Psychology* 67 (November 1963): 422–36.

Costello, John M., and Lee, Sang M., "Needs Fulfillment and Job Satisfaction of Professionals," *Public Personnel Management* 3 (September/October 1974): 454–61.

Dyer, Lee; Schwab, Donald P.; and Fossum, John A., "Impacts of Pay on Employee Behaviors and Attitudes: An Update," in Glueck, William F., *Personnel: A Book of Readings,* Dallas: Business Publications, 1979. pp. 270–78.

Goodman, Paul S., and Friedman, Abraham, "An Examination of Adams's Theory of Inequity," *Administrative Science Quarterly* 16 (September 1971): 271–88.

Keevey, Richard F., "State Productivity Improvements: Building on Existing Strengths," *Public Administration Review* 40 (September/ October 1980): 451–58.

Kerr, Steven, "On the Folly of Rewarding A While Hoping for B," *Academy of Management Journal* 18 (December 1975): 769–83.

King, Nathan, "Clarification and Evaluation of the Two-Factor Theory of Job Satisfaction," *Psychological Bulletin* 74 (July 1970): 18–31.

McClelland, David, "That Urge to Achieve," in Natemeyer, Walter E., ed., *Classics of Organizational Behavior,* Oak Park, Ill.: Moore Publishing Co., 1978. pp. 88–94.

Meyer, Herbert H., "The Pay-for-Performance Dilemma," in Glueck, William F., *Personnel: A Book of Readings,* Dallas: Business Publications, 1979. pp. 259–70.

Nord, Walter R., "Job Satisfaction Reconsidered," *American Psychologist* 32 (December 1977): 1026–35.

Orr, Daniel, "Public Employee Compensation Levels," in Chickering, A. Lawrence, *Public Employee Unions,* San Francisco: Institute for Contemporary Studies, 1976. pp. 131–44.

Podsakoff, Philip M., "Satisfaction and Performance Measures of Personnel Effectiveness," in Schuler, Randall S.; McFillen, James M.; and Dalton, Dan R., *Applied Readings in Personnel and Human Resource Management,* St. Paul: West Publishing Co., 1981. pp. 3–19.

Umstot, Denis D.; Bell, Cecil H., Jr.; and Mitchell, Terrence R., "Effects of Job Enrichment and Task Goals on Satisfaction and Productivity: Implications for Job Design," *Journal of Applied Psychology* 61 (August 1976): 379–94.

9

A Campaigner for Equal Rights

Dawson Bryan had worked ten years in the building-construction trade in Parkhurst when he joined the Code Enforcement Department of the city as a code-compliance inspector. In a few years he had worked up through the two grades of compliance inspector and the positions of safety officer and assistant director of the department and last year he was named director.

By city ordinance, the duties of the department were to inspect construction, alteration, or remodeling of any buildings and the installation of electric wiring, gas and water lines, plumbing, and air conditioning; to act as designee of the county Health Department for the enforcement of health provisions in the city code; and to enforce housing regulations, safety regulations, and sign regulations.

A big, burly man, Bryan took a no-nonsense attitude toward his job and the fifteen employees in the department. Tact was not a word in his vocabulary. When he gave instructions, he was inclined to shout as he had done when working outdoors in the building trade. The men in the department were used to his high-decibel communication and paid no attention to it. On the whole, the department was well managed, was strict in enforcing the codes despite being understaffed, and worked very well as a team. It was an all-male enclave in a city government that since the adoption of an equal-opportunity and affirmative-action ordinance had been increasingly infiltrated in recent years by women employees in departments, like street cleaning and maintenance, that had never seen them before.

The male stronghold in code enforcement was breached when the Department of Personnel sent Bryan a new Compliance Inspector

Grade 1 named Kate Grunwald. Bryan immediately got on the telephone to protest to Martin Everest, director of personnel, that the work of inspection was so specialized no woman could handle it. Everest replied that Grunwald was fully qualified, in fact better qualified than some of the male inspectors because she had studied electrical engineering in a university for two years and only three or four of his present staff had any college work. "Anyway," Everest said, "read Articles III and IV of our union contract dealing with nondiscrimination and affirmative action. You'll see why we were glad to hire Grunwald." (See Exhibit 1 at the end of this case.) Bryan replied he did not need to read a book to learn that a woman in his department meant trouble.

Kate Grunwald was not the type to ask any special favors on the job. She had quit the university after two years when she married and her husband, a petroleum-engineering senior, upon graduation had taken a job in Iran. Five years later their marriage ended in divorce, and Grunwald, who gained custody of their boy, was irregularly employed for a time in construction work, where she encountered difficulty because of being a woman. She had noted the subordinate position of women in the Iranian society and had suffered from sex bias on the job in the United States. She therefore became an ardent activist in the women's movement and took part in rallies and demonstrations of the National Organization for Women (NOW) in support of the Equal Rights Amendment (ERA). She had adopted a belligerent attitude toward what she perceived as sex bias.

On the job, Grunwald was first assigned to checking on complaints, most of them reports of health nuisances, and not on routine inspection of the electrical wiring, gas and water lines, and plumbing in new construction that she considered herself best qualified to do. She was reliable and competent, and Bryan could not find any reasonable fault with her work. Nevertheless, the relationship between the two might be accurately described as restrained hostility.

After Grunwald had been six months on the job, a vacancy occurred for a Grade 2 compliance inspector. She mentioned to Bryan that she intended to apply for the job, but he tried to discourage her by saying she ought to have more experience before seeking a promotion. Nevertheless, Grunwald submitted an application to the Personnel Department. When asked for a report on her work, Bryan told Everest, the personnel director, that she was doing all right as far as he could see, but disrupted the peace of the department by expressing her views on women's rights and ERA and had taken time off during a busy spring-inspection season to attend a regional convention of NOW. "All the more reason for promoting her," Everest said. "We don't want a bunch of women libbers picketing City Hall on her behalf."

A few months after receiving her promotion, Grunwald decided to apply for another vacancy in the department, that of safety officer, a supervisory position with a higher salary. She was dissuaded from doing so by Bryan on the ground that two other compliance inspectors with more seniority were already applicants. A year later the safety-officer position became vacant again and Grunwald, against the advice of Bryan, applied for it.

A week later she obtained sick leave, but it was soon revealed publicly there was nothing wrong with her health: television news reports showed her in the forefront of a large crowd demonstrating for passage of the ERA on the steps of the state capitol. A resolution approving the ERA was being debated in the legislature and was the focus of national attention. Women's-rights leaders from around the state and country had gathered to push for a favorable vote in the legislature, motion-picture and television celebrities urged adoption at rallies on the capitol steps and in newspaper and television interviews, and supporters filled the statehouse corridors and legislative offices lobbying for the measure. Grunwald did not miss a day taking part in this activity.

When she returned to her job, Bryan angrily told her she had no business taking sick leave to engage in political activity, which was forbidden in the city charter. Equally angry, Grunwald told Bryan that he was a sexist and that most city departments were in violation of the equal-rights and affirmative-action provisions of the charter in respect to the employment of women. The only political activity forbidden in the city charter, she said, was a prohibition against employees taking part in city elections.

A few days after this confrontation, the most heated that had taken place between Grunwald and Bryan, she learned that she had not received the promotion to safety officer.

Shortly afterward, Grunwald filed a complaint with the Equal Employment Opportunity Commission alleging that she had been passed over for promotion on grounds of sex discrimination. She charged that she had been discouraged from seeking promotions by the head of her department and that she was a victim of discrimination when she failed to get promoted when she had applied for a higher position. She also questioned the qualifications of a male who, she alleged, was given the job of safety director without applying for it. She cited her department head's criticism of her support for ERA as prima facie evidence of discrimination. She asked for advancement in position equal in pay and authority to past positions she had sought and for assurances there would be no retaliation resulting from her complaint.

Questioned by a newspaper reporter about her complaint, Grunwald said, "Women are not hired by the city for managerial positions on an equal basis with men. I'm interested in seeing more women selected as department heads. I'm going all the way with this complaint for the good of all women."

Questions and Instructions

1. Was the personnel director remiss in failing to do more than tell Bryan to read the union contract clauses on affirmative action to help prepare for the acceptance of a woman in the Code Enforcement Department?
2. What decision do you think the Human Rights Commission will reach on Grunwald's complaint under the Civil Rights Act of 1964? (See Exhibit 1 in Case No. 23, "The Prank That Misfired.")
3. Is the fact that Grunwald took sick leave to lobby for the ERA sufficient grounds for a reprimand or denial of a promotion?
4. Do you think Grunwald was right in going directly to the EEOC with her complaint instead of seeking redress through grievance procedures outlined in the city's contract with the American Federation of State, County, and Municipal Employees Union? Explain.
5. Do you think Grunwald would make a good department head or supervisor?

Selected Bibliography

Brown, Marsha, "Getting and Keeping Women in·Non-Traditional Jobs," *Public Personnel Management* 10 (No. 4, 1981): 408–11.

Burns, Ruth Ann, "Women in Municipal Management: Opportunities and Barriers," in *The Municipal Year Book 1981,* Washington, D.C.: International City Management Association, 1981. pp. 167–74.

Cayer, N. Joseph, and Sigelman, Lee, "Minorities and Women in State and Local Government: 1973–1975," *Public Administration Review* 40 (September/October 1980): 443–50.

Cruz, Nestor, " 'Realpolitik' and Affirmative Action," *Public Personnel Management* 9 (No. 3, 1980): 192–95.

Gettings, Robert, "Litigation as a Tool for Social Change," *Journal of Health and Human Resources Administration* 2 (February 1980): 313–19.

Hackman, J. Richard, and Lawler, Edward E., III, "Employee Reactions to Job Characteristics," *Journal of Applied Psychology* 55 (June 1971): 259–86.

Holley, William H., and Feild, Hubert S., "Equal Employment Opportunity and Its Implications for Personnel Practices," in Glueck, William F., *Personnel: A Book of Readings,* Dallas: Business Publications, 1979. pp. 349–58.

Kovach, Kenneth A., "Women in the Labor Force: A Socio-Economic Analysis," *Public Personnel Management* 9 (No. 4, 1980): 318–26.

Menges, Edward H., Jr., "The Lakewood, Colorado, Personnel System: Creating an Environment for Productivity," *Public Personnel Management* 9 (No. 4, 1980): 257–67.

Rosen, Benson, and Jerdee, Thomas H., "On-the-Job Sex Bias: Increasing Managerial Awareness," *Personnel Administrator* 22 (January 1977): 15–18.

Ruzicho, Andrew J., "The Weber Case—Its Impact on Affirmative Action," *Personnel Administrator* 25 (June 1980): 69–72.

Schleh, Edward C., "Using Central Staff to Boost Line Initiative," *Management Review* 65 (May 1976): 17–23.

Smith, Russel A.; Edwards, Harry T.; and Clark, Theodore R., *Labor Relations in the Public Sector: Cases and Materials,* 2nd ed., Indianapolis, Ind.: Bobbs-Merrill, 1979.

Tomkins, Adrienne, "Sex Discrimination: Adrienne Tomkins, Stenographer," *Civil Liberties Review* 5 (September/October 1978): 19–24.

Exhibit 1. Union Contract Articles on Civil Rights

Article III

Non-Discrimination

Section 1. No employee or an individual being considered for employment shall be favored or subjected to discrimination by management or by the Union because of race, creed, color, sex, or national origin, relationship to any person or persons, or political or union activities, other than those prohibited by this Agreement.

Section 2. Management and the Union agree not to interfere with the right of employees to become or not to become members of the Union and further, will urge the employees that there will be no discrimination or coercion against any employee because of Union membership or non-membership.

Article IV

Affirmative Action

Section 1. The City and the Union are committed to the concept and practice of equal employment opportunity as a necessary component of merit principles, which is a phase of affirmative action.

Section 2. The Affirmative Action commitment will be supported by positive and aggressive practices and procedures, which will insure non-discrimination and equal-employment opportunity for racial and ethnic minorities, the disadvantaged, and women in securing admission in the City employment force and promotional opportunities at all job levels.

Section 3. The general objectives of the City and the Union in affirmative-action practice will be:

a. to engage in continuous planning and monitoring of the effects of practices in order to eliminate and prevent the occurrence of arbitrary, discriminatory practices and policies related to employment, membership, and promotion; and

b. to take positive steps to solicit applicants for employment and membership from minority groups and women's organizations.

10

Parking Meters—A Perennial Problem

Once again the town of San Juan looked forward to the annual show put on by the City Council. The *Evening Gazette* printed the agenda for the next meeting, which included the item "Replacement of Parking Meters," and the bulletin board of San Juan Cable Television announced that it would cover the meeting. The show, which occurred as regularly as the Pioneer Days festival and was almost as much fun, always packed the council chamber.

The issue over the parking meters was whether to keep the seven hundred old and obsolete meters, which frequently were inoperable and which accepted only pennies and nickels, or to replace them with new meters that would accept pennies, nickels, dimes, and quarters. The question of whether to install new meters taking coins of larger denomination that would produce more revenue was almost as controversial as that raised twenty-five years before when the installation of the meters was first considered. The council had brought up the matter of replacing the old meters on five previous occasions, and the debate had always resulted in a stalemate.

Mayor Arthur Enriquez wanted to avoid the circus atmosphere of previous discussions of the parking-meter problem. When he called the council to order with a rap of the gavel, he was a little dismayed by the television cameras and lights and the standing-room-only crowd in the chamber. After approval of the minutes, the mayor introduced the second item on the agenda, "Replacement of Parking Meters."

"The discussion of the advantages and disadvantages surrounding the parking meters has been going on for five years," Enriquez said.

"The debate is not on whether San Juan will have meters, for that has been established. The debate centers on whether we will replace the old meters with new ones—meters that will accept larger coin denominations. This is no time to become angry over the meters. Let us reason together and resolve our differences in a manner that will benefit the citizens of San Juan."

Enriquez then introduced the new city manager, Joseph Stevenson, who would make a preliminary report on the question of replacing the meters. Stevenson was aware that his predecessor had been fired by a vote of three to two because of his support of replacement. He did not intend to get into similar trouble by submitting a proposal either for or against the meters.

He began by saying that to an outsider the controversy over the parking meters might appear inflated and unnecessary, but to the citizens of San Juan it was a matter of principle. He related that more than twenty-five years before, when the city first considered installing meters, citizens were outraged. They felt that the streets belonged to the public and they should not be charged for using them. But after the installation of the meters, drivers got accustomed to putting their pennies in the slot and thought nothing of it. But about fifteen years ago parking in the downtown district became a serious problem because the population had grown from 10,500 to more than 25,000 people. Today, Stevenson continued, the penny cost for parking was no deterrent to misuse of parking space. Spaces that should be open to customers and clients of downtown stores and firms were taken up by the cars of business and professional men and their employees. The downtown parking problem went beyond the question of replacement of meters. "In the early days," he said, "meters were used to regulate parking and were not an instrument of city-revenue enhancement." There might be other solutions to the problem, such as municipal or privately operated parking lots or garages. He did not believe the meter question could be answered this evening. The air had to be cleared and he would have to develop a plan for the council to consider. To this end, he had developed an "Administrative Plan of Action." He then distributed to the council members and the audience a list of objectives and studies that should be made. (See Exhibit 1 at the end of this case.)

Stevenson's temporizing proposal was effective, and those who had come to the council meeting expecting fireworks were disappointed. Several of the council members briefly stated their points of view and only a few of the people in the audience were sufficiently aroused to take the floor.

Adam McKnight, a businessman and council member from a ward that included the downtown area, said, "Parking meters are merely devices that regulate the use of limited parking space in high-use parts of the town. We're a friendly town. We want farmers and people from neighboring towns and small communities to come to San Juan and shop. We're not money-hungry people. We don't need new and more expensive gadgets complicating our way of life. Leave the more expensive meters to those who live in big cities."

Elizabeth Howard, a council member from a well-to-do residential district, disagreed with McKnight. She saw "no reason why San Juan should remain stagnant or not keep up with the demands of the time." Revenue was generated from parking meters, she said, and this revenue would purchase the new meters and increase the city's coffers as well. "Who among us can't afford to spend a dime or fifteen cents a half-hour for parking these days?" she asked rhetorically.

Philip Hemphill, a council member and an implement dealer, reported the complaint of a rancher who had recently priced a John Deere tractor. "He would like to purchase the tractor from my dealership," Hemphill said, "but he was angry over receiving a parking ticket last Saturday. It seemed like every time he came to town he got a parking ticket."

After forty-five minutes of comment from the council members and members of the public, Mayor Enriquez entertained a motion to table the parking-meter issue until the next monthly meeting. It carried unanimously. City Manager Stevenson breathed a sigh of relief. He had a little time left to survey the situation, find out the facts and figures, and come up with proposals to solve the problem.

Questions and Instructions

1. If you were Stevenson, what would you do first? Why? Is the administrative plan of action an adequate one? Have any factors been overlooked? If so, what are they?
2. What would you do to keep a good relationship with the council?
3. The day after the council meeting, you go into the Rainbow Cafe next to City Hall. Council members Howard and Hemphill are sitting in a booth and they invite you to join them for a cup of coffee. In the course of the conversation Hemphill turns to you and asks, "How do you personally stand on the meter question?" What will be your response? What are the implications associated with your response? Discuss.
4. What methods will you use to obtain public opinion about the parking meters? Telephone survey, mailed questionnaires,

newspaper poll, or some other form of survey method? What are
the advantages and limitations associated with random versus
nonrandom sampling techniques?

5.   Evaluate the outcome possibilities presented in objective four of
Exhibit 1 at the end of this chapter. What assumptions are
reflected in the entries? Do you agree or disagree with their
stated impact? What other impacts might be added to the outcome table? Elaborate.

6.   Develop a model by which parking-meter policies may be evaluated in the future. What are the assumptions upon which the
model is based and what are their implications? Explain.

Selected Bibliography

Davidson, Dan H., and Bennett, Solon A., "Municipal Purchasing
Practices," *The Municipal Year Book 1980,* Washington, D.C.:
International City Management Association, 1980.

Etzioni, Amitai, "Mixed Scanning: A Third Approach to Decision-
Making," *Public Administration Review* 27 (December 1967):
387–88.

Fitz-Gibbon, Carol Taylor, and Morris, Lynn Lyons, *How to Design a
Program Evaluation,* Beverly Hills, Calif.: Sage Publications, 1978.

Hatry, Harry P.; Winnie, Richard E.; and Fisk, Donald M., *Practical
Program Evaluation for State and Local Governments,* 2nd ed.,
Washington, D.C.: The Urban Institute Press, 1981. Ch. 2,
"What's the Program All About? Identifying Program Objectives,
Evaluation Criteria, and Clientele Groups," pp. 13–24, and Ch. 4,
"The Dirty Job—Data Collection," pp. 57–71.

Lathan, Gary P., and Yukl, Gary A., "A Review of Research on the
Application of Goal Setting in Organizations," *Academy of Management Journal* 18 (December 1975): 824–45.

Meltsner, Arnold J., *Policy Analysts in the Bureaucracy,* Berkeley,
Calif.: University of California Press, 1976. Ch. 7, "Communication," pp. 229–64, and Ch. 8, "Predicaments," pp. 265–94.

Merget, Astrid E., "The Era of Fiscal Restraint," in *The Municipal Year
Book 1980,* Washington, D.C.: International City Management
Association, 1980. pp. 178–91.

Morgan, David R., *Managing Urban America: The Politics and Administration of America's Cities,* North Scituate, Mass.: Duxbury
Press, 1979. Ch. 1, "The External World of the Urban Manager,"
pp. 12–40, and Ch. 3, "Urban Policy Making," pp. 68–95.

Murphy, Jerome T., *Getting the Facts, A Fieldwork Guide for Evalua-*

tors and Policy Analysts, Santa Monica, Calif.: Goodyear Publishing Co., 1980. Ch. 7, "Summing Up and Applying Standards," pp. 161–80.

Odiorne, George S., "How to Succeed in MBO Goal Setting," *Personnel Journal* 57 (August 1978): 427–29.

Quade, E. S., *Analysis for Public Decisions,* New York: Elsevier North Holland, 1975. Ch. 1, "Analysis and Public Decisions," pp. 1–12; Ch. 2, "What Sort of Problem? What Sort of Analysis?" pp. 13–31; and Ch. 7, "Effectiveness and Benefits," pp. 103–15.

Rice, Mitchell F., and Jones, Woodrow, Jr., "Municipal Service Suits, Local Public Services and Service Equality," *Midwest Review of Public Administration* 14 (March 1980): 29–39.

Steiner, Richard, "Communication between Government and Citizen: Open or Closed Book?" *Southern Review of Public Administration* 1 (March 1978): 542–61.

Weiss, Carol H., *Evaluation Research,* Englewood Cliffs, N.J.: Prentice-Hall, 1972. pp. 1–59.

Wesemann, H. Edward, "Innovative Revenue Sources: The Entrepreneurial Municipality," *Public Management* 63 (January/February 1981): pp. 21–23.

Wikstrom, Nelson, "The Mayor as a Policy Leader in the Council-Manager Form of Government: A View From the Field," *Public Administration Review* 39 (May/June 1979): 270–76.

Exhibit 1. Administrative Plan of Action on Parking Meters

Objectives:

1. To assess the need for new parking meters as indicated by the cost of scheduled and unscheduled maintenance over a five-year period.
2. To analyze the economic advantages associated with the purchase and installation costs projected to the end of the next fiscal year.
3. To determine public attitudes on parking meters by conducting a poll or by using some other means of measuring public opinion.
4. To prepare a table of possible outcomes based on usage levels.

NEW METERS

Low Usage	*High Usage*
Medium revenue receipts	High revenue receipts
Satisfied auto owners	Dissatisfied auto owners
Low maintenance costs	Average maintenance costs

OLD METERS

Low Usage	*High Usage*
Low revenue receipts	Average revenue receipts
Satisfied auto owners	Satisfied auto owners
High maintenance costs	High maintenance costs

5. To prepare a proposal for the disbursement of meter revenue obtained from the present system and from a new metered system.
6. To examine the possibility of municipal parking lots or privately operated lots.
7. To prepare a final report and to make recommendations to the City Council.

11

Leonard Davis's Dilemma

Leonard Davis was the warden of Thornton Maximum Security Prison in a southern state. He was fifty-five years old and had a master's degree in clinical psychology. Davis had been involved in correctional work for nearly twenty-five years. During his fifteen years of service at Thornton, Davis worked for five years as captain of the guard, six years as the deputy warden, and the last four years as the warden. He had proved to be a competent administrator. More important, there had not been a major incident at the prison while he had been in charge. One reason for this record seems to have been the attitude he projected and instilled in his staff. He treated every inmate with respect and dignity and demanded that his staff do the same. "Never forget we are working with human beings," he frequently reminded them.

Over the years Davis had sent many proposals for penal reform to the governor and to the Board of Corrections and Pardons—none of which had been acted upon. His major concerns were rehabilitation and therapeutic treatment for inmates. He requested greater freedom in work-release programs and argued for the development of educational and job-training programs within the prison. He often expressed to the governor his concern that the prison had been intended to house a maximum of 350 prisoners, yet the current population was about 750. Davis worried that this overcrowding would have a devastating effect on first-term inmates who were forced into daily contact with hard-core criminals.

Davis felt that although he had not accomplished everything he desired, he had contributed to the advancement of humane treatment of the inmates and as a result the prison was safer for both the guards and the inmates. With this feeling of accomplishment Davis was looking forward to a meeting with the new director and superintendent of the state's Department of Corrections, Thomas Brown. Davis knew very little about Brown other than that he was a political appointee of the new governor and his very close friend.

The main topic of the first meeting between Brown and Davis concerned the proposal that the prison budget be reduced by ten percent. Davis argued vehemently that his budget was currently inadequate and that it was preposterous to suggest a reduction. Davis stated that he had a responsibility to the public and to the inmates to offer a minimal amount of rehabilitative treatment. He concluded by warning Brown that reducing the budget would be equivalent to setting a match to a powder keg, that the deprivation to the inmates would be real.

Brown countered by stating, "I appreciate your theatrics, Davis, but let's face the facts. We don't rehabilitate anyone. Who are you trying to kid? Our primary, if not total, emphasis has always been custody and not treatment. We have a big warehouse here and don't forget it. Rehabilitation and therapeutic treatment, if not actually ploys used to inflate your budget, are at best a waste of money. The governor promised cutbacks in spending, and frankly a reduction in correction expenditures is politically safe. We did not violate the law; the inmates did. Let them pay the fiddler. It is the governor's belief that a reduction can and will be made in this institution. I suggest you prepare for the reduction in your budget because, like it or not, you will face a substantial reduction in the governor's proposed budget."

Questions and Instructions

1. Comment on Brown's statement that a reduction in correction expenditures was politically safe.
2. Explain why you agree or disagree with Davis's philosophy of prison administration.
3. Would it be appropriate for Davis to lobby key legislators about the governor's proposed budget?
4. Would it be wise for Davis to contact the news media in an effort to gain public backing for his viewpoint?
5. Do the states have the political will and resources to fund prisons adequately or should this be partly a federal matter?

Selected Bibliography

Barton, Rayburn, "Roles Advocated for Administrators by the New Public Administration," *Southern Review of Public Administration* 3 (March 1980): 463–86.

Bennett, Stephen A., "Rehabilitation in Check," in MacNamara, Donald E. J., *Readings in Criminal Justice 78/79,* Guilford, Conn.: Dushkin Publishing Group, 1978. pp. 228–30.

Carter, Robert M.; McGee, Richard A.; and Nelson, E. Kim, *Corrections in America,* Philadelphia: J. B. Lippincott, 1975.

Cochran, Clark E.; Mayer, Lawrence C.; Carr, T. R.; and Cayer, N. Joseph, *American Public Policy: An Introduction,* New York: St. Martin's Press, 1982. Ch. 6, "Crime and Criminal Justice: Dilemmas of Social Control," pp. 155–95.

Cressey, Donald R., "Sources of Resistance to Innovation in Corrections," *Offenders as a Correctional Manpower Resource,* Washington, D.C.: Joint Commission on Correctional Manpower and Training, June 1968. pp. 31–49.

Dunn, William N., *Public Policy Analysis: An Introduction,* Englewood Cliffs, N.J.: Prentice-Hall, 1981.

Glaser, Daniel, *The Effectiveness of a Prison and Parole System,* Indianapolis, Ind.: Bobbs-Merrill Educational Publishing, 1977 (Abridged ed.) Ch. 10, "Work in Prison," pp. 156–72; Ch. 11, "Education in Prison," pp. 173–93; and Ch. 15, "Easing the Post Prison Problem," pp. 265–88.

Hatry, Harry P.; Winnie, Richard E.; and Fisk, Donald M., "How to Design a Program Evaluation," in Lane, Frederick S., *Managing State and Local Government: Cases and Readings,* New York: St. Martin's Press, 1980. pp. 368–87.

Kerrigan, John E., and Hinton, David W., "Knowledge and Skills Needs for Tomorrow's Public Administrators," *Public Administration Review* 40 (September/October 1980): 469–73.

Keve, Paul W., "Toward More Corrective Work in Prison," in Carter, Robert M.; Glaser, Daniel; and Wilkins, Leslie T., *Correctional Institutions,* 2nd ed., New York: J. B. Lippincott, 1977. pp. 289–92.

Nachmias, David, *Public Policy Evaluation: Approaches and Methods,* New York: St. Martin's Press, 1979. Ch. 2, "Policy Experimentation," pp. 21–46, and Ch. 3, "Quasi-Experimental Evaluations," pp. 47–73.

Ohlin, Lloyd E., "Correctional Strategies in Conflict," *Proceedings of the American Philosophical Society* 118 (June 1974): 248–53.

Palumbo, Dennis, and Sharp, Elaine, "Process Versus Impact Evaluation of Community Corrections," in Nachmias, David, ed., *The Practice of Policy Evaluation,* New York: St. Martin's Press, 1980. pp. 288–304.

Reid, Sue Titus, *Crime and Criminology,* 2nd ed., New York: Holt, Rinehart and Winston, 1979. Ch. 16, "The Modern Prison: Progress Toward Treatment and Rehabilitation,'' pp. 646–86, and Ch. 18, ''Release from Prison,'' pp. 727–81.

Rourke, Francis E., *Bureaucracy, Politics, and Public Policy,* 2nd ed., Boston: Little Brown, 1976. Ch. 3, ''The Mobilization of Political Support,'' pp. 42–80, and Ch. 4, ''Differentials in Agency Power,'' pp. 81–105.

Wildavsky, Aaron, *The Politics of the Budgetary Process,* 3rd ed., Boston: Little Brown, 1979. Ch. 3, ''Strategies,'' pp. 63–126.

12

Does That Design Belong to Us?

Rex Hegg and Mark Walters were about to hit their drives on the first tee when General James Snyder arrived at the clubhouse. Walters motioned to Snyder, who was looking for them.

"Over here, General," called Walters.

"Sorry I'm late," Snyder said as the two men shook hands, "but I got hung up in a meeting back at the office."

"No problem, General. We've only been here a couple of minutes ourselves. General, I'd like you to meet Rex Hegg, our director of security and internal control."

Hegg and Snyder shook hands and then all three hit their drives and began walking down the fairway.

Hegg and Walters worked for the Alaska State Engineering and Design Agency, and Snyder was on active duty with the U.S. Air Force in charge of the Office of Special Investigation (OSI).

"General, a situation has developed within the agency that worries Rex and me," Walters said. "We talked at length the other day and decided we need the advice of a professional."

"Be happy to help if I can," replied Snyder. "What seems to be the problem?"

"It concerns one of the designers on our staff," Walters went on. "It started out innocently enough. Two months ago I was having a casual conversation with Terry Hofer about how we spent our free evenings and weekends. Hofer told me he had recently been working evenings with his neighbor on a project of mutual interest. Hofer is an excellent electronics designer and we have a good rapport, so I pursued the subject a little further. I inquired as to the nature of the project and Hofer said it was an electronical device that could activate street lights to flash for twenty-four hours when the bulb was about to burn out."

Snyder interrupted, "You mean Hofer was designing and building this device with his neighbor?"

"Apparently so," replied Walters. "Hofer told me his neighbor was a successful inventor who had a number of patents to his credit. Now retired, the neighbor spends most of his time in his basement shop and had been working on the device for a considerable length of time. Hofer helps whenever he has the time to spare." The three men stopped and Walters lighted a cigarette before he continued, "I thought little of it at the time. In fact, I almost envied Hofer because it sounded like something I might enjoy doing myself if I had a neighbor with that kind of talent. A month later I asked Hofer how his project was coming along and he said the work had progressed to the point where he and his neighbor had formed a corporation to market the device."

Snyder asked, "This was a corporation in name only since the product had to be perfected before it was ready for manufacturing and marketing?"

"That's right," said Walters. "My first concern was that the agency was going to lose a top-notch electronics designer."

"Are you concerned about an employee conflict of interest in terms of Hofer moonlighting or has he been using agency time and components to work on his outside project?" asked Snyder.

"I must emphasize," Walters replied, "that I see no evidence so far that suggests Hofer is using agency time and material for a personal effort, but . . . "

"Then, you'll have to assume he isn't," Snyder said. "I'm afraid I don't quite see the issue as yet."

"We think the issue is privileged data," said Hegg, "but we can't prove it yet and we are unsure of the best approach to take at this point."

"Please explain," replied Snyder.

"In long talks with Hofer about the experimental device, he told me more than I think he meant to. I believe part of Hofer's electronics design for the flasher copies a design that another of our engineers has developed. In essence, I believe he is stealing agency data for his own monetary gain."

"I see," Snyder replied. "Have you confronted Hofer yet?"

"No, we haven't. We thought it would be unwise to do anything until we got an outside perspective, something a little more objective. We don't want to make any unfounded accusations and offend a valuable employee. At the same time we just can't sit back and let the agency get ripped off."

Questions and Instructions

1. As General Snyder, what would you advise them to do?
2. Would it be appropriate to seek legal advice? Why?
3. Who should own the rights to a technological design developed by a person while working for a government agency?
4. Assume you are the director of the Alaska State Engineering and Design Agency. Prepare a policy statement that clearly defines the rights and duties of state employees in situations such as this.

Selected Bibliography

Bailey, Stephen K., "Ethics and the Public Service," *Public Administration Review* 24 (December 1964): 235–43.

Banfield, Edward C., "Corruption as a Feature of Governmental Organization," *Journal of Law and Economics* 18 (December 1975): 587–605.

Beard, Edmund, "Conflict of Interest and the Public Sector," in deGeorge, Richard T., and Pichler, Joseph A., *Ethics, Free Enterprise, and Public Policy,* New York: Oxford University Press, 1978. pp. 232–47.

Boling, T. Edwin, and Dempsey, John, "Ethical Dilemmas in Government: Designing an Organizational Response," *Public Personnel Management* 10 (1981): 11–19.

Bowman, James S., "The Management of Ethics: Codes of Conduct in Organizations," *Public Personnel Management* 10 (1981): 59–66.

Burnett, Arthur L., "Management's Positive Interest in Accountability Through Whistle-Blowing," *Bureaucrat* 9 (Summer 1980): 5–10.

Hays, Steven W., and Gleissner, Richard R., "Codes of Ethics in State Government: A Nationwide Survey," *Public Personnel Management* 10 (1981): 48–58.

Patriarche, John M., "Ethical Questions Which Administrators Face," *Public Management* 57 (June 1975): 17–19.

Peters, Charles, and Branch, Taylor, eds., *Blowing the Whistle: Dissent in the Public Interest,* New York: Praeger, 1972.

Rohr, John, *Ethics for Bureaucrats: An Essay on Law and Values,* New York: Marcel Dekker, 1978.

Wakefield, Susan, "Ethics and the Public Service: A Case for Individual Responsibility," *Public Administration Review* 36 (November/December 1976): 661–66.

Waldo, Dwight, "Reflections on Public Morality," *Administration and Society* 6 (November 1974): 267–82.

13

An Instance of
Racial Bias?

Union City advertised for a secretary-receptionist who could type forty-five words a minute and take shorthand. The advertisement required that the applicant be pleasant, well-groomed, and willing to perform housekeeping duties. The advertisement stated that the salary was negotiable, depending on experience.

Among the applicants was Lani Kolini, a male Iranian and naturalized citizen who lived in Union City. He was thirty years old and a college graduate. While at college, Kolini held office in several social and honor organizations. He had received no job offers upon graduation.

Kolini was interviewed by Roger Clark, the city manager. Clark, a staunch patriot, served in World War II and was still active in the army reserve and veterans' organizations. He was in his mid-fifties and the father of four boys. Although Clark had an uncanny way of letting everyone know he was the boss on all decisions, he got along well with city employees.

Kolini appeared for the interview with a small, well-groomed beard. When asked about the beard, he explained to Clark that he wore it because he wished to preserve his cultural heritage. Clark then questioned him about his connections with his native country and why he became a citizen of the United States. Kolini refused to answer the questions because he felt they were not job-related. Clark then told Kolini that if he were hired he would be expected to "perform some housekeeping duties" and "dress up the office." Kolini informed Clark that he always tried to be well groomed and pleasant but preferred not to wear a suit and tie or be someone's personal maid.

68

Kolini left the interview feeling that Clark had not treated him as a serious applicant for the position. He told his wife that the interview had been biased because he had not been questioned about his excellent credentials.

Kolini was not hired. Instead, Clark hired Rebecca Schlick, a 21-year-old high-school graduate with two years' experience as a receptionist-typist at a local Hilton Hotel. She had minimal secretarial skills but was attractive and had a winning personality.

Questions and Instructions

1. List several reasons why you would have hired Kolini for the job. List several reasons why you would not have done so.
2. What advice would you give Kolini regarding his next job interview?
3. Does an employer have a duty to hire an overqualified applicant rather than one who is minimally qualified?
4. What legal remedies are available to Kolini?
5. Does sexual discrimination extend to males in jobs that may have been traditionally held more often by women?

Selected Bibliography

Carlson, Robert E.; Thayer, Paul W; Mayfield, Eugene C.; and Peterson, Donald A., "Improvements in the Selection Interview," *Personnel Journal* 50 (April 1971): 268–75.

Clark, Alfred W., and Wotherspoon, Judith A., "Manager's Conflict: Democratic Management Versus Distrust of People's Capacity," *Psychological Reports* 32 (June 1973); 815–19.

Cohen, Stephen L., and Bunker, Kerry A., "Subtle Effects of Sex Role Stereotypes on Recruiters' Hiring Decisions," *Journal of Applied Psychology* 60 (October 1975): 566–72.

Dipboye, Robert L.; Arvey, Richard D.; and Terpstra, David E., "Equal Employment and the Interview," *Personnel Journal* 55 (October 1976): 520–22.

Gilmore, David C., and Ferris, Gerald R., "Effects of Mode of Information Presentation, Sex of Applicant, and Sex of Interviewer on Simulated Interview Decisions," *Psychological Reports* 40 (April 1977): 566.

———, "Problems in the Employment Interview," in Rowland, Kendrith M.; London, Manuel; Ferris, Gerald R.; and Sherman, Jay L., *Cur-

rent Issues in Personnel Management, Boston: Allyn and Bacon, 1980. pp. 51–58.

Greenlaw, Paul S., and Kohl, John P., "National Origin Discrimination and the New EEOC Guidelines," *Personnel Journal* 60 (August 1981): 634–36.

———, "Selection Interviewing and the New Uniform Federal Guidelines," *Personnel Administrator* 25 (August 1980): 74–80.

London, Manuel M., and Hakel, Milton O., "Effects of Applicant Stereotypes, Order and Information on Interview Impressions," *Journal of Applied Psychology* 59 (April 1975): 157–62.

Mitnick, Margery Manesberg, "Equal Employment Opportunity and Affirmative Action: A Managerial Training Guide," *Personnel Journal* 56 (October 1977): 492–97.

Morishima, James, "The Special Employment Issues for Asian Americans," *Public Personnel Management* 10 (No. 4, 1981): 384–92.

Rosen, Bernard, and Jerdee, Thomas H., "Influence of Sex-Role Stereotypes on Personnel Decisions," *Journal of Applied Psychology* 59 (February 1974): 9–14.

Simon, William A., Jr., "A Practical Approach to the Uniform Selection Guidelines," *Personnel Administrator* 24 (November 1979): 75–80.

14

A Leave of Absence

John Harris, head of the Second Regional Office of the State Service Bureau, had decided to take a leave of absence to assume a temporary position on the governor's task force on reorganization. He estimated that he would be gone for nine months. He had been in charge of the regional office since it was created ten years before.

In the past, Harris had received excellent performance evaluations from his supervisors and was respected for his administrative ability. He felt that recently he had not been getting the support from the central office he had once received. He attributed this to his office's high turnover and decreased productivity for the past two years and feared that his superiors believed he had lost his administrative talent. He was beginning to think he had been selected for the task force so that he could be replaced in an indirect manner. Since he had worked with the bureau for seventeen of its twenty years, he could not believe he would be asked to transfer or resign.

Two weeks before he was to report to the task force, he asked Richard Rhodes, chief administrator of the central office, how his replacement would be selected. Rhodes told Harris that he could select his own replacement from a list of candidates submitted by the bureau and from Harris's qualified subordinates.

Harris decided to examine the qualifications of each candidate and select the one with the weakest background. This, he thought, would enable him to return to his old job when his assignment on the task force was completed. After reviewing the list of candidates, Harris narrowed his choice to three people: Linda Smith, administrative assistant from Region One; Maxwell Jones, administrative assistant from Region Seven; and William Marx, from Harris's office.

71

In reviewing Linda Smith's and Maxwell Jones's files, Harris decided that they were very ambitious young people who might become a threat to his position. Both Smith and Jones had a master's degree and Harris feared that they might be thought more competent than he. Therefore, he decided to appoint Marx, who, he felt, had an adequate background and qualifications that would satisfy his superiors but who would not pose a serious threat. Marx had been loyal to him for years and always seemed to display great respect. Thus Harris believed Marx would hesitate before attempting to undermine him. Harris left for his new assignment confident that he had made the right decision.

When Marx assumed Harris's position, he directed his efforts toward achieving efficiency. He reorganized the structure of the office and specified distinct work assignments for each employee. He appointed a personnel assistant and an administrative assistant.

Marx thus assumed a rigid and highly structured approach in his new managerial capacity and achieved excellent results after only two months. These were noted by his superiors, who expressed their appreciation for this attention to increased efficiency. However, after five months, problems began to develop that were unnoticed by Marx. Many of his subordinates begin to feel they were being worked too hard. They believed that Marx was overly rigid and that a break was developing in their communications with one another.

Before two more months had passed, Richard Rhodes, chief administrator at the central office, received a message informing him that Harris would complete his assignment in two weeks and was preparing to resume his position at the Second Regional Office. Rhodes was faced with the problem of deciding whether to replace Harris with Marx. He had never had a problem with Harris in the past and still thought Harris was capable of resuming his old post. But, unaware of the staff criticism of Marx, he believed Marx had been doing a better job.

Rhodes realized he would never have thought of replacing Harris had the task-force assignment not come up, putting Marx in Harris's place. Rhodes was also aware of the problems confronting Harris's office at the time Harris was there but had passed them off believing they were caused by some external or coincidental factors—nothing Harris could not handle. However, when Marx's reorganization and strict managerial approach were implemented and highly positive results appeared, he began to question Harris's ability. He thought that perhaps Marx's approach was necessary at this time to correct the office's problems.

Questions and Instructions

1. Compare and contrast Harris's and Marx's management styles. For whom would you rather work?

2. Discuss several choices available to Rhodes in resolving the problem. What are some of the things Rhodes should consider before making a final decision?
3. How could Rhodes have prevented this problem from occurring?
4. Discuss the ethical implications of Harris's decision to choose the least-qualified person as his temporary successor?

Selected Bibliography

Balk, Walter L., "Toward a Government Productivity Ethic," *Public Administration Review* 38 (January/February 1978): 15–18.

Bavelos, Alex, and Barrett, Dermot, "An Experimental Approach to Organizational Communication," in Mankin, Don; Ames, Russell E., Jr.; and Gordsky, Milton A., eds., *Classics of Industrial and Organizational Psychology,* Oak Park, Ill.; Moore Publishing Co., 1980. pp. 476–94.

Bok, Sissela, *Lying: Moral Choice in Public and Private Life,* New York: Pantheon Books, 1978.

Boling, T. Edwin, and Dempsey, John, "Ethical Dilemmas in Government: Designing an Organizational Response," *Public Personnel Management* 10 (1981): 11–19.

Bowman, James, "Managerial Ethics in Business and Government," *Business Horizons* 19 (October 1976): 48–54.

Churchman, C. West, "The Myth of Management," in Matteson, Michael T., and Ivancevich, John M., eds., *Management Classics,* Santa Monica, Calif.: Goodyear Publishing Co., 1977. pp. 406–14.

Hurka, Slavek J., "Managers of Professional Departments in Teaching Hospitals: A Study of Satisfaction," *Journal of Health and Human Resources Administration* 3 (November 1980): 192–200.

Mosher, Frederick C., "Some Notes on Reorganizations in Public Agencies," in Lane, Frederick S., *Managing State and Local Government: Cases and Readings,* New York: St. Martin's Press, 1980. pp. 117–37.

Prudent, H. O., "The Upward Mobile, Indifferent and Ambivalent Typology of Managers," *Academy of Management Journal* 16 (September 1973): 454–64.

Van Maanen, John; Lotte, Bailyn; and Schein, Edgar H., "The Shape of Things to Come: A New Look at Organizational Careers," in Hackman, J. Richard; Lawler, Edward E., III; and Porter, Lyman W., *Perspectives on Behavior in Organizations,* New York: McGraw-Hill, 1977.

15

Public Safety vs. Union Labor

The late-November weather was beautiful as the city manager, Carla James, settled down to work on a Friday morning. However, the forecast called for rain with scattered light snow flurries by nightfall. By midafternoon, a full-scale blizzard was in the making. James began outlining plans for snow removal. Her job as city manager included handling public emergencies, and she was determined that no one would have cause to accuse City Hall of negligence.

By Saturday morning the blizzard was going full force. City policy dictated that the street crew not work while the wind was still blowing. Clearing the streets would be useless, since the snow would be blown into drifts that would block traffic. James and a few staff members who could get to work sought to assure citizens in news broadcasts that the roads would be cleared as soon as possible. Final schedules were prepared for overtime work for the regular street crew and as soon as the snow stopped blowing the crew was dispatched. After they had worked a sixteen-hour shift, James asked employees from other departments to help remove snow so that the street crew could rest. Several employees and a city councilman, Joe Carleton, volunteered their services. All except Carleton were to be compensated at their usual overtime rate. Everything was operating as planned until the new crew was preparing to take over the snow-removal process.

James received a frantic call from Carleton. The AFL-CIO Municipal Workers Union, which represented Street Department employees, was refusing to let volunteers replace the street crew. James headed for the Municipal Service Center where the dispute was taking place. She had talked with union leaders barely two hours before and had reassured

74

them that bringing in other workers was not meant to weaken union influence. Union officials had told her they had no objection to the plans for a relief crew, but now they were refusing to cooperate.

When James arrived at the center the situation was tense. Carleton was jumping up and down yelling, "To hell with your damn union!" James's first task was to calm Carleton. No understanding could be reached if he continued to insult the union. After all rational methods of placating the councilman failed, James took him aside. As Carleton continued to fume, James said decisively, "All further discussions of this problem will be conducted between the union representative and myself."

James reminded the union officials that this was a public emergency. They responded by accusing her of using the emergency to deprive Street Department employees of earning additional overtime. They also said they would not allow nonunion city employees to perform the designated work of union workers. James argued that several of the volunteers, although not employed by the Street Department, were union members. James replied, "This is not just a union matter! We have a matter of public safety that must be swiftly dealt with." The union officials agreed, but felt that transferring union workers outside their regular job classifications would establish an undesirable precedent.

James knew that union membership had been declining over the last few years. Only 30 percent of the city employees eligible for membership belonged to it. Since the union contract was to be negotiated in three weeks, she felt that union officials were using this incident to impress their members and to gain leverage at the bargaining table.

Questions and Instructions

1. Did James make adequate preparations for dealing with emergency snow removal? What factors should she have considered and planned for?
2. What course of action is available to James in dealing with the snow-removal problem once the union has entered the scene?
3. How should James deal with the union representative?
4. If you were a union representative, what course of action would you plan to take during this crisis?
5. Should the city manager consult with other council members or the city attorney before making a decision about assigning nonunion employees to the street crew?
6. Do you think that other city employees share the sentiments of the union officials?

7. Are the union officials justified in their demands? What is the potential impact of the union's position on public support for the union's actions?

Selected Bibliography

Atwood, Jay F., "Collective Bargaining's Challenge: Five Imperatives for Public Managers," *Public Personnel Management* 5 (January/ February 1976): 24–31.

Dyer, Lee; Schwab, Donald P.; and Fossum, John A., "Impacts of Pay on Employee Behaviors and Attitudes: An Update," in Glueck, William F., *Personnel: A Book of Readings,* Dallas: Business Publications, 1979. pp. 270–78.

Hampton, David R.; Summer, Charles E.; and Webber, Ross A., *Organization Behavior and the Practice of Management,* 3rd ed., Glenview, Ill.: Scott, Foresman, 1978. Ch. 10, "Leadership," pp. 595–661.

Long, Norton E., "Public/Private Coalition: Hope for Urban Survival," *National Civic Review* 69 (October 1980): 484–90.

Martin, James E., and Biasatti, Lawrence L., "A Hierarchy of Important Elements in Union-Management Relations," *Journal of Management* 5 (Fall 1979): 299–40.

Mathis, Robert L., and Jackson, John H., *Personnel: Contemporary Perspectives and Applications,* 3rd ed., St. Paul: West Publishing Co., 1982. Section VII, "Organization/Union Interfaces," pp. 465–518.

Nigro, Felix A., and Nigro, Lloyd G., "Public Sector Unionism," in Levine, Charles, ed., *Managing Human Resources: A Challenge to Urban Governments,* Beverly Hills, Calif.: Sage, 1977.

Stanley, David T., *Managing Local Government Under Union Pressure,* Washington, D.C.: The Brookings Institution, 1972. Ch. 1, "Public Administration and Unions in Nineteen Local Governments," pp. 1–15, and Ch. 5, "Effect on Work Management and Working Conditions," pp. 89–111.

Wellington, Harry H., and Winter, Ralph K., Jr., "The Limits of Collective Bargaining in Public Employment," in Chickering, A. Lawrence, *Public Employee Unions: A Study of the Crisis in Public Sector Labor Relations,* San Francisco: Institute for Contemporary Studies, 1976. pp. 51–75.

16

Old Friendships

Two months ago, Tom Gordon was promoted to manager of operations of the Kennedy Recreation Center in Unionville. Gordon and his staff had been working overtime in planning the summer program. After discussing staffing requirements with the city's director of the Parks and Recreation Department, Gordon was granted an additional position. According to department policy, Gordon would be responsible for interviewing applicants and selecting the person to fill the new position.

Gordon was somewhat insecure in his job. His promotion had involved a transfer from another recreation center and he was relatively unacquainted with staff members at the Kennedy Center. He had recently learned that several of his colleagues had sought the position he now held. Other than that, nothing had occurred that would indicate there was any opposition to his appointment. Thinking he had to develop more self-confidence to become an effective leader at Kennedy, Gordon felt he should make his decision without consulting anyone else.

There were five applicants on the eligibility list. Gordon recognized one familiar name, Sam Cook. Gordon and Cook had been close friends several years before but had not kept in contact for some time. Gordon was aware that Cook had had some trouble with the law in his youth. When he was sixteen he had stolen a car and while being pursued by the police had had an accident in which several people were seriously injured. The accident occurred in the same minority community that the Kennedy Center served. Cook's employment record in the intervening years had been exemplary, however, and his employers had praised his job performance. He was married and had begun a family since Gordon last saw him.

The other applicants did not appear so well qualified as Cook. One who worked as a student intern in the Parks and Recreation Department received an unfavorable report from the manager of another recreation center. Another with previous experience had been discharged several years earlier and was reputed to have strong racial biases. The remaining two were college graduates with no work experience. While this lack of experience did not eliminate them, Gordon preferred a person with some on-the-job training.

After interviewing all of the applicants and checking their references, Gordon was convinced that Cook was the most qualified candidate. He felt that he could work best with Cook but was concerned about community reaction because of the incident in Cook's youth. Even if he had not been Cook's friend, Gordon would be inclined to hire him because he believed people were capable of rehabilitation and should not be denied equal consideration.

Questions and Instructions

1. Is Gordon unfair to those without experience?
2. Is Gordon too concerned with doing a favor for an old friend? Would choosing an old friend be a good idea?
3. Should Cook's past prevent him from being considered for the position? Would the fact that he now has a good work record be a point in his favor in the community?
4. Would Cook be best advised to seek a job at another location where his past would not be known?
5. Since Gordon has so many doubts about hiring Cook, should he reconsider his decision not to consult the Parks and Recreation director about the appointment?

Selected Bibliography

Blake, Robert R., and Mouton, Jane S., "Grid Organizational Development," in Mankin, Don; Ames, Russell E., Jr.; and Grodsky, Milton A., *Classics of Industrial and Organizational Psychology,* Oak Park, Ill.: Moore Publishing Co., 1980. pp. 540–55.

Cronback, Lee J., "Selection Theory for a Political World," *Public Personnel Management* 9 (January/February 1980): 37–50.

"Ethics: Dictates and Dilemmas," *Public Management* (Special Issue on ICMA Code of Ethics), 63 (March 1981): 2–22.

Klinefelter, John, and Thompkins, James, "Adverse Impact in Employment Selection," *Public Personnel Management* 5 (May/June 1976): 199–204.

Korman, Abraham K., "Personnel Selection: The Traditional Models," in Korman, Abraham K., *Industrial and Organizational Psychology,* Englewood Cliffs, N.J.: Prentice-Hall, 1971. pp. 179–204.

Madden, Carl, "Forces Which Influence Ethical Behavior," in Walton, Clarence, *The Ethics of Corporate Conduct,* Englewood Cliffs, N.J.: Prentice-Hall, 1977. pp. 31–78.

Shoop, Robert, "Public Personnel Selection: A Matter of Consistency," *Public Personnel Management* 3 (July/August 1974): 341–43.

17

No Clean Sweep in Winchester

Under attack from a newly formed Tax Reduction League, inspired in part by the success of the Proposition 13 agitation in California, the city of Winchester in 1980 reduced the ad valorem tax by a rate that amounted to a municipal budget cut of 5 percent. Winchester is a city of 150,000 population in the upper Midwest. It is the center of a rich agricultural district but also is highly industrialized with a serious air-pollution problem.

Faced with instructions from the City Council to effect savings in the Department of Public Works in order to reduce fuel consumption and keep within the smaller budget, Superintendent Fleming Hartman thought hard about what services could be eliminated and what maintenance costs could be cut. He decided that major savings could be made in the street-cleaning department. Clean streets were desirable, he thought, but they were not essential as were other maintenance services. With the approval of the mayor and City Council he relegated the sweeping schedule on a regular basis to the downtown streets and main thoroughfares. Residential streets were cleaned only in response to complaints and then only if they were close to an arterial street. He was able to sell four sweepers and two flushers and cut the work force from twenty-four to twelve. Fuel consumption was substantial in street cleaning—each sweeper used 5,000 gallons of fuel a year—and the sale of the equipment saved about 20,000 gallons.

The new street-cleaning plan went into operation in February. The first adverse reaction came after the last snowfall in late March. The sweepers took several days to clean up the sand and other abrasives, curb-deep in some places, that had been spread to improve driving conditions. Complaints poured into the office of the Public Works Department, the two local television stations showed films of the accumulated grit, the *Daily Bulletin* editorialized against the inefficiency of the street department, and the mayor telephoned Superintendent Hartman demanding that something be done immediately to reverse the usual complaint and get the public off his back.

The complaints did not end after the clean-up of sand. As spring advanced, unsightly litter accumulated, paper was blown into yards and against buildings and fences, beer and soft-drink cans tinkled as they were propelled down the street by the wind, and dust and soot sometimes filled the air. Moreover, the lake in Winchester's large Greenbriar Park became increasingly polluted from the streams and storm drainage flowing into it.

In 1980 the Tax Reduction League had been the voice of the people. As 1981 progressed it was replaced by environmental groups and neighborhood associations crying out against the dirt and litter. "Clean Up Winchester" was the slogan adopted by these various groups. As a result the City Council gave street sweeping a high priority in drawing up the budget for 1982–83. But though many were concerned about municipal aesthetics, many also were concerned about high taxes. A state-mandated property-reassessment program that would raise ad valorem taxes, the loss of federal funds in the New Federalism program of the national administration, and finally inflationary costs made it difficult for the City Council to provide a balanced budget without a tax increase, anathema to the people. To avoid or minimize a tax increase, the council ordered department heads to develop user fees in budget areas where rates could be established to pay for programs.

Public Works Superintendent Hartman received an extra instruction in formulating his proposal: he was to do everything possible about meeting the pressures to keep Winchester's streets clean.

Questions and Instructions

1. What fees could a municipal public-works department propose? Should there be a special fee for street cleaning or could the fee be collected from other services performed by the city?
2. What street-cleaning program, including number of sweepers, flushers, and other equipment, work and supervisory force, and frequency of cleaning, would you propose for Winchester?
3. Discuss the possibility of contracting with a private firm for performing the street-cleaning job.
4. In what other areas of municipal management might private con-

tractors replace city employees in performing services and maintenance?

Selected Bibliography

Ahlbrandt, Roger S., Jr., "Implications of Contracting for Public Service," *Urban Affairs Quarterly* 9 (March 1974): 337–58.

Florestano, Patricia S., and Gordon, Stephen B., "Public vs. Private: Small Government Contracting with the Private Sector," *Public Administration Review* 40 (January/February 1980): 29–34.

———, "Private Provision of Public Services: Contracting by Large Local Governments," *International Journal of Public Administration* 1 (1979): 307–27.

———, "Contracting with the Private Sector," *National Civic Review* 71 (July–August 1982):350–57.

Hayes, Frederick O., "City and County Productivity Programs," *Public Administration Review* 38 (January/February 1978): 15–18.

Honadle, Beth Walter, "Interlocal Cooperation," *National Civic Review* 71 (July–August 1982): 362–64.

Mehavy, Stephen L., "Intergovernmental Contracting for Municipal Police Services: An Empirical Analysis," *Land Economics* 55 (February 1979): 59–72.

Morgan, David R.; Meyer, Michael E.; and England, Robert E., "Alternatives to Municipal Service Delivery: A Four-State Comparison," *Southern Review of Public Administration* 5 (Summer 1981): 184–98.

Pitt, Robert, "Why Street Cleaning Is Worth the Effort," *American City and County* 95 (April 1980): 41–43.

Ridings, Richard L., " 'User Fee' Pays for Clean Streets," *American City and County* 97 (February 1981): 43–44.

Savas, E. S., "An Empirical Study of Competition in Municipal Service Delivery," *Public Administration Review,* 37 (November/December 1977): 717–24.

———, "Policy Analysis for Local Government: Public vs. Private Refuse Collection," *Policy Analysis* 3 (Winter 1977): 49–74.

Sonenblum, Sidney; Kirlin, John J.; and Ries, John C., *How Cities Provide Services: An Evaluation of Alternative Delivery Structures,* Cambridge, Mass.: Ballinger Publishing Co., 1977.

"Street Sweeping Blues? Try Contracting the Service Out," *American City and County* 96 (September 1981): 55–61.

18

Preservation of Public Lands

The Department of the Interior was considering whether to act on a proposal by James Carlson, director of the western regional agency of the National Park Service, that 20,000 square miles of park land be designated as a habitat reserve for the protection of endangered animals. It would include all the area within Glacier National Park in Montana, the Yellowstone–Grand Teton National Parks in Wyoming, and about 50 percent of the mountain region between the parks. Part of this land was located in the mineral-rich Western Overthrust Belt.

The western regional agency had existed for only six months and had been established to coordinate operations of National Park offices in the western part of the country. Carlson's appointment surprised many people in the Department of the Interior. Although Carlson had an excellent record, many thought that at age thirty-six he was too young and inexperienced to assume such a responsible position. Carlson came from a socially prominent family in the East, was well educated, and viewed himself as an advocate of change.

Because he had been in his new position for a short time, Carlson did not have the opportunity to discuss his proposal with John Stevens, director of Yellowstone–Grand Teton National Park, and Guy Williams, director of Glacier National Park.

Stevens had been the National Park director in Wyoming for twenty-six years. Over the years he had developed a network of close ties with the state's political leaders and was on a first-name basis with most of the public officials. As director, he had advocated the expansion of business enterprises throughout the natural wonderland. Even though economic and tourist-trade functions were not within the scope of his responsibilities, he felt that more businesses in the area would attract more tourists to the park and thus bring more money into the state.

Guy Williams, on the other hand, was interested in preserving the original purpose in the development of national parks in this country. He felt that Glacier Park and the surrounding mountain regions should remain "just as men like Jim Bridger and John Colter found them." He viewed his responsibility as centering on park preservation and effective game management. Citing income from nonresident hunters as a prime example, he argued that proper game management could be as economically healthy to the state as the expansion of commercial businesses in the park area.

When Stevens read about Carlson's proposal for the special habitat reserve in the newspaper, he immediately telephoned Williams. "What the hell is that idiot Carlson up to?" he asked Williams. "Doesn't he know what his stupid proposal will do to the tourist business in our states?"

"Take it easy, John," said Williams. "Carlson knows what he is doing. His proposal will be good for the tourist business. It will help preserve the status of our parks for years to come."

"You're as crazy as Carlson," said Stevens. "I've had farmers and ranchers calling me all morning. They're scared that the federal government is going to take away their federally owned or leased land and are worried about what's going to happen to their livestock if we turn this area into an African game refuge. Owners of motels, restaurants, souvenir shops, and gas stations need customers to make a living, not game animals. They're livid. This young fellow comes out here and doesn't know either the politics or the economics that are affected by his environmental proposal. This whole project is a waste of the taxpayers' money."

"Get with the times, John," said Williams. "Environmentalism is an important issue today. We need to protect this land because it's unique. Carlson is just responding to public demand."

"You two were together in this all the time," screamed Stevens. "I'll nail both your hides to the wall before this is over."

Questions and Instructions

1. What is your opinion of Carlson's proposal? Would it be beneficial to the region in terms of the people and economy of the area?
2. Do you think Carlson's proposal is likely to be approved? What effect will it have on Carlson's career if it fails?
3. Was Carlson's surprise statement the best way to announce the

refuge proposal? What could Carlson have done to increase the probability of success for his proposal?

4. How sensitive should federal administrators be to the needs and concerns of people affected by their decision? Is there anything in Carlson's proposal that shows federal-state cooperation? federal-state competition?

5. Should a decision on the use of this land be based on a cost-benefit analysis? What are the advantages or disadvantages of employing a cost-benefit analysis in this matter? What information would you need to make a cost-benefit analysis?

Selected Bibliography

Filley, Alan C.; House, Robert J.; and Kerr, Steven, *Managerial Process and Organizational Behavior,* 2nd ed., Glenview, Ill.: Scott, Foresman, 1976. Ch. 17, "Professionals in Organizations and Line-Staff Relationships," pp. 380–409, Ch. 9, "Conflict Resolution and Problem Solving," pp. 162–82.

Hanke, Steven H., "On the Feasibility of Cost Benefit Analysis," *Public Policy* 29 (Spring 1981): 147–57.

Hardin, Garrett, "The Tragedy of the Commons," *Science* 162 (1968): 1243–48.

Leavitt, Harold J., *Managerial Psychology,* 4th ed., Chicago: University of Chicago Press, 1978. Ch. 13, "Power Tactics, Pressure and Coercion: A Second Model for Influence," pp. 148–55.

Likert, Rensis, *New Patterns of Management,* New York: McGraw-Hill, 1961. See "The Principle of Supportive Relationships," pp. 103–18.

Mishan, Edward J., *Cost Benefit Analysis: An Introduction,* New York: Praeger Press, 1976.

Peters, B. Guy, "Insiders and Outsiders: The Politics of Pressure Group Influence on Bureaucracy," *Administration and Society* 9 (August 1977): 191–218.

Tannenbaum, Robert, and Schmidt, Warren H., "How to Choose a Leadership Pattern," *Harvard Business Review* 51 (May/June 1973); 162–72.

19

An Authoritarian Approach to Management

Richard Patton had grown up in a small town in a largely rural Midwestern state whose economy was based on agriculture. His parents were hard-working and devout and subjected their children to severe discipline. As a boy Patton did odd jobs to pay for his own clothes and school supplies. He was a typical product of a society that valued the work ethic: disciplined, conservative, industrious, and respectful of authority.

At the university, where he studied public administration, Patton was mainly interested in those aspects of courses that he considered down-to-earth. He found theoretical and philosophical propositions boring, because he had difficulty in applying the abstract to practical matters.

Upon graduation Patton got his first job in his own state as an assistant to the director of the Social Welfare Department in Jefferson County, a rural county with about 40,000 people that was neither wealthy nor poor. Demands on social-welfare services were not great, and the problems facing the department staff of ten were readily taken care of. Patton won the respect of his director and coworkers by his conscientious work and reliability. When the director moved on after a year, Patton succeeded him in the post.

A year later Patton accepted an offer to direct a department in a large county with more industry, a more varied economy, and a more diverse population than Jefferson County. Patton became head of a department with forty staff members that was governed by the Polk County Board of Commissioners and the county Social Service Commission. Though the county had a mixed population that included Indians, Chicanos, and blacks, no members of these groups worked at the department. It was a typical public-welfare agency, administered by the county, supervised by the state, and funded by the county, state, and federal governments. Its program included Aid for Families with Dependent Children (AFDC), Work Incentive (WIN), Supplemental Security Income (SSI), and Medicaid, administered under guidelines set by the state and federal governments.

The staff members, Patton soon discovered, frequently failed to follow guidelines and even appeared unfamiliar with them, applied rules inconsistently, and were sometimes indifferent to their clients' needs. Employees often arrived late at the office, took time off without permission to take care of personal matters, left clients waiting while getting coffee or chatting with fellow employees, and in general were inefficient and lackadaisical. Patton found few of them had the education and training for their work and quickly discovered the reason: qualified people were hard to obtain because of the low pay scale, the minimum acceptable by state requirements. The county commissioners, all conservative politically and economically, held budgets to the lowest possible level. Salary levels in all county offices were not competitive with those in the private sector.

Patton's initial review of the agency revealed that three persons appeared potentially useful in establishing an organizational structure to replace the present slipshod operation. They were the assistant director and two others who had ill-defined supervisory powers.

The course of action to reform the agency appeared clear to Patton. What was needed was a highly structured and disciplined organization. He envisioned himself as keeping a finger on all the programs administered by the agency. Supervisors would be selected from within the organization. Authority would be delegated to the supervisors, and line workers would be classified according to a strict hierarchy. Jobs would be highly specialized and all employees would be trained to do their job in a prescribed manner. Weekly staff meetings would be used to review and modify work styles and to inculcate respect for authority.

In putting his plans into effect Patton rejected suggestions of the workers. He felt that their ideas on pay, job design, and office procedures had no place in a well-run operation. "If they don't like the way the office is run, they can work some other place," he said. Despite Patton's authoritarian approach to management, some improvement was beginning to be made. The office was brightened by fresh paint and the furniture was rearranged so that counselors had more privacy in discussing problems with their clients. Responsibility for certain tasks was assigned to specific people, files were kept up-to-date, and client requests were handled more quickly. Patton and his supervisors, carefully chosen from among the staff, seemed to receive proper respect from other employees.

But dissatisfaction and dissent soon boiled over. Line workers challenged Patton's edicts at staff meetings, complained about many of the imposed rules and regulations, wrangled over policies and goals, and threatened to appeal to the governing boards.

Patton's supervisors periodically approached him with suggestions for changes. Patton was upset and felt they were interfering with his prerogatives as an administrator, yet he was willing to listen to their opinions, especially because he began to fear losing his job if the extent of the objections among the staff reached the agency's governing boards.

The supervisors explained to him that many improvements had been made in the department, but they believed the administrative structure had to be made more responsive to staff personnel. They suggested that staff input in salary plans, office-procedural policies, and staff meetings be increased and that a program of upgrading jobs and pay be introduced. They thought that an administrative system could be too strict. The department under the former director had not been tightly controlled but the work got done and the public seemed satisfied as to the level of service delivery.

It was hard for Patton to believe he had been wrong in thinking the welfare department needed the imposition of a more rigid system, but he now recognized that his reforms had failed and that there were aspects of management to which he had been blind.

Questions and Instructions

1. Granted that the welfare department needed to be made more efficient, what course could Patton have followed to make his reforms more acceptable to his staff?
2. What needed changes in the department did Patton overlook?
3. What courses of action would you recommend for Patton to correct his mistakes?
4. Would another organizational theory and management practice have been more appropriate for the welfare department than that followed by Patton? Explain.
5. What are some of the organizational factors that can impede change? facilitate change? How can resistance to change be overcome?

Selected Bibliography

Adizes, Ichak, and Borgese, Elisabeth Mann, eds., *Self-Management: New Dimensions to Democracy,* Santa Barbara, Calif.: Clio Press, 1975, pp. 3–37.

Carroll, Stephen J., and Tosi, Henry L., *Organizational Behavior,* Chicago, St. Clair Press, 1977. Ch. 13, "Managing Human Resources in the Hierarchical Organization," pp. 365–98.

Drucker, Peter F., "The Deadly Sins in Public Administration," *Public Administration Review* 40 (March/April 1980): 103–6.

Gortner, Harold F., *Administration in the Public Sector,* 2nd ed., New York: John Wiley and Sons, 1981. Ch. 11, "Control: Planning's Other Face," pp. 242–63.

Latham, Gary P., and Wexley, Kenneth N., *Increasing Productivity Through Performance Appraisal,* Reading, Mass.: Addison-Wesley Publishing Co., 1981. Ch. 7, "Conducting Formal and Informal Performance Appraisals," pp. 149–73.

Lawler, Edward E., III, "Should the Quality of Work Life Be Legislated?" in Glueck, William F., *Personnel: A Book of Readings,* Dallas: Business Publications, 1979. pp. 76–82.

Likert, Rensis, *New Patterns of Management,* New York: McGraw-Hill, 1961.

Locke, Edwin A., "The Case Against Legislating the Quality of Work Life," in Glueck, William F., *Personnel: A Book of Readings,* Dallas: Business Publications, 1979. pp. 83–85.

Natemeyer, Walter E., ed., *Classics of Organizational Change,* Oak Park, Ill.: Moore Publishing Co., 1978. Section VI, "Organizational Change and Development," pp. 298–362.

Present, Phillip E., *People and Public Administration,* Pacific Palisades, Calif.: Palisades Publishers, 1979. See Topic 3, "The Individual and the Organization," pp. 95–130.

Siedman, Harold, *Politics, Position, and Power,* 3rd ed., New York: Oxford University Press, 1980. See pp. 24–30 for a discussion of the strategic and tactical uses of reorganization, and pp. 191–92 for an analysis of local governmental agency response.

Terpstra, David E., "Theories of Motivation—Borrowing the Best," *Personnel Journal* 58 (June 1979): 376–83.

20

A Question of Contamination

Henry Erickson had been assistant to the director of the State Department of Environmental Protection for eight years. In addition to his regular duties, he had been recently assigned by the department director, Mark Simpson, to serve as public relations representative. His new assignment was the result of a memo received from the governor's office. The governor, attempting to improve the public image of officials, directed all departments to appoint a senior employee to be responsible for improving the relationship between state government and the public. His memo emphasized the importance of providing accurate and complete information to the public with minimal delay. In addition, the public was to be informed of the responsibilities and operation of each major department. The governor hoped that his campaign of "selling government to the people" would reverse the growing trend of public criticism of state officials.

Erickson was impressed by the governor's new policy. He felt that too often government failed to be responsive to the public. However, he was aware of the difficulties of his task. To be truly effective required a great deal of time. On occasion it seemed to him that officials spent more time polishing their image than providing the basic services of their department. Despite these difficulties, Erickson felt the new policy was desirable and decided he would make every effort to comply.

About eight months later, the governor's new policy seemed to be succeeding. The press was becoming less critical, and Erickson noticed a slight change of attitude in people requesting information from his department. The governor had just successfully completed a primary election battle, helped, Erickson thought, by his slogan calling for "open government."

About this time, Erickson received a request for assistance from a rancher, Oscar Walton, in the western part of the state who said that in the past two weeks nearly two hundred of his cattle had mysteriously died. The rancher explained that he had analyzed the water sources on his land and the cattle's feed but could not determine the cause of death. He was afraid of losing the rest of his herd.

Erickson told the rancher that he would use all of the department's resources to help him solve the problem. During the course of his investigation, Erickson uncovered an apparent conflict of interest involving Ralph Fitzgerald, the attorney general. Fitzgerald had a large investment in a chemical company, the Fast Grow Corporation, that produced fertilizer. A year and a half before, the Department of Environmental Protection had investigated possible water pollution caused by use of the firm's fertilizer. Although there was no conclusive evidence, it was strongly suspected that certain chemicals in the fertilizer could contaminate local water-drainage areas. However, the department decided to stop its investigation. It was rumored that Fitzgerald and the Environmental Protection director, Mark Simpson, had come to an agreement.

Erickson consulted with some colleagues in his office concerning this matter. He was uncertain as to the amount of information he should provide his constituent. If the fertilizer was contaminating water-drainage areas, it would provide at least a partial explanation of the rancher's problem. If, however, he was wrong, he might face a possible damage suit from the fertilizer company. In addition, Director Simpson soon learned that new inquiries were being made into this matter and called on Erickson to ask him about the investigation. Simpson opened the meeting by saying, "I hear you have reopened the investigation on the cattle deaths at the Walton ranch." Erickson replied that he had and that it was in response to the governor's policy.

After some further talk, Simpson told Erickson, "Look, I can't go into the details, but there are too many people involved in the Fast Grow Corporation who are either prominent Democrats or large financial contributors to the governor's campaign. We cannot afford to be open on this one. There could be too many heads to roll including mine and perhaps yours. We are fortunate that Fitzgerald, who wants to run against the governor next time, is involved." Erickson's dilemma had increased; he wondered if he should pursue the investigation or drop it.

Questions and Instructions

1. Where does Erickson's loyalty lie in this situation—with the public, with his department, or with his own integrity?

2.   If Erickson decides to blow the whistle in this case, what would be his best course of action?
3.   On the evidence he now has of the possible environmental dangers of the fertilizer, should Erickson inform the public? If so, should he leak the information to the press or identify himself as the source? What would be the likely consequences of each action?
4.   In view of the governor's campaign slogan of "open government," do you think his chance for reelection would be harmed by disclosure?

Selected Bibliography

Aldrich, Howard, "Organization Boundaries and Inter-organizational Conflict," *Human Relations* 24 (August 1971): 279–93.

Aram, John D., *Dilemmas of Administrative Behavior,* Englewood Cliffs, N.J.: Prentice-Hall, 1976.

Armstrong, DeWitt C., III, and Graham, George A., "Ethical Preparation for the Public Service," *Bureaucrat* 4 (April 1975): 5–22.

Bailey, Stephen K., "Ethics and the Public Service," *Public Administration Review* 24 (December 1964): 234–43.

Blake, Eugene Carson, "Should the Code of Ethics in Public Life Be Absolute or Relative?" *Annals of the American Academy of Political and Social Science* 363 (January 1966): 4–11.

Boling, T. Edwin, "Organizational Ethics: Rules, Creativity, and Idealism," in Sutherland, John W., *Management Handbook for Public Administrators,* New York: Van Nostrand Reinhold, 1978. pp. 221–53.

Caiden, Gerald E., "Ethics in the Public Service: Codification Misses the Real Target," *Public Personnel Management* 10 (1981): 146–52.

Cooper, Melvin G., "Administering Ethics Laws: The Alabama Experience," *National Civic Review* 68 (February 1979): 77–81.

Dometrius, Nelson C., "State Government Administration and the Electoral Process," *State Government* 53 (Summer 1980): 129–34.

Fletcher, Thomas W., and McGwire, John M., "Government and Private Business: New Relationships Emerging," *National Civic Review* 69 (October 1980): 491–96.

Foster, Gregory D., "Legalism, Moralism, and the Bureaucratic Mentality," *Public Personnel Management* 10 (1981): 93–97.

Frome, Michael, "Blowing the Whistle," *The Center Magazine* 11 (November/December 1978): 50–58.

Lovrich, Nicholas P., "Professional Ethics and the Public Interest: Sources of Judgment," *Public Personnel Management* 10 (1981): 87–92.
Rohr, John A., "Financial Disclosure: Power in Search of Policy," *Public Personnel Management* 10 (1981): 29–40.
"Symposium: Public Administration as a Profession," *Southern Review of Public Administration,* 5 (Fall 1981): 237–391.
Walton, Richard E.; Dutton, John M.; and Cafferty, Thomas P., "Organizational Context and Interdepartmental Conflict," *Administrative Science Quarterly* 14 (December 1969): 522–42.

21

Unifying the Department of Corrections

Matt Steele was employed by the State Department of Corrections and Public Safety. This department provided the administrative support staff to the State Criminal Justice Commission, which had final authority over the distribution of federal funds to state and local criminal-court agencies. In addition to its fiscal function, the commission served as an administrative body in developing criminal-justice policy in the state.

Steele, as the court program administrator, was responsible for planning and coordinating the activities of the prosecution and defense agencies. In addition, he was responsible for informing the commission of pending criminal-justice legislation and was periodically required to testify before legislative committees on criminal-justice policy issues.

Steele had been working for the Department of Corrections and Public Safety for six years. Initially, his efforts were frustrating and fruitless. He found that the relationship between the court agencies and the Department of Corrections and Public Safety was strained and at times dysfunctional. Only during the past year had he been able to make progress in improving the relationship. He was excited about some new and much-needed programs that he planned to implement with the cooperation of state and local court agencies.

For several years the State Criminal Justice Commission had been concerned with the delivery of correctional services in the state. One year before, the commission funded a study of state correctional services that was conducted and prepared by a nationally known consulting firm. The report concluded that correctional services in the state were fragmented and inefficient. As a result of this study, the commission recommended legislation to the governor establishing a unified Department of Corrections. The governor endorsed the recommendation in his State of the State address. He pointed out that the state's Criminal Justice Commission supported the concept of a unified Department of Corrections and that federal funds would be available to defer the state's cost for the first three years of the department's operation.

One week later legislation establishing a unified Department of Corrections was introduced in the Senate and House. The legislation called for consolidating the correctional services provided by the Department of Social Services, the Unified Judicial System, and the Board of Charities and Corrections into one department. The proposed department would be responsible for all correctional services under the direction of a new cabinet-level secretary.

There was an immediate backlash from the affected agencies. Since the courts were currently responsible for probation services provided by court service workers, there was an intense feeling that this legislation was a direct attempt by the governor to circumvent the independent power of the courts. As the legislative session progressed, the issue became more controversial and the judges were openly campaigning against the legislation. The commission and the governor would not compromise their position concerning adult and juvenile probation. It was apparent that bitter feelings would result on both sides of the issue regardless of the outcome of the legislation.

Steele was in the center of the controversy. He knew he would be required to testify in support of the legislation, yet he felt his testimony would ruin the progress he had already made with the courts as court program administrator. He strongly believed in the concept of unified corrections because he had worked as a juvenile probation officer and was aware of the fragmentation in the corrections system. However, his primary responsibility as court program administrator required a good working relationship with the courts.

Questions and Instructions

1. Explain what you would do if you were in Steele's position.
2. Is there any way that Steele can bring about legislative changes that will result in a favorable policy for his department?
3. What are some advantages and limitations associated with cen-

tralization by function? some advantages and disadvantages associated with decentralization?
4. Should probation service be an executive or a judicial function?
5. If Steele argues for the administrative position, what data and information would enhance that position?

Selected Bibliography

Graham, George A., "Ethical Guidelines for Public Administrators: Observations on Rules of the Game," *Public Administration Review,* 34 (January/February 1974): 90–92.

Khandwalla, Pradip N., *The Design of Organizations,* New York: Harcourt Brace Jovanovich, 1977.

Koontz, Harold, "The Management Theory Jungle," in Matteson, Michael T., and Ivancevich, John M., eds., *Management Classics,* Santa Monica, Calif.: Goodyear Publishing Co., 1977. pp. 19–33.

Leavitt, Harold J., *Managerial Psychology,* 4th ed., Chicago: University of Chicago Press, 1978. See "The Jigsaw Puzzle of Individual Responsibility," pp. 321–23.

Lorsch, Jay W., "Introduction to the Structural Design of Organizations," in Dalton, G. W.; Lawrence, P. R., and Lorsch, Jay W., *Organizational Structure and Design,* Homewood, Ill.: Richard D. Irwin, 1970. pp. 1–16.

Porter, David O., and Olsen, Eugene A., "Some Critical Issues in Governmental Centralization and Decentralization," *Public Administration Review* 36 (January/February 1976): 72–84.

Salamon, Lester M., "The Goals of Reorganization: A Framework for Analysis," *Administration and Society* 12 (February 1981): 437–46.

Scott, W. Richard., *Organizations: Rational, Natural and Open Systems,* Englewood Cliffs, N.J.: Prentice-Hall, 1981. Ch. 6, "Goal Setting in Organizations," pp. 261–74.

Sherman, Harvey, *It All Depends: A Pragmatic Approach,* University of Alabama Press, 1975. Chs. 1 and 2, pp. 74–82.

Simon, Herbert A., *Administrative Behavior: A Study of Decision-Making Processes in Administrative Organizations,* 3rd ed., New York: The Free Press, 1976. Ch. 2, "Some Problems of Administrative Theory," pp. 20–44.

Stern, Louis W.; Sternthal, Brian; and Craig, C. Samuel, "Strategies for Managing Interorganizational Conflict: A Laboratory Paradigm," *Journal of Applied Psychology* 60 (August 1975): 472–82.

Walton, Richard E., and Dutton, John M., "The Management of Inter-departmental Conflict: A Model and Review," *Administrative Science Quarterly* 14 (March 1969): 73–84.

Zald, Mayer N., "Power Balance and Staff Conflict in Correctional Institutions," *Administrative Science Quarterly* 7, (June 1962): 22–49.

22

A Problem of Motivation

Two years before, the Department of Human Services had hired six new employees with the assistance of the federal government's Work Incentive (WIN) program. Under the program, the federal government paid the employees' salaries for a six-month training period, after which the department had the option of hiring or releasing the employees based on their performance and the recommendations of their supervisors.

Julie Davis, one of the WIN employees, was placed in the Child Welfare Department. Initially she was very industrious and suggested several improvements in procedures relating to her job. She exhibited a high degree of initiative and performed her duties efficiently. After about six weeks, though, Jeff Baker, her supervisor, noticed that she was developing poor working habits, such as long coffee breaks, tardiness, and absenteeism.

Baker felt Davis's low performance had resulted from her association with two employees in the adoption unit of the department. Baker arranged a meeting with her and advised her of the unacceptability of her work behavior. He had received complaints from other employees that she was not carrying her share of the load. "Julie," he said, "generally your work has been very good but lately your job performance has not lived up to expectations. Although our standards are higher than other sections of this department, the chances for promotion and career advancement are a lot better for the hard-working employee. You can do a lot better than you have been doing!" After the session with Baker, Davis's work and behavior immediately improved. She volunteered to assist others whenever her own work was completed and quickly acquired the necessary skills for several other positions in the section. She often worked as a substitute in the absence of other employees.

At the end of the training period Baker recommended that the agency hire Davis at the level of Grade 5. The quality of her work remained consistently high and she continued to assist others willingly. Six months later, when she had completed a year with the agency, she was promoted to Grade 6 and assigned additional responsibilities. Indeed, a bright future seemed on the horizon.

About two months later, one of the employees Davis had been assisting resigned because of a death in her family. The announcement for the newly opened position emphasized it was limited to employees of the department. Since Davis was familiar with many aspects of the position, she discussed applying for it with Baker, who advised her that even though she was the only staff member familiar with the job her chance of being on the list of applicants supplied by the Bureau of Personnel was small because she had only fourteen months' experience instead of the required two years. He said she would make the list only if there were no applicants with the required experience. This was possible, though unlikely. Davis decided to apply and hope for the best. There were several applicants with the required experience and she did not make the list.

Davis's attitude changed immediately. She became irritable and her relationship with other staff members deteriorated. She developed intense feelings of insecurity. Each time a new employee was hired she felt as though she might be replaced. As a result of this constant fear she developed an ulcer. In another meeting with her, Davis reassured her of her abilities, explained the steps involved in employee termination, and outlined the grievance procedures available to employees should termination occur. Initially, she seemed to gain confidence and her work improved, though not to the level of her previous performance. Davis had become confused and felt angry toward Baker for what she considered to be unwarranted encouragement.

Since Baker felt he could no longer adequately motivate Davis, he recommended that she be transferred to another supervisor, Malcolm Tate. After a few weeks, her work performance and attitude improved considerably, and Tate soon considered her among the best employees he had ever supervised.

The problem in the department appeared to be resolved, but Tate might be faced with the same problem as Baker. In the next four months two employees under Tate's supervision were to retire. Both positions were at the Grade 7 level. Davis was now qualified for both, but there were others in the agency better qualified. Even if she made the list, there was a good possibility she would not be selected for the position.

Questions and Instructions

1. Was transferring Davis the best course of action Baker could have taken? What other choices did he have?
2. Do rules stating that a person must have two years' experience bear any relationship to the realities of an employee's efficiency and the needs of an organization? Should the rules be reviewed?
3. Do you feel that the manner in which Davis was hired affected her job performance?
4. Should Tate encourage Davis to apply for a new position when the possibility of not being selected exists?
5. What can Tate do to prevent the recurrence of the previous situation if Davis is not selected for one of the Grade 7 positions?
6. Davis seems to be experiencing stress. What do you think could be the main cause of the stress? Is the stress-risk behavior related to the actions of others, or is it related to her own expectations? What can Baker do to reduce the level of personal stress that Davis is experiencing? What can Davis do about her own situation?
7. Does Davis appear to be internally or externally motivated? What are the implications associated with both of these motivations?

Selected Bibliography

Brass, Daniel J., "Structural Relationships, Job Characteristics, and Worker Satisfaction and Performance," *Administrative Science Quarterly* 26 (September 1981): 331–48.

Filipowicz, Christine, "The Troubled Employee: Whose Responsibility?" *Personnel Administrator* 24 (June 1979): 17–22.

Glisson, Charles A., and Martin, Patricia Yancey, "Productivity and Efficiency in Human Service Organizations as Related to Structure, Size, and Age," *Academy of Management Journal* 23 (March 1980): 21–37.

Goodman, Paul S.; Salipante, Paul; and Paransky, Harold, "Hiring, Training, Retaining the Hard Core Unemployed: A Selected Review," *Journal of Applied Psychology* 58 (August 1973): 23–33.

Herzberg, Frederick, "One More Time: How Do You Motivate

Employees?'' *Harvard Business Review* 46 (January/February 1968): 53–62.

House, Robert J., and Mitchell, Terence R., ''Path-Goal Theory of Leadership,'' *Contemporary Business* 3 (Autumn 1974): 81–97.

Lutz, Carl F., ''Efficient Maintenance of the Classification Plan,'' *Public Personnel Management* 2 (July/August 1973): 232–41.

Maslow, Abraham H., ''A Theory of Human Motivation,'' *Psychological Review* 50 (July 1943): 370–96.

Mealiea, Laird W., and Duffy, John F., ''An Integrated Model for Training and Development: How to Build on What You Already Have,'' *Public Personnel Management* 9 (No. 4, 1980): 336–43.

Paul, William J., Jr.; Robertson, Keith B.; and Herzberg, Frederick, ''Job Enrichment Pays Off,'' *Harvard Business Review* 47 (March/April 1969): 61–78.

Radin, Beryl A., ''Leadership Training for Women in State and Local Government,'' *Public Personnel Management* 9 (No. 2, 1980): 52–60.

Schulkind, Gilbert A., ''Monitoring Position Classification—Practical Problems and Possible Solutions,'' *Public Personnel Management* 4 (January/February 1975): 32–37.

White, Robert N., ''State Grievance and Appeals Systems: A Survey,'' *Public Personnel Management* 10 (No. 3, 1981): 313–23.

23

The Prank That Misfired

Phoebe Palmer, a GS-4 clerk-stenographer at Beckworth Air Force Base, was as cheerful as the small bird after which her parents had named her. Young, pretty, and friendly, she was treated as something of a pet by the twenty men, all civilians, in the office in which she had worked for three years. They would frequently tease her in a playful, good-natured way. They delighted in playing jokes on her, for she was somewhat naive and easily fooled. She seemed to enjoy the pranks as much as the perpetrators. She was mature enough to know there was nothing malicious in their banter or jokes that reflected on her ability as a secretary. She considered herself, and was, an efficient worker.

One Friday morning shortly after Phoebe—everyone called her by her first name—reported for work, the telephone rang and a male voice asked, "What about that ad in this week's *Beckworth Bulletin?* I think we might be interested in a trade for our office."

Puzzled, Phoebe replied, "Ad? I don't know anything about an ad in the *Bulletin.*"

The man on the other end of the line laughed and said, "Look it up in the want ads and you'll see." Still laughing he hung up the receiver.

Almost immediately the phone rang again. This time it was a woman. "I'm interested in that job in your office. Could you tell me about it? I think I might want to make a change."

"There's no position open in this office," Phoebe replied. "I think you must have made a mistake."

"Is this 9555?" the voice asked. "This week's *Bulletin* says to call this number about a job exchange."

Replying that there must be some mistake, Phoebe hung up and hurried to look in the *Bulletin,* the base newspaper published every Friday, which she had picked up from a stack on the floor when she entered the building. On page seven among the classifieds she found the following notice:

WANTED TO TRADE
ONE FS-4 Clerk-Steno for a GS-3
Clerk-Typist who is quiet, reserved,
uses telephone to minimum extent
and has no personal problems. No
deposit, no return. Call 9555 for
details.

Phoebe, reading the notice, was slightly puzzled and also somewhat amused. It was, she thought, just another joke perpetrated by the men in the office.

But it soon ceased to be a joke. The first two calls were the opening of a floodgate. As soon as Phoebe got rid of one caller, the phone rang again. Some of the callers, like the second one she had spoken to, did not see the want ad as a prank and seriously sought details about the position. Most of the callers were male employees or airmen at the base who recognized the advertisement as a prank and used it as an occasion to display their wit or to ask for a date. A few of the calls were obscene.

Almost in tears after an hour of constant telephone calls, Phoebe refused to answer the phone and the men in the office began handling this chore. What had been intended as fun had become an embarrassment both for her and for the men. Everyone was uncomfortable at the end of the day, but the young woman was angry and determined to find out who had inserted the want ad. She went to the *Beckworth Bulletin* office and complained to the editor. Copy for the paper was not thrown away until a month after publication and the want ad, which was hand-written and had been mailed in, was available. Phoebe recognized the handwriting immediately as being that of one of the men in her office.

On Monday, Phoebe made an appointment with the director of her division, Houston Turner, and complained that the want ad in the *Bulletin* had made her the laughingstock of the entire base. It was well known that she was the only stenographer-clerk in her office. The incessant telephone calls and the wisecracks and obscenities she had had to listen to had so upset her that she could not sleep at night and she was too embarrassed to leave the house over the weekend. She did not see how she could face friends and acquaintances on the base.

A little later in the morning Turner received a telephone call from Imogene Dexter, president of the local chapter of the National Organization for Federally Employed Women. Quick to spot anything that might involve mistreatment of women, Dexter had noticed the *Bulletin* want ad and on investigation had found out about Phoebe's traumatic experience. She told Turner that the want ad had caused embarrassment to the victim of the prank, that it gave negative implications about her work performance and personal life, and that she felt that the prank constituted sexual harassment about which her organization had taken a very hard line. "We will pursue this matter vigorously," she asserted in closing, "and will expect the fullest cooperation from you in handling this matter."

Questions and Instructions

1. Assume that you are Houston Turner. What would you say to Phoebe to ease her mind about the prank? Would you suggest that she take a leave to let the matter die down?
2. What action should be taken against the perpetrators of the prank?
3. Libel is defined in one state statute as "a false and unprivileged publication by writing, printing, picture, effigy, or other fixed representation to the eye that exposes any person to hatred, contempt, ridicule, or obloquy, or that causes him or her to be shunned or avoided, or that tends to injure a person in his or her occupation." Do you think the want ad libels Palmer even though she was not mentioned by name? Do you think she should demand a printed apology from the *Beckworth Bulletin*? Would it be advisable for her to see a lawyer about a possible libel suit?
4. Do you think Dexter's charge that the prank constituted sexual harassment is accurate? (See Exhibits 1 and 2 at the end of this case.) Would it be advisable for Phoebe Palmer to file a complaint of sexual harassment?

Selected Bibliography

Biles, George E., "A Program Guide for Preventing Sexual Harassment in the Workplace," *Personnel Administrator* 26 (June 1981): 49–56.

Driscoll, Jeanne Bosson, "Sexual Attraction and Harassment: Management's New Problems," *Personnel Journal* 60 (January 1981): 33–36.

Farley, Lin, *Sexual Shakedown: Sexual Harassment of Women at Work,* New York: McGraw-Hill, 1979.

Gordon, Francine E., and Strober, Myra H., eds., *Bringing Women into Management,* New York: McGraw-Hill, 1975. Chs. 1, 2, and 3, pp. 7–58.

Hoyman, Michelle, and Robinson, Ronda, "Interpreting the New Sexual Harassment Guidelines," *Personnel Journal* 59 (December 1980): 996–1000.

James, Jennifer, "Sexual Harassment," *Public Personnel Management* 10 (No. 4, 1981): 402–7.

Kronenberger, George K., and Rourke, David L., "Effective Training and the Elimination of Sexual Harassment," *Personnel Journal* 60 (November 1981): 879–83.

MacKinnon, Catharine A., *Sexual Harassment of Working Women,* New Haven, Conn.: Yale University Press, 1979.

Neugarten, Dail Ann, and Shafritz, Jay M., *Sexuality in Organizations: Romantic and Coercive Behaviors at Work,* Oak Park, Ill.: Moore Publishing Co., 1980. See Section II, "Sexual Harassment: The Problem," pp. 57–77 and Section IV, "The Legal Status: Sexual Harassment Under Title VII," pp. 109–57.

Quinn, Robert E., "Coping with Cupid: The Formation, Impact, and Management of Romantic Relationships in Organizations," *Administrative Science Quarterly* 22 (March 1977): 30–45.

Renick, James C., "Sexual Harassment at Work: Why It Happens, What to Do About It," *Personnel Journal* 59 (August 1980): 658–62.

Somers, Patricia A., and Clementson-Mohr, Judith, "Sexual Extortion in the Workplace," *Personnel Administrator* 24 (April 1979): 23–28.

Thurston, Kathryn A., "Sexual Harassment: An Organizational Perspective," *Personnel Administrator* 25 (December 1980): 59–64.

Exhibit 1. Excerpt from Civil Rights Act of 1964

TITLE VII—EQUAL EMPLOYMENT OPPORTUNITY
DISCRIMINATION BECAUSE OF RACE, COLOR,
RELIGION, SEX, OR NATIONAL ORIGIN

Section 703.

a. It shall be an unlawful employment practice for an employer—

1. to fail or refuse to hire or to discharge any individual, or otherwise to discriminate against any individual with respect to his compensation, terms, conditions, or privileges of employment, because of such individual's race, color, religion, sex, or national origin; or

2. to limit, segregate, or classify his employees in any way which would deprive or tend to deprive any individual of employment opportunities or otherwise adversely affect his status as an employee, because of such individual's race, color, religion, sex, or national origin.

b. It shall be an unlawful employment practice for an employment agency to fail or refuse to refer for employment, or otherwise to discriminate against, any individual because of his race, color, religion, sex, or national origin, or to classify or refer for employment any individual on the basis of his race, color, religion, sex, or national origin.

c. It shall be an unlawful employment practice for a labor organization—

1. to exclude or to expel from its membership, or otherwise to discriminate against, any individual because of his race, color, religion, sex, or national origin;

2. to limit, segregate, or classify its membership, or to classify or fail or refuse to refer for employment any individual, in any way which would deprive or tend to deprive any individual of employment opportunities, or would limit such employment opportunities or otherwise adversely affect his status as an employee or as an applicant for employment, because of such individual's race, color, religion, sex, or national origin; or

3. to cause or attempt to cause an employer to discriminate against an individual in violation of this section.

d. It shall be an unlawful employment practice for any employer, labor organization, or joint labor-management committee controlling apprenticeship or other training or retraining, including on-the-job training programs, to discriminate against any individual because of his race, color, religion, sex, or national origin in admission to, or employment in, any program established to provide apprenticeship or other training.

e. Notwithstanding any other provision of this title, (1) it shall not be an unlawful employment practice for an employer to hire and employ employees, for an employment agency to classify, or refer for employment any individual, for a labor organization to classify its membership or to classify or refer for employment any individual, or for an employer, labor organization, or joint labor-management committee controlling apprenticeship or other training or retraining programs to admit or employ any individual in any such program, on the basis of his religion, sex, or national origin in those certain instances where religion, sex or national origin is a bona fide occupational qualification reasonably necessary to the normal operation of that particular business or enterprise, and (2) it shall not be an unlawful employment practice for a school, college, university, or other educational institution or institution of learning to hire and employ employees of a particular religion if such school, college, university, or other educational institution or institution of learning is, in whole or in substantial part, owned, supported, controlled, or managed by a particular religion or by a particular religious corporation, association, or society, or if the curriculum of such school, college, university, or other educational institution or institution of learning is directed toward the propagation of a particular religion.

f. As used in this title, the phrase "unlawful employment practice" shall not be deemed to include any action or measure taken by an employer, labor organization, joint labor-management committee, or employment agency with respect to an individual who is a member of the Communist Party of the United States or of any other organization required to register as a Communist-action or Communist-front organization by final order of the Subversive Activities Control Board pursuant to the Subversive Activities Control Act of 1950.

g. Notwithstanding any other provision of this title, it shall not be an unlawful employment practice for an employer to fail or refuse to hire and employ any individual for any position, for an employer to discharge any individual from any position, or for an employment agency to fail or refuse to refer any individual for employment in any position, or for a labor organization to fail or refuse to refer any individual for employment in any position, if—

1. the occupancy of such position, or access to the premises in or upon which any part of the duties of such position is performed, or is to be performed, is subject to any requirement imposed in the interest of the national security of the United States under any security program in effect pursuant to or administered under any statute of the United States or any Executive order of the President; and

2. such individual has not fulfilled or has ceased to fulfill that requirement.

h. Notwithstanding any other provision of this title, it shall not be an unlawful employment practice for an employer to apply different standards of compensation, or different terms, conditions, or privileges of employment pursuant to a bona fide seniority or merit system, or a system which measures earnings by quantity or quality of production or to employees who work in different locations, provided that such differences are not the result of an intention to discriminate because of race, color, religion, sex, or national origin, nor shall it be an unlawful employment practice for an employer to give and to act upon the results of any professionally developed ability test provided that such test, its administration or action upon the results is not designed, intended, or used to discriminate because of race, color, religion, sex, or national origin. It shall not be an unlawful employment practice under this title for any employer to differentiate upon the basis of sex in determining the amount of the wages or compensation paid or to be paid to employees of such employer if such differentiation is authorized by the provisions of section 6(d) of the Fair Labor Standards Act of 1938, as amended (29) U.S.C. 206(d).

Exhibit 2. Directive on Sexual Harassment Issued by the Equal Employment Opportunity Commission

Section 1604.11 Sexual harassment.

a. Harassment on the basis of sex is a violation of Sec. 703 of Title VII. Unwelcome sexual advances, requests for sexual favors, and other verbal or physical conduct of a sexual nature constitute sexual harassment when (1) submission to such conduct is made either explicitly or implicitly a term or condition of an individual's employment, (2) submission to or rejection of such conduct by an individual is used as the basis for employment decisions affecting such individual, or (3) such conduct has the purpose or effect of unreasonably interfering with an individual's work performance or creating an intimidating, hostile, or offensive working environment.

b. In determining whether alleged conduct constitutes sexual harassment, the Commission will look at the record as a whole and at the totality of the circumstances, such as the nature of the sexual advances and the context in which the alleged incidents occurred. The determination of the legality of a particular action will be made from the facts, on a case by case basis.

c. Applying general Title VII principles, an employer, employment agency, joint apprenticeship committee or labor organization (hereinafter collectively referred to as "employer") is responsible for its acts and those of its agents and supervisory employees with respect to sexual harassment regardless of whether the specific acts complained of were authorized or even forbidden by the employer and regardless of whether the employer knew or should have known of their occurrence. The commission will examine the circumstances of the particular employment relationship and the job functions performed by the individual in determining whether an individual acts in either a supervisory or agency capacity.

d. With respect to conduct between fellow employees, an employer is responsible for acts of sexual harassment in the workplace where the employer (or its agents or supervisory employees) knows or should have known of the conduct, unless it can show that it took immediate and appropriate corrective action.

e. An employer may also be responsible for the acts of non-employees, with respect to sexual harassment of employees in the workplace, where the employer (or its agents or supervisory employees) knows or should have known of the conduct and fails to take immediate and appropriate corrective action. In reviewing these cases the Commission will consider the extent of the employer's control and any other legal responsibility which the employer may have with respect to the conduct of such non-employees.

f. Prevention is the best tool for the elimination of sexual harassment. An employer should take all steps necessary to prevent sexual harassment from occurring, such as affirmatively raising the subject, expressing strong disapproval, developing appropriate sanctions, informing employees of their right to raise and how to raise the issue of harassment under Title VII, and developing methods to sensitize all concerned.

g. Other related practices: Where employment opportunities or benefits are granted because of an individual's submission to the employer's sexual advances or requests for sexual favors, the employer may be held liable for unlawful sex discrimination against other persons who were qualified for but denied that employment opportunity or benefit.

24

The Parking-Ticket Ledger

For the past five years Ronald Hughes had been employed as a radio dispatcher for the 35-member police force of Madison. Although Madison was a fairly small and quiet town, the job of radio dispatcher was demanding. Hughes was a responsible employee who had worked well under stress and equally well during occasional lulls. The duties of a dispatcher as described in Hughes's job description were:

1. monitoring and recording radio conversations with various law-enforcement agencies
2. receiving and recording police-related information on the telephone
3. typing and filing police and fire reports
4. assisting in the processing of offenders, such as fingerprinting
5. monitoring security alarms
6. maintaining security for jailed offenders

Hughes, along with four other radio dispatchers, was responsible for performing each of these duties as they arose. Hughes was also responsible for keeping the parking-ticket ledger in order. Tickets were registered and records kept of warrants and payments.

Hughes was employed Monday through Friday on the day watch (8 A.M. to 4 P.M.), which was considered the best shift by the entire department. Little police activity occurred during this shift, and most of the dispatcher's time was spent on the telephone routing incoming calls to various city offices. However, emergency situations calling for quick thinking and action did arise from time to time.

At first Hughes accepted his assignment to the day watch happily. But after five years at the same position, he had begun to feel that he was stagnating rather than developing his potential. Hughes decided to do something about his problem and conferred with Barry Grant, the city manager. "I really wish I could help you, Ron," Grant told him, "but you know what a bureaucratic mess the police force is. You go through channels, get involved in red tape, and then you end up where you started. Stick it out, Ron, your day will come." Although sympathetic, Grant's advice made Hughes feel even more discontented.

Hughes began to think he was not being fairly compensated for his work because of the extra duty of keeping the parking-ticket ledger. Each year the city set the hourly wage rates paid city employees based on their position. Only one class of dispatcher was recognized and longevity and merit were considered in the pay rate. Hughes believed his position carried more of a load than the other four dispatcher assignments and that therefore he was entitled to a higher rate of pay. If not paid more, Hughes felt he should not have to perform the extra duty of keeping the ledger.

When Hughes took this new problem to the city manager, Grant's sympathy had dwindled considerably. "I don't know exactly what to say," Grant said. "Obviously the keeping of the parking-ticket ledger is the responsibility of the department issuing the tickets. Who the department assigns to take care of it is their decision. I'm afraid, Ron, we're stuck with their decision." Hughes then took his problem to the police chief, who told him that the bookkeeping fell within the duties required of a dispatcher and that it was not an extra burden meriting additional compensation.

In general, the other dispatchers supported the city administrator and police chief's view. They insisted that the day watch involved no more work than the night watch. The late-night personnel pointed out that their shift involved activities not included in the day watch, including the booking of offenders and the maintenance of prisoners. The night people also mentioned that the work they were involved in was more stressful and required more effort and intelligence.

No agreement was reached and the conflict within the department grew as employees took sides. Finally Hughes had "had enough" and believed the only answer was to resign. He gave his two-weeks' notice and began looking for a new job.

Questions and Instructions

1. What aspects of a career civil-service system or merit system does Madison lack?

2. Would a grievance procedure be helpful to Tom Hughes?
3. Were Grant's comment about the "bureaucratic mess in the police force" and advice to "stick it out" wise?
4. If there is a "bureaucratic mess" in the police department, does the city manager have any responsibility to straighten it out?
5. Hughes appears to be a good employee. Should the city have a career-development program for employees?

Selected Bibliography

Alber, Antone F., "How (and How Not) to Approach Job Enrichment," *Personnel Journal* 58 (December 1979): 837–41.

Britton, Donald E., "Are Job Descriptions Really Necessary?" *Personnel Administrator* 20 (January 1975): 47–50.

———, "Common Practices in Wage and Salary Competition," *Personnel Administrator* 19 (January/February 1974): 19–24.

Cohen, Stephen L., and Meyer, Herbert H., "Toward a More Comprehensive Career Planning Program," *Personnel Journal* 58 (September 1979): 611–15.

Dyer, Lee; Schwab, Donald P.; and Fossum, John A., "Impacts of Pay on Employee Behaviors and Attitudes: An Update," *Personnel Administrator* 23 (January 1978): 51–58.

Dyer, Lee, and Theriault, Roland, "The Determinants of Pay Satisfaction," *Journal of Applied Psychology* 61 (October 1976): 596–604.

Ellig, Bruce R., "Salary Surveys: Design to Application," *Personnel Administrator* 22 (October 1977): 41–48.

Fredlund, Robert R., "Criteria for Selecting a Wage System," *Public Personnel Management* 5 (September/October 1976): 323–27.

Greiner, John M., "Incentives for Municipal Employees: An Update," in *The Municipal Year Book 1980*, Washington, D.C.; International City Management Association, 1980. pp. 192–209.

Hackman, J. Richard; Oldham, Greg; Janson, Robert; and Purdy, Kenneth, "A New Strategy of Job Enrichment," *California Management Review* 27 (1975): 57–71.

Howell, Jon P., and Dorfman, Peter W., "Substitutes for Leadership: Test of a Construct," *Academy of Management Journal* 24 (December 1981): 714–28.

Lawler, Edward E., III, "New Approaches to Pay: Innovations That Work," *Personnel* 53 (September/October 1976): 11–23.

Locke, Edwin A.; Sirota, David; and Wolfson, Alan D., "An Experimental Case Study of the Successes and Failures of Job Enrichment in a Government Agency," *Journal of Applied Psychology* 61 (December 1976): 701–11.

Luthans, Fred, *Organizational Behavior,* New York: McGraw-Hill, 1973. Ch. 22, "Modern Behavioral Applications to Management," pp. 508–36.

Newstrom, John W.; Reif, William E.; and Monczka, Robert M., "Motivating the Public Employee: Fact vs. Fiction," *Public Personnel Management* 5 (January/February 1976): 67–72.

Schonberger, Richard J., and Hennessey, Henry W., Jr., "Is Equal Pay for Comparable Work Fair?" *Personnel Journal* 60 (December 1981): 964–71.

Simpson, Karl F., "Job Enrichment: Just Another Half-Truth?" *Personnel Administrator* 20 (November 1975): 42–45.

Terpstra, David E., "Theories of Motivation—Borrowing the Best," *Personnel Journal* 58 (June 1979): 376–79.

Whisemand, Paul M., and Ferguson, Fred R., *The Managing of Police Organizations,* Englewood Cliffs, N.J.: Prentice-Hall, 1978. Ch. 11, "Job Enrichment," pp. 375–406.

25

Affirmative-Action Pressures

Southwestern State University carried on its letterheads and printed in its catalogs and other publications the notice: "Southwestern State University Is an Equal Opportunity Institution." Following such a policy was important to it financially because otherwise it would not be entitled to federal funds for research, aid to students, and various special programs. Hence it engaged in vigorous affirmative-action efforts to recruit members of minorities as students and faculty members and to fill positions in administration and maintenance.

In the late 1970s and early 1980s declines in enrollment and reductions in state appropriations along with increased costs in everything placed the university in a serious financial bind. A freeze was placed on new programs and increases in the administrative, maintenance, and instructional staffs, and an order was pending against filling vacancies created by retirement or resignation. The situation grew more serious in that the university had failed to meet its goals in employing members of minorities, and it faced a federal affirmative-action compliance audit. The word went out that any vacancies had to be filled by members of minorities.

In these circumstances Dwight Garfield, chief of campus security, and Captain Paul Rossi, head of campus police, were faced with the problem of finding a replacement for a black police officer who had resigned. Already understaffed, campus security would be severely handicapped if a replacement were not found before the freeze on filling vacancies was invoked. In seeking another black, Garfield had advertisements inserted in the state's one newspaper published primarily for

114

blacks, the *Afro-American,* and in commercial spots on radio stations directed toward a black listenership.

Because the eligibility standards for the campus police were high—a bachelor's degree was required—and university pay scales were low, there were only a few applicants for the vacancy. After checking out the applications, Captain Rossi discovered there was only one black candidate, Charles Blakemore, a student in a community college in the nearby town of Riverview. At his interview with Garfield and Rossi, Blakemore impressed them favorably. Dressed in coat and tie and with trimmed hair, he was neat in appearance; he appeared to be above average in intelligence; and he was eager to get the job because it would enable him to continue his college education. Garfield and Rossi agreed that the requirement of a degree for the job might be waived, but a more serious block to his employment turned up—a criminal-record check revealed that there was a fugitive warrant out for Blakemore in California.

Blakemore acknowledged the charge against him—statutory rape involving a 16-year-old girl. Blakemore explained that his arrest was the result of a "setup" by the girl's mother who had tried to extort $500 from him. He now realized that he had been wrong in leaving the state, that he should have faced up to the charge against him. But because he was young—only eighteen—and frightened, with no money to hire an attorney, he had gone to live with relatives in Riverview. Recently he had heard from home that the district attorney was prepared to drop charges against him because the complaining witnesses had disappeared, but he would have to return to California. He assured Garfield and Rossi that if hired he would return to California to clear himself of his legal difficulties.

Garfield and Rossi were convinced that Blakemore had had a "raw deal," as Rossi put it, but they could hardly appoint a person with a felony charge against him to the campus police. They would have told Blakemore of this but then they began to receive pressure to hire him from the director of Black Studies, the student organization the Black People's Union, and the university vice-president in charge of minority affairs. In the past three years Blakemore had proved himself worthy of consideration by earning his high-school diploma, attending the community college, and working part-time. It would be wrong to hold the dubious criminal charge in California against him. With the proviso that Blakemore, before his six-month probationary period of employment was completed, would return to California and take care of the legal charges against him, Garfield and Rossi decided to hire him. After five months, Blakemore returned to California to face the charges.

They were indeed dropped by the district attorney but Blakemore was sentenced to ninety days in the Los Angeles County Jail for contempt of court in not showing up for his arraignment.

Questions and Instructions

1. Were Garfield and Rossi right in hiring Blakemore? Discuss fully.
2. Should employment standards be waived or lowered to provide more jobs for members of minority groups?
3. Should members of minorities be hired before or instead of better-qualified nonminority people?
4. How fair is adopting a quota system in carrying out an equal-opportunity or affirmative-action policy?
5. Do you believe that reverse discrimination is a serious problem in government employment?

Selected Bibliography

Bellone, Carl J., and Darling, Douglas H., "Implementing Affirmative Action Programs: Problems and Strategies," *Public Personnel Management* 9 (No. 3, 1980): 184–91.

Foster, Gregory D., "Law, Morality, and the Public Servant," *Public Administration Review* 41 (January/February 1981): 29–33.

Grossman, Harry, "The Equal Employment Opportunity Act of 1972: Its Implications for the State and Local Government Manager," *Public Personnel Management* 2 (September/October 1973): 370–79.

Jreisat, J. E., and Swierczek, F. W., "Affirmative Action in Public Administration in the South: A Human Resources Approach," *Southern Review of Public Administration,* 5 (Summer 1981): 148–61.

Mintzberg, Henry, *The Nature of Managerial Work,* New York: Harper and Row, 1973.

Palmer, J. David, "Recruitment and Staffing," in Crouch, Winston W., ed., *Local Government Personnel Administration,* Washington, D.C.: International City Management Association, 1976.

Renick, James C., "The Impact of Municipal Affirmative Action Programs on Black Representation in Government Employment:

Reality or Rhetoric?'' *Southern Review of Public Administration* 5 (Summer 1981): 129–46.

Sherman, Mitchell, ''Equal Employment Opportunity: Legal Issues and Societal Consequences,'' *Public Personnel Management* 7 (March/April 1978): 127–33.

26

Biting the Bullet

Governor James Oliver appeared on the state's public television network to announce that the state's income could be $24 million short of projections by the end of the fiscal year. Not wishing to increase taxes in a declining economy and prohibited by the constitution from incurring a deficit of more than $100,000, the governor said he was ordering a 5 percent cut in the budgets of all government departments and agencies.

"I want the cuts to be uniformly made so that nobody can say I'm picking on one department or one state agency," said Governor Oliver. "Department heads will decide cuts within the agencies, and outlines of planned cuts must be in my office within three weeks."

The governor's announcement shocked Vincent Scotch, chairman of the state's Board of Regents for Higher Education. The board was responsible for the administration of the state's seven universities and colleges. Scotch called an emergency meeting of the board and outlined the problems of cutting $2.6 million from the college and university budgets. "Eighty-two percent of our funds are spent on employees," he reported, "and a labor contract with the union representing the faculty at colleges and universities forbids us from laying off tenured faculty members during the term of the contract."

The board members agreed that the best way to implement Governor Oliver's budget cuts was to order each of the seven college presidents to formulate a 5-percent cut at his institution. But after the meeting, Robert Lewis, director of the faculty union, stated: "We'll go to court if necessary to prevent the regents or presidents from laying off faculty members in the current fiscal year regardless of whether they are tenured. The union contract specifically says that in all cases tenured faculty members will complete their existing appointment contracts and that nontenured faculty members may have their contracts terminated this fiscal year only if there is an emergency financial exigency. This hardly qualifies as an emergency financial exigency."

The day following the regents' meeting, Thomas T. Yarberry, president of Central State University, met with his vice-presidents for academic affairs, administration, and student services. He handed them a copy of the school's current budget and told them to formulate a plan showing a 5-percent budget reduction in each of their respective areas. (See Exhibit 1 at the end of this case.)

Carl Nute, vice-president of academic affairs, felt across-the-board cuts for each area were unfair. "Not every unit in this university contributes equally to the goals, purposes, and basic function of the university," he declared. "Before cuts can be made, priorities must be established and programs examined on a university-wide basis to determine the impact the cuts will have on the students, the employees, the people of the state, and the primary purposes of a university, which are teaching and research. Intercollegiate athletics and administrative-support services are secondary and they should bear the brunt of the cuts."

"I couldn't agree with you more," responded President Yarberry. "I'd like to sit down with the three of you and establish program priorities on a university-wide basis. However, I have only one week left to get these budget-reduction plans back to the regents, and participatory management doesn't work when you're dealing with budget cuts."

President Yarberry then handed each vice-president a copy of the budget cuts he had prepared for his own office. (See Exhibit 2 at the end of this case.)

"It's not easy cutting your own budget," he said at the end of the meeting, "but we're not being paid to make easy decisions."

The next day Vice-President Nute met with the deans of Arts and Sciences, Business, Education, Fine Arts, and Law. He informed them of President Yarberry's order and passed out a copy of their total budget classified by tenured faculty salaries, nontenured faculty salaries, and uncommitted salaries.* (See Exhibit 3 at the end of this case.) Nute then requested suggestions from the deans as to which programs and areas were of lowest priority and therefore should absorb the greatest share of the 5-percent cut.

Dean Walter Stark of the School of Business was quick to respond. "The first reduction has to come from uncommitted salaries," he said.

---

*Budgeted salaries for positions not filled due to late resignations or difficulty in finding qualified people.

"Those cuts could absorb over two-thirds of the reduction allocated to us."

"Taking $111,235 of budgeted salaries would cost Arts and Sciences four teachers of professorial rank," Dean Dale Schultz said. "We're up for accreditation this year and we need those slots filled."

"You haven't filled those positions in two years," replied Dean Stark. "Uncommitted salaries indicate waste and should always be the first target for budget cuts."

"Uncommitted salaries don't always indicate waste," retorted Dean Caxton Turner of Fine Arts. "In the past Dean Schultz and I were conserving our resources and now you want to penalize us for it."

The meeting soon degenerated into loud argument, but finally Nute was able to bring the group back to order. "This is getting us nowhere," he said. "I want each of you to draw up a plan to reduce your budget by 10 percent. Tomorrow we'll meet again and together prioritize your proposed budget reduction from the first to go to the last to go till we hit our target 5-percent reduction."

"That's not fair," said Dean Philip Carter of the School of Education. "Some of us will end up having our budgets reduced by 10 percent while others may have no reduction."

"Meeting adjourned," Nute said firmly.

The next day Nute met with the deans and reviewed their planned budget reductions. Not one of them had reduced his or her budget by even 5 percent. (See Exhibits 4–8 at the end of this case.)

Questions and Instructions

1. Assume you are Vice-President Nute. What would you do next?
2. Compare President Yarberry's approach to the budget-reduction problem with Vice-President Nute's approach. Which do you prefer?
3. Do you feel the regents should have participated more in deciding specific budget cuts? Why or why not?
4. What type of contingency plan, if any, should President Yarberry prepare in the event of future budget cuts?
5. What is cutback management? What are some of the implications associated with cutting back? Explain.
6. What cutback tactics might be used in addition to mandating an across-the-board 5-percent budget reduction?
7. Are there any functions, projects, or activities that the colleges and schools might stop completely? that they can get other agencies or levels of government to carry out? Are there any areas where labor costs might be reduced by capital investment

in labor-saving forms of technology? What activities might be done more efficiently at Central State University? at your own university or college? Prepare a list and discuss.

8. Social scientists have extensively researched the subjects of motivation and barriers to organizational change. Cutting back during a period of resource scarcity may bring about changes in the level of resource consumption, number of employees, level of job satisfaction and employee morale, level of employee productivity, and the attitude of employees and clients toward support of government. Is there anything known about the characteristics and dynamics of change that might make it easier for Vice-President Nute to get the reduction he has asked for? Explain.

9. Are there any ethical implications associated with cutback management and politics? Does the university or any other organization or agency of government have an ethical responsibility toward its terminated employees? toward the clients it serves? Explain.

Selected Bibliography

Behn, Robert D., "How to Terminate a Public Policy: A Dozen Hints for the Would-Be Policy Terminator," *Policy Analysis* 4 (Summer 1978): 393–413.

Blair, John P., and Nachmias, David, *Fiscal Retrenchment and Urban Policy,* Beverly Hills, Calif.: Sage Publications, 1979.

Boje, David M., and Whetten, David A., "Effects of Organizational Strategies and Contextual Constraints on Centrality and Attributions of Influence in Interorganizational Networks," *Administrative Science Quarterly* 26 (September 1981): 378–95.

Brewer, Garry D., "Termination: Hard Choices—Harder Questions," *Public Administration Review* 38 (July/August 1978): 338–44.

Cyert, Richard M., "The Management of Universities of Constant or Decreasing Size," *Public Administration Review* 38 (July/August 1978): 344–49.

Flentje, H. Edward, "Governor as Manager: A Political Assessment," *State Government* 54 (No. 3, 1981): 76–81.

Glassberg, Andrew, "Organizational Responses to Municipal Budget Decreases," *Public Administration Review* 38 (July/August 1978): 325–32.

Krebill, J. Robert, and Mosher, Ronald F., "Delaware Budgets for Productivity," *State Government* 53 (Winter 1980): 17–21.

Levine, Charles H., "Organizational Decline and Cutback Management," *Public Administration Review* 38 (July/August 1978): 316–25.

——, "More on Cutback Management: Hard Questions for Hard Times," *Public Administration Review* 39 (March/April 1979): 179–83.

Levine, Charles H.; Rubin, Irene S.; and Wolohojian, George G., *The Politics of Retrenchment: How Local Governments Manage Fiscal Stress,* Beverly Hills, Calif.: Sage Publications, 1980. Especially Chs. 2, 7, and 8.

Lindblom, Charles E., "The Science of Muddling Through," *Public Administration Review* 19 (Spring 1959): 79–88.

Pfeffer, Jeffrey, and Moore, William L., "Power in University Budgeting: A Replication and Extension," *Administrative Science Quarterly* 25 (December 1980): 637–53.

Rubin, Irene S., "Retrenchment and Flexibility in Public Organizations," in Charles H. Levine and Irene S. Rubin (eds.), *Fiscal Stress and Public Policy,* Beverly Hills, Calif.: Sage Publications, 1980. pp. 159–78.

——, "Retrenchment, Loose Structure, and Adaptability in the University," *Sociology of Education* 52 (October 1979): 211–22.

Simon, Herbert A., "Administrative Decision Making," *Public Administration Review* 25 (March 1965): 31–37.

Williams, John J., "Designing a Budgeting System with Planned Confusion," *California Management Review* 24 (Winter 1981): 75–85.

Exhibit 1. Total Budget of Central State University

ACADEMIC AFFAIRS	
College of Arts and Sciences	$ 3,430,865
School of Business	855,831
School of Education	1,536,452
College of Fine Arts	852,652
School of Law	982,287
Vice President of Academic Affairs	64,503
Subtotal—Vice President Nute	$ 7,722,590
ADMINISTRATION	
Intercollegiate Athletics	$ 291,179
Business/Finance/Personnel	570,430
Computer Center	732,288
Educational Media Center	166,997
Central State University Research Institute	25,652
Physical Plant	2,075,491
Statewide Education Services	53,599
Vice President for Administration	37,630
Affirmative Action	15,583
Legal Counsel	5,866
Subtotal—Vice President Steel	$ 3,974,715
STUDENT SERVICES	
Student Services Administration	$ 61,048
Admissions	120,276
Alumni	10,000
Financial Aids	86,266
Registrar	128,107
University Counseling Center	97,777
University Relations	65,171
Subtotal—Vice President Ore	$ 568,645
Office of the President	$ 143,129
Convocations/Memberships	13,620
Subtotal—President Yarberry	$ 156,749
TOTAL	$12,422,699
PROPOSED REDUCTION: 5%	$ 621,135

Exhibit 2. Budget Cuts in the Office of the President

Item	Amount	Consequences
Harvard Seminar for College Presidents	$ 3,500	Breaking from policy of building professional development into the operating budget.
University Hospitality	$ 9,133	Reduce the level of hosting institutional donors, regents, legislators, lecturers, commencement hospitality, etc.
Retirement Seminars	$ 2,000	Discontinue a service that has been provided for individuals approaching retirement.
Campus Sign	$ 7,000	Abandon, again, a project that has been planned for four years, a project that would give attention to special campus events, etc.
Equipment Match	$ 8,000	Federal equipment funds will not be available as the result of not being able to provide matching funds.
TOTAL	$29,633	

Exhibit 3. Total Budget for Academic Affairs

	Total Budget	Tenured Faculty Salaries	Nontenured Faculty Salaries	Uncommitted Salaries	Remainder
CAS	$3,430,865	$2,000,030	$ 900,900	$ 111,235	$ 418,700
SB	855,831	600,004	196,830	1,204	57,793
SE	1,536,452	1,016,780	228,947	24,491	266,234
CFA	852,652	592,108	58,974	101,848	99,722
SL	982,287	586,371	52,124	20,469	323,323
VPAA	64,503	47,861			16,642
TOTAL	$7,722,590	$4,843,154	$1,437,775	$ 259,247	$1,182,414

CAS-College of Arts & Sciences, Dean Schultz
SB-School of Business, Dean Stark
SE-School of Education, Dean Carter
CFA-College of Fine Arts, Dean Turner
SL-School of Law, Dean Samuelson
VPAA-Vice President of Academic Affairs, Dr. Carl Nute

Exhibit 4. Dean Schultz's Proposed Budget Reduction for the College of Fine Arts and Sciences

Faculty Salaries	$32,761
Contractual Services	8,000
Supplies & Materials	5,000
Capital Assets	8,000
TOTAL	$53,761

A late faculty resignation in political science resulted in salary salvage of $20,761. Faculty turnover from a number of positions, either opened or filled at a lower salary level, resulted in salary salvage of $10,000. The money normally would be used to fulfill the necessary requests for added sections in English, communications, and mathematics. The sections simply will not be taught, which may mean that students cannot take the courses during the second semester. Faculty turnover in psychology resulted in salary salvage of $2,000. This money would have been used to hire additional teaching assistants in the psychology department with its two graduate degrees. Failure to provide it will mean that some potential assistants will do without or that other assistants will operate on a lower stipend. The elimination of matching funds for federal equipment grants will create a serious risk in providing these funds from remaining departmental resources if the grant applications are funded. Loss of additional operating and maintenance funds in the amount of $13,000 will greatly reduce the potential of the college to fund a great many activities, including travel and speakers.

Exhibit 5. Dean Stark's Proposed Budget Reduction for the School of Business

Faculty Salaries	$1,204

Impact:

Loss of these uncommitted salary funds would make it impossible to hire student labor.

Exhibit 6. Dean Carter's Proposed Budget Reduction for the School of Education

Faculty Salaries	$27,800
Part-Time Temporary Services	2,809
Contractual Services	2,000
TOTAL	$32,609

Impact:

A resignation in a recreation position resulted in salary salvage of $27,800. We will ease attempts to fill this vacancy created by a resignation after the start of this school year. Classes for second semester will be covered by part-time faculty and teaching assistants, as is being done in the first semester with funds budgeted for the position. Labor budget would be reduced by $2,809. Grants and external funding will be sought to accomplish the tasks expected to be covered in this funding during this year. This is a one-year reduction unless new funding sources are found, which appears very difficult for the tasks expected from these funds. The planned addition of another computer terminal for student use in the School of Education will be delayed for this academic year.

Exhibit 7. Dean Turner's Proposed Budget Reduction for the College of Fine Arts

Faculty Salaries	$37,514
Travel	1,000
Supplies & Materials	3,486
TOTAL	$42,000

Impact:

Salary salvage in the amount of $23,465 in music will be generated due to open visiting artist positions and one faculty member on leave without pay. These funds have been identified for translation into partial payment for a Steinway "B" piano. The department does not own one of these essential instruments and this was seen as an exceptional opportunity to acquire an expensive piece of equipment otherwise unattainable. This money must be returned to music-department personnel next year to return professors currently on leave to their contracted salary base. Failure to do so would necessitate terminating part-time faculty and graduate assistants. Open visiting-artist positions in art will generate salary salvage in the amount of $14,049. Loss of these funds would destroy departmental efforts to bring in artists of regional and national reputation as a supplement to the skills and experiences of the resident exposure of art students to the dynamics of the contemporary art world. This money must be available next year to cover sick-leave payment obligations. A reduction in operating and maintenance in art would impede faculty development by restricting attendance of all professional meetings and workshops. A reduction in operating and maintenance in theater would curtail faculty development, departmental outreach, and business operations. It would delay the replacement of worn and outmoded equipment and further restrict departmental ability to prepare theater majors with professional skills and knowledge.

Exhibit 8. Dean Samuelson's Proposed Budget Reduction for the School of Law

Travel	$6,000

Impact:

Travel by law-school personnel is essential for recruiting students, recruiting faculty, and keeping current in developments of the law. Loss of this money will require disapproval of some travel requests already submitted for out-of-state attendance at law institutes, workshops or professional meetings on new legislation, court decisions, and development in the field of administrative law. Travel for recruiting and instate continuing legal education will not be reduced.

27

The Irate Police Chief

Charles Wilson was hired as Fairview's first city manager one year ago. Wilson had previously served as an assistant city manager of a large eastern city for six years. Initially, he thought he would miss the challenges and excitement associated with big-city government and handling the problems of a large city. Instead, he found that small-city management could be just as stimulating and satisfying. He was particularly pleased at the chance to apply big-city management techniques to Fairview.

Fairview was governed by a seven-member council. The mayor, Elmer Scott, was the presiding officer. Scott had been mayor for the past nine years. He was the first to suggest that Fairview needed a city manager. He felt that Fairview, with a population of six thousand, needed the expertise of a professional to administer its daily operations. "Don't worry about a thing," he told Wilson. "The city council is one hundred percent behind the idea of a city manager. Don't be afraid to make any changes you think will benefit our city."

Wilson was elated. He immediately began to reorganize city government and instituted several new administration policies. One involved the establishment of an exit interview for city employees leaving their jobs. These interviews had been used successfully by his former employer in the East. Under this procedure, a person leaving city employment was required to have a conference with the city manager to discuss the job, the department, and the reasons for leaving. Wilson felt that the information obtained would be useful in improving efficiency.

After a year as city manager, Wilson held his first exit interview, one with a city police patrol officer. "The city Police Department is a joke," stated the officer. "Morale is deteriorating. No one gives a damn anymore. The department rarely follows any standard rules or procedures. Money that was allotted by the City Council for training was spent by the police chief to remodel his office. Three weeks ago, the chief hired his nephew as a patrolman when there were three other, more qualified people applying for the job." When the interview was completed, Wilson thanked the officer for being so candid.

The next day Wilson called the police chief, Grady O'Brien, and told him that his department had been criticized by an officer leaving the police force in an exit interview. The chief became outraged. "Quit meddling in my department," he demanded. "If there are any problems in the police department, I'll take care of them."

Wilson did not know what to do. He knew that O'Brien had been a resident of Fairview all his life. He had joined the police force twenty-four years before and was promoted to chief within ten years. He was a popular figure in the community as a member of the volunteer fire department, an officer in the VFW and Elks, a deacon in his church, and a Boy Scout leader.

The next morning Wilson received a call from Elmer Scott. "Chief O'Brien called me last night," Scott said. "He told me you were accusing him of all kinds of things. Chuck, I've never heard him as angry as this before. If you know what's good for you, keep your nose out of Police Department business."

Questions and Instruction

1. Are there any different expectations of roles and management style for a manager in a small city as compared with those in a large city?
2. Should Wilson have revealed to the police chief information contained in the exit interview? Should statements made in such an interview be held confidential? What use should be made of information so gained?
3. The interview contained allegations of unethical and very likely illegal actions by the police chief. Should Wilson take any action in regard to these allegations? What courses of action are open to him?
4. Was Wilson, presumably a sophisticated big-city official, naive in accepting the assurances of the mayor that he had a free hand in administering city affairs? Should he now obtain a written statement of his powers and authority?

Selected Bibliography

Banovetz, James M., ed., *Managing the Modern City,* Washington, D.C.: International City Managers Association, 1971. See "Leadership Styles and Strategies," pp. 108–33.

Boynton, Robert Paul, and Wright, Deil S., "Mayor-Manager Relationships in Large Council-Manager Cities: A Reinterpretation," *Public Administration Review* 31 (January/February 1971): 28–36.

Carrell, Jeptha J., "The City Manager and His Council: Sources of Conflict," *Public Administration Review* 22 (December 1962): 203–8.

Hilb, Martin, "The Standardized Exit Interview," *Personnel Journal* 56 (June 1978): 327–29.

Lahiff, James M., "The Exit Interview: Antiquated or Underrated?" *Personnel Administrator* 21 (May 1976): 55–60.

Leavitt, Harold J., *Managerial Psychology,* 4th ed., Chicago: University of Chicago Press, 1978. Ch. 12, "Authority: One Model for Influence," pp. 136–47.

Likert, Rensis, and Likert, Jane G., *New Ways of Managing Conflict,* New York: McGraw-Hill, 1976.

Loveridge, Ronald O. "The City Manager in Legislative Politics: A Collision of Role Conceptions," *Polity* 1 (Winter 1968): 213–36.

———, *City Managers in Legislative Politics,* Indianapolis: Bobbs-Merrill, 1971.

Presthus, Robert V., "Authority in Organizations," *Public Administration Review* 20 (Spring 1960): 86–91.

Schmidt, Warren H., "Conflict: A Powerful Process for (Good or Bad) Change," *Management Review* 63 (December 1974): 4–10.

Stone, Clarence N.; Whelan, Robert K.; and Murin, William J., *Urban Policy and Politics in a Bureaucratic Age,* Englewood Cliffs, N.J., Prentice-Hall, 1979. Ch. 7, "Suburban Politics: Change and Paradox," pp. 87–97.

Tannenbaum, Robert, and Schmidt, Warren H., "How to Choose a Leadership Pattern," *Harvard Business Review* 51 (May/June 1973): 162–72.

28

A Matter of Relief

For the third time in a year, Mildred Barnes, office manager of the Bryanville Department of Public Works, was faced with the task of screening applicants for the position of PBX operator-receptionist. She believed the job had a high turnover because it was tedious and offered little challenge or opportunity for advancement.

From among the applicants, Barnes hired Sue Simpson, who was young, energetic, and attractive, with a vivacious personality. Barnes congratulated herself on having filled a difficult position.

Gail Collins, Barnes's assistant, had been with the agency for fifteen years. She had initially worked as a PBX operator for ten years before being promoted. She was respected by her fellow workers for her quiet, methodical manner. One of Collins's duties was to relieve the regular switchboard operator.

After two months, Simpson, the new PBX operator, began to complain to Barnes about Collins, contending that she did not relieve her as soon as she was supposed to. She hinted that Collins behaved like a martyr when she had to work the board. Barnes knew that Collins's work load was heavy and that she frequently stayed in the office through her lunch hour to complete her tasks. Nevertheless, Collins's negative attitude toward working the board was apparent.

Office practice had called for the relief operator to eat lunch at the same time as the others and then to relieve the regular operator, who took a late lunch hour. As a result, the regular switchboard operator had had little chance to socialize with the other workers during the lunch hour. Collins began to trade off lunch schedules with Simpson to allow her to have a regular lunch period every other day. Collins also relieved Simpson on several occasions so that she could attend office birthday, holiday, and retirement parties.

Nevertheless, Simpson still continued to complain to fellow workers about Collins, and soon others in the office began to criticize her attitude. Resentment against Collins became undisguised and one day Collins heard Simpson say, "Even though she relieves me now, she acts put out about the work arrangement!" Mildred Barnes heard several complaints and was not quite sure what to do. Since Collins all this time had said nothing, Barnes decided to do nothing and see what happened. She noticed, though, that Collins's attitude toward her job had deteriorated even though her work remained well above average. She mentioned this to Collins. "Certainly I feel different now about taking over the board," said Collins. "Wouldn't you feel the same way if everyone had it in for you?"

Questions and Instructions

1. Is this office conflict serious enough for Barnes to take action?
2. What may have indicated to Barnes that she made a mistake when she hired Sue Simpson?
3. Why do you think that Gail Collins adopted the policy of trading off lunch schedules with Simpson? If you were Collins, would you tell Barnes what is going on?
4. What is causing the problem, Simpson's complaining and gossiping or Collins's lack of assertive behavior?
5. Since both parties, Collins and Simpson, have complaints, should a confrontation/conciliation meeting be arranged by Barnes?
6. If placed in Barnes's position, how would you go about the task of determining whether Collins is late in relieving Smith? Do you think Collins has too heavy a work load and needs to use part of her lunch period to keep up with her assignments?

Selected Bibliography

Burke, Ronald J., "Methods of Resolving Superior-Subordinate Conflict: The Constructive Use of Subordinate Differences and Disagreements," *Organizational Behavior and Human Performances* 5 (No. 4, 1970): 393–411.

Burke, Ronald J., and Wilcox, Douglas S., "Absenteeism and Turnover Among Female Telephone Operators," *Personnel Psychology* 25 (Winter 1972): 639–48.

Dunnette, Marvin D.; Arvey, Richard D.; and Banas, Paul A., "Why Do They Leave?" *Personnel* 50 (May/June 1973): 25–38.

Filley, Alan C., *Interpersonal Conflict Resolution,* Glenview, Ill.: Scott Foresman, 1975.

Kelly, Joe, "Make Conflict Work for You," *Harvard Business Review* 48 (July/August 1970): 103–13.

Klingner, Donald E., *Public Personnel Management,* Englewood Cliffs, N.J.: Prentice-Hall, 1980. Ch. 21, "Discipline and Grievances," pp. 381–402.

Likert, Rensis, "The Principle of Supportive Relationships," in Likert, Rensis, *New Patterns of Management,* New York: McGraw-Hill, 1961. pp. 103–18.

Maier, Norman Raymond, *Problem Solving Discussions and Conferences: Leadership Methods and Skills,* New York: McGraw-Hill, 1963.

Maslow, Abraham H., "On Low Grumbles, High Grumbles, and Metagrumbles," in Maslow, Abraham H., *The Farther Reaches of Human Nature,* New York: Viking Press, 1971. pp. 239–48.

Mathis, Robert L., and Jackson, John H., *Personnel: Contemporary Perspectives and Applications,* 3rd ed., St. Paul: West Publishing Co., 1982. See "Legal vs. Behavioral Grievance Resolution," pp. 512–14.

Morano, Richard A., "Managing Conflict for Problem Solving," *Personnel Journal* 55 (August 1976): 393–94.

Pursley, Robert D., and Snortland, Neil, *Managing Government Organizations,* North Scituate, Mass.: Duxbury Press, 1980. See "Discipline and Grievances," pp. 272–75.

U.S. Office of Personnel Management, *Employee Performance Evaluation—A Practical Guide to Development and Implementation for State, County, and Municipal Governments,* Washington, D.C.: U.S. Government Printing Office, 1979. pp. 8–22.

29

A New Director at Hillside Children's Center

The Hillside Children's Center provided detention-care services for juveniles arrested for criminal offenses or because of parental request, court order, social-agency referral, or pending court disposition. They were also held for such minor offenses as running away, unruliness, incorrigibility, disobedience, loitering, truancy, curfew violations, and having undesirable associations or because they were deprived and neglected.

Hillside was chiefly a reception and diagnostic center and not a correctional institution. Children might be kept there from a few days to two and a half months while a decision was made to return them to the community or send them to a training or correctional institution, a court, a day-care center, a foster home, or a private institution. The capacity of the center was limited to twenty-five children.

The center was established by the county commissioners in 1970 during a wave of reforms in the juvenile criminal-justice system begun by the United States Supreme Court in two decisions of 1966 and 1967. In *Kent* v. *U.S.,* the court extended limited due-process guarantees to juveniles, and in *Re Gault* it held that juveniles were entitled to the rights to have counsel, invoke the privilege against self-incrimination, confront and cross-examine witnesses, and have adequate notice given to both parents and child, including a precise statement of the charge, so that a defense could be reasonably prepared.

Established in this new era of children's rights, Hillside had enunciated the following goals:

1. To reduce the number of juvenile cases ending in court.

2. To reduce the length of detention.
3. To provide intake diagnostic and emergency treatment.
4. To reduce recidivism.
5. To provide referral to community agencies for services needed by juvenile offenders.
6. To mobilize community resources to help solve youth problems.
7. To provide programs to help alleviate conditions that encourage juvenile delinquency.
8. To accomplish all the goals listed above at a cost equal to or less than that required to process regular juvenile cases.

Over the years, the staff of Hillside had lived up to these goals fairly well and until recently had reduced the average stay of children in need of supervision, or CHINS as they were called, to ten days. Some were completely processed in half this time.

But two years ago, partly in reaction to the increase in juvenile crime and the growing addiction to drugs among young people, the county commissioners, upon the retirement of the woman who had been director of Hillside since its founding, appointed a new director who was unsympathetic to what he termed "mollycoddling" of youthful delinquents. He was Adam Mathers, untrained in criminal-justice administration but with fifteen years of experience as a military policeman and ten years as assistant director of the Midstate School for Boys. In taking over a different type of juvenile facility, Mathers introduced stricter discipline of the children and indicated he would like to run the home like an army barracks.

As could be expected, the new harsh regime violated many of the principles of juvenile care espoused by the trained professionals at Hillside—two psychologists, two social workers, two teachers, and four counselors. They found that their charges were more intractable and that their stay at the center lengthened. Attempts to escape increased, fights broke out among the inmates, two of the live-in counselors were attacked, and one boy committed suicide. When staff members protested that Mathers's strict rules interfered with the diagnosis and disposition of cases, the director told them not to be bleeding hearts—a little discipline was good for the detention-center inmates.

Two years after Mathers took over, there was an almost complete turnover in staff. Newcomers to the staff did not find the efficiently operated institution that one might expect of a man of Mathers's character. Work schedules were erratically planned, job roles were ill-defined, there was no performance and evaluation system, and morale was low. What was worse, because of frequent resignations of the staff members, the program of services for the center's children lacked continuity. On one occasion staff members met with Mathers to consider the problems at Hillside, but he was unreceptive to their suggestions. They had their own jobs to do, he told them, and should leave management decisions to management.

Questions and Instructions

1. What official courses of action are open to the professional staff to effect changes in Mathers's management of the center?
2. Should staff members present their case to the American Civil Liberties Union or a local group called the Coalition for Children, Youth, and Families?
3. Should staff members discuss the situation at Hillside with the press?

Selected Bibliography

Bohlander, George W., "Fair Representation: Not Just a Union Problem," in Schuler, Randall S.; McFillen, James M.; and Dalton, Dan R.; eds., *Applied Readings in Personnel and Human Resource Management,* St. Paul: West Publishing Co., 1981, pp. 284–92.

Bolles, Blair, "Correctives for Dishonest and Unfair Public Administrators," *Annals of the American Academy of Political and Social Science* 363 (January 1966): 23–27.

Briscoe, Dennis R., "Toward an Individual Strategy for Coping with Change," *Personnel Administrator* 22 (September 1977): 45–48.

Dwoskin, Robert P., *The Rights of the Public Employee,* Chicago: American Library Association, 1978.

Fisher, Cynthia D., "On the Dubious Wisdom of Expecting Job Satisfaction to Correlate with Performance," *Academy of Management Review* 5 (October 1980): 607–11.

Fisher, John E., "The Authoritarian as Anti-Manager," *Public Personnel Management* 7 (January/February 1978): 3–41.

Grant, Jack E., "Tell the Boss—Don't Ask," in Hills, William G.; Scurlock, Voyle C.; Viaille, Harold D.; and West, James A., *Conducting the People's Business: The Framework and Functions of Public Administration,* Norman, Okla.: University of Oklahoma Press, 1973. pp. 404–05.

Greiner, Larry E., "Patterns of Organizational Change," *Harvard Business Review* 45 (May/June 1967): 119–28.

Hopkins, James H., and Binderup, Robert D., "Employee Relations and Union Organizing Campaigns," in Schuler, Randall S.; McFillen, James M.; and Dalton, Dan R., *Applied Readings in Personnel and Human Resource Management,* St. Paul: West Publishing Co., 1981. pp. 275–83.

Newstrom, John W.; Reif, William E.; and Monczka, Robert M., "Motivating the Public Employee: Fact vs. Fiction," *Public Personnel Management* 5 (January/February 1976): 67–72.

Peters, Charles, and Branch, Taylor, eds., *Blowing the Whistle: Dissent in the Public Interest,* New York: Praeger, 1972.

Rosenblum, David H., "Public Personnel Administration and the Constitution: An Emergent Approach," *Public Administration Review* 35 (January/February 1975): 52–59.

Scheffer, Walter F., "The Clienteles of Executive Branch Agencies," in Vocino, Thomas, and Rabin, Jack, comps., *Contemporary Public Administration,* New York: Harcourt Brace Jovanovich, 1981. pp. 119–43.

Stanton, Roger R., "Professional Managers and Personal Liability," *Public Personnel Management* 7 (January/February 1978): 43–48.

White, Orion, and McSwain, Cynthia J., "The Issue of Authority and the Learning Process: Founding Theory in Myths," *Southern Review of Public Administration* 3 (December 1979): 309–22.

30

Supervising Job Trainees

Under a new job-training program established by the state, Layton County had received $100,000 to hire disadvantaged young people in county offices and agencies. Eligible youths were assigned to positions by the county commissioners upon the request of officials and agency heads.

Under this plan, trainees received the minimum wage for one year and then were considered qualified to hold jobs in government or private industry or business. To increase the number of people taken into the program, a time-sharing arrangement was permitted; that is, individual trainees could work half-days five days a week. Two trainees, one working in the morning and one in the afternoon, would be the equivalent of a full-time employee.

Evelyn Madison, court clerk, was assigned two trainees, Juanita Gomez and Wilma Rutledge, certified to her as competent typists. Both were attending Layton County Vo-Tech School and had completed courses in typing. If they proved satisfactory, they would be of inestimable help in the court clerk's office, which was understaffed and falling behind in record keeping.

Madison, known as a demon for efficiency, met with each trainee when she reported for work and carefully explained office procedures and regulations. The new workers were to become members of the typing pool and were expected to do the same work as regular employees: type case background summaries for reference during judicial proceedings and civil- and criminal-case action summaries, transcribe recorded dictation, and do other legal typing. Madison emphasized the need for absolute accuracy because often the documents and papers they typed

138

would constitute permanent court records. One of the full-time secretaries of the office would supervise them during their first two weeks on the job.

After the trainees had been working three weeks, it became apparent that their performance was unsatisfactory. Unfamiliar with such legal terms as habeas corpus, nolo contendere, affidavit, and writ of mandamus, the trainees did not comprehend the matter they were copying and submitted "finished" material full of typing and transcription errors. Both girls took up the time of other staff members asking questions and sometimes giggled over material they were copying because it seemed so outlandish. Much of Madison's time, as well as that of other staff members, was spent in checking and correcting the trainees' typing, and thus they hampered rather than helped production.

Her patience wearing thin after several weeks, Madison called the young women separately into her office and lectured them about their performance. Their typing was careless and their work was full of errors that they themselves should have been able to spot. Moreover, their behavior was not proper for a well-run office and they disrupted the routine of other employees. Unless they improved at once they might be released from the program.

Both girls were apologetic and expressed anxiety over the possibility of being dismissed, but each tended to blame the other for the errors and slow production rate. As a partial solution to the problem, Madison assigned separate "in" and "out" boxes to each, and they seemed pleased with this new arrangement.

In the next few weeks Rutledge increased the volume of her work but continued to make many typographical and transcription errors. Gomez's typing improved in accuracy and she took greater pains, but her output fell off and so her contribution to office productivity was minuscule.

Deciding that the trainees were taking up too much of her own and her staff's time, Madison informed them that they would be relieved of their current duties and be assigned to answering telephones and running errands. Rutledge protested, asserting that she had entered the program to develop marketable skills. In her opinion, the program was not keeping its promise and the new duties did not represent worthwhile training.

Questions and Instructions

1. Do you think Madison was justified, in the interest of office productivity, in reassigning the trainees to work involving no special ability?

2. What leadership principles might Madison have followed in dealing with the trainees to improve their work? How could she have motivated them to improve?
3. Who was at fault in assigning the two girls to positions they were not qualified to fill? How could such misassignments be avoided?
4. What responsibilities do office managers and supervisors have toward people in training programs? Should Madison, for example, have introduced an instructional program to improve the office skills of the trainees assigned to her?

Selected Bibliography

Argyris, Chris, "Leadership, Learning and Changing the Status Quo," *Organizational Dynamics* 4 (Winter 1976): 29–43.

Committee for Economic Development, *Improving Management of the Public Work Force,* New York: Committee for Economic Development, 1978. Ch. 5, "The Role of the Manager," pp. 91–102.

Giglioni, Giovanni B.; Giglioni, Joyce B.; and Bryant, James A., "Performance Appraisal: Here Comes the Judge," *California Management Review* 24 (Winter 1981): 14–23.

Janka, Katherine; Luke, Robert; and Morrison, Charles, *People, Performance . . . Results!* Washington, D.C.: National Training and Development Service Press, 1977. Ch. 2, "Program Options and Elements," pp. 23–38.

Katzell, Raymond A.; Beinstock, Penney; and Faerstein, Paul H., *A Guide to Worker Productivity Experiments in the United States 1971–75,* Scarsdale, N.Y.: Work in America Institute, 1977. See Program 3, "Training and Instruction," pp. 13–15, for a listing of studies related to training and turnover, job success, absenteeism, attitudes, and a number of other variables.

Lee, Robert D., Jr., *Public Personnel Systems,* Baltimore: University Park Press, 1979. See "Training and Education," pp. 176–87.

Levinson, Harry, "Appraisal of What Performance?" *Harvard Business Review* 54 (July/August 1976): 125–34.

———, "Asinine Attitudes Toward Motivation," *Harvard Business Review* 51 (January/February 1973): 70–76.

Robison, David, *Alternative Work Patterns: Changing Approaches to Work Scheduling,* Scarsdale, N.Y.: Work in America Institute, 1976. pp. 17–19.

Schneier, Craig Eric, "Training and Development Programs: What Learning Theory and Research Have to Offer," in Schneier, Craig

Eric, and Beatty, Richard W., *Personnel Administration Today: Readings and Commentary,* Reading, Mass.: Addison-Wesley, 1978. pp. 326–47.

Schockley, Pamela S., and Staley, Constance M., ''Women in Management Training Programs: What They Think About Key Issues,'' *Public Personnel Management* 9 (No. 3, 1980): 214–24.

31

Documentary Evidence

It was an exciting moment for Royfield Puckett as he drove his Volkswagen into the Deep Valley Children's Center parking lot with its sign: Doctors and Administrative Staff Only. Before him stood the 65-bed hospital of which today he would become the chief administrator—a modernistic structure of glass, concrete, and steel.

Only thirty-five years old, Puckett had a feeling of accomplishment as he viewed the hospital and its landscaped grounds. Only a few years before, after receiving his master's degree in public administration, he had joined the staff of a 250-bed hospital and worked his way up to assistant director. Now he had assumed the responsibility of operating an institution serving about eight hundred disabled children across the state, providing physical, occupational, and speech therapy; social services; and dental, recreational, and dietary programs.

Yet he also felt apprehensive. Was he really qualified by experience for the top administrative post in such a center? It looked open and welcoming as he approached the entrance, but more from instinct than from knowledge he suspected it was not all it seemed to be—a happy place providing humanitarian services to young people.

His predecessor, Lester Morton, had resigned unexpectedly upon his father's death to manage a family business, Puckett had been told when interviewed by the hospital board. Puckett felt, however, that he had heard only part of the story. The guarded manner in which staff members talked with him when he was taken on a tour led him to feel that below the surface problems lurked. Well, he was in charge now, he thought as he entered the building, and he would soon find out.

In his first few days Puckett devoted his efforts to familiarizing him-

142

self with hospital policies and procedures, its printed rules and regulations, and the minutiae of day-to-day operations, and to getting acquainted with staff members. All those he conferred with were friendly but hesitant in talking about the two-year administration of Lester Morton. Puckett decided that he might find out more if he read the minutes of staff meetings and of the hospital board of directors.

The minutes of the Morton staff meetings were contained in a single manila folder, and it did not take Puckett long to review them since only eight had been held, each one featuring a guest speaker or theme. Morton appeared to dominate the sessions, his remarks being reported in full. He concluded the meetings with exhortatory pep talks devoted to platitudes about the need for teamwork and good public relations. The staff was seldom consulted about policy matters and problems and there appeared to be little general discussion.

In contrast to Morton's staff meetings, those of his predecessor, Alfred Kahn, had been held weekly. Kahn would summarize any hospital news, training programs, or developments and then ask department heads to discuss their projects or problems. Puckett disliked clichés, but he decided that under Kahn the administrative staff was a team, whereas under Morton it was always being urged to become one.

Puckett also researched the rate of turnover during the Morton and Kahn administrations. He asked the personnel department to draw up a list of all positions vacated during the last three months of the Morton administration, the reasons employees gave their supervisor for leaving the center, and the reasons they gave in an anonymous questionnaire.

Meanwhile Puckett sought more information from department heads about their operations and problems. Among the first he interviewed was Martha Ritter, director of public relations. He found her friendly but somewhat cynical. After they had chatted a few minutes, Puckett asked, "Well, Martha, I'd like to know what you think we can do to improve the hospital."

Ritter looked surprised and then, stifling a giggle, replied: "Excuse me, it's just that, well, I wouldn't know where to begin."

"Don't worry," Puckett said. "Please feel free to tell me what is on your mind."

"Well, my latest nightmare is the donor list—you know, the list of four thousand people who have made contributions to the hospital," Ritter said. "It's gone."

"Gone?"

"Gone. I called up the computer center and the woman who used to run the list for me said she doesn't even work with the computer any more since they put in a new machine. 'New computer?' I said. 'No one told me about changing computers.' Needless to say the list is gone. Oh, if I'd only known we were going to change systems. But who was going to tell me? No one ever saw Mr. Morton. We rarely had staff meetings."

Ritter looked out the window and adjusted her glasses. "No, Mr. Puckett, things started going downhill the first week Mr. Morton was here and especially after he put in the time clocks. It doesn't seem to matter any more how much you actually work so long as you're not two and a half minutes late in checking in."

Chats with other department heads confirmed what Ritter had told Puckett—Morton's administration had been a disaster. The best description of the situation came from Hester Wilson, head of nursing services: "We were a team, or better still, more like a family before Mr. Morton became the administrator. I suppose things were going too smoothly. Have you ever been in a boat, Mr. Puckett, on a calm sea? Well, you'd swear the boat is just standing still. The fact is the current below the surface is moving you right along. It must have looked to the Board of Directors like we were moving too smoothly to be making progress. They wanted a new administrator with—what's the word— pizazz, somebody who could get the center known in the state. Well, he was a good advertisement—for himself. Our duty is to handicapped children, and our services to them suffered."

Returning to his office after talking with Wilson, Puckett found a report on his desk prepared by the Department of Personnel on the employees who had left the center in the last three months. (See Exhibits 1 and 2 at the end of this case.) He studied the reasons given supervisors for leaving and the reasons given in the anonymous questionnaire. Here was documentary evidence of a situation not fully revealed in his interviews. He had inherited a real administrative problem.

Questions and Instructions

1. If you were Puckett, what are the first changes you would make as the new hospital administrator?
2. What are some of the underlying reasons for the job dissatisfaction at the hospital?
3. What generalizations can be drawn from Exhibits 1 and 2 at the end of this case that might be beneficial in reducing the level of employee turnover? How would you classify the fourteen reasons given in Exhibit 1? in Exhibit 2? Develop a classification scheme and be prepared to discuss its strengths and weaknesses in class.
4. Item 7 on the "Employee Notice of Separation" form in Exhibit 3 at the end of this case lists items that employees might con-

sider among the three most important "factors that contributed to your decision to leave Deep Valley Children's Center." Use this list to develop a workable classification scheme that would be useful in analyzing the reasons for employee turnover. Are there any factors that are missing? What are they and why are they important?

5. What are some of the advantages and disadvantages associated with employee separations?

Selected Bibliography

Augustine, Joseph C., "Personnel Turnover," in Famularo, Joseph J., ed., *Handbook of Modern Personnel Administration,* New York: McGraw-Hill, 1972. Ch. 62, pp. 1–12.

Dalton, Dan R.; Krackhardt, David M.; and Porter, Lyman W., "Functional Turnover: An Empirical Assessment," *Journal of Applied Psychology* 66 (December 1981): 716–21.

Dixon, Andrew L., "The Long Goodbye," *Supervisory Management* 27 (January 1982): 26–29.

Dunham, Randall B., and Smith, Frank J., *Organizational Surveys: An Internal Assessment of Organizational Health,* Glenview, Ill.: Scott, Foresman, 1979. Ch. 3. "Organizational Surveys: The Purposes," pp. 36–60.

Gellerman, Saul W., *The Management of Human Resources,* Hinsdale, Ill.: Dryden Press, 1976. pp. 121–46.

March, James G., and Simon, Herbert A., *Organizations,* New York: John Wiley and Sons, 1966. Ch. 4, "Motivational Constraints: The Decision to Participate," pp. 83–111.

Martin, Thomas N., and Hunt, J. G., "Social Influence and Intent to Leave: A Path-Analytic Process Model," *Personnel Psychology* 33 (Autumn 1980): 505–28.

Meyer, C. Kenneth, and Beville, Mitchel J., Jr., "Turnover in State Government: A Regional Assessment," *Midwest Review of Public Administration* 14 (March 1980): 51–63.

Meyer, C. Kenneth; Beville, Mitchel J., Jr.; Magedanz, Thomas C.; and Hackert, Ann M., "South Dakota State Government Employee Turnover and Work Related Attitudes: An Analysis and Recommendation," *Midwest Review of Public Administration* 13 (June 1979): 88–118.

Peters, Lawrence H.; Bhagat, Rabi S.; and O'Connor, Edward J., "An Examination of the Independent and Joint Contributions of Organizational Commitment and Job Satisfaction on Employee Intentions to Quit," *Group and Organization Studies* 6 (March 1981): 73–81.

Price, James L., *The Study of Turnover,* Ames, Iowa: The Iowa State University Press, 1977.

Stone, Eugene, *Research Methods in Organizational Behavior,* Santa Monica, Calif.: Goodyear Publishing Co., 1978. Ch. 2, "The Research Process," pp. 15–34, and Ch. 4, "Measurement Methods," pp. 61–76.

Whitsett, David A., "Where Are Your Unenriched Jobs?" *Harvard Business Review* 53 (January/February 1975): 74–80.

Exhibit 1. Item 1 of the Supervisors' Report on Employee Separation

Item 1. Information concerning the separation of this employee is necessary for the purpose of processing unemployment insurance claims. Please obtain information from the employee concerning his or her reasons for termination. Involuntary terminations must contain information supporting the reasons for termination. Voluntary terminations must include information as to why the individual has terminated and what the individual is going to do after termination. If he or she is separating to accept other employment, information is necessary indicating the type of new employment.

REASONS FOR TERMINATION

Employee 1
"Lack of job satisfaction. Frustration due to discrepancies in administrative practices. Some personal problems, but for the most part Mary was the first counseling therapist to tackle some of the demanding tasks associated with intake diagnostics. Nothing could have been done to prevent her from leaving."

Employee 2
"Henry was asked to resign for failure to obey a direct order given to him by a supervisor. He left the area telling the ward staff to call the supervisor's office telling them that he refused to work in the area. He left without reporting in with the supervisor's office."

Employee 3
"Mr. Jones left to accept a position in the private sector with greater promotion possibilities and a higher starting salary."

Employee 4
"Leaving due to better employment opportunities in the city and an opportunity to work on a special-education certification."

Employee 5
"This counselor was terminated for unnecessary roughness with the patients, agitating children by teasing them, and unacceptable work performance while on duty."

Employee 6
"Mary came into my office tearful, stating that she felt that she was not able emotionally to continue her work in caring for clients in the area to which she was assigned. She said the center was becoming a depressing place to work and she needed a little time to think about where she was going with her career."

Employee 7
"Herriott drives 56 miles to work a day and is finding that with the cost of gas it is terribly expensive. In fact, it is so expensive that she has to resign. She also is planning on the foster care facility which she has been working on for the past few months in her home, and will be providing some meals, housing, etc., for elderly persons."

Employee 8
"It was my understanding that she requested to transfer to the 8:00 A.M. to 4:30 P.M. shift. I was also informed it might be beneficial for her to work in a more closely supervised situation due to questionable job practices. Also, she

needs to improve her communication skills. She also needs to set priorities that are in greater accordance to the needs of the center. She generally complied to what was requested of her, but frequently voiced discontent with numerous center policies, procedures, management, personnel etc. She did not convey a genuinely sincere, enthusiastic, and motivated attitude. In turn, she tends to function in a rather regimented, authoritarian manner and will continue to need to strengthen her communication skills. With added experience she has the potential of becoming a more effective counselor."

Employee 9
"Voluntary termination. She stated that she only wanted to work during the week so that she would have more time to spend on extracurricular affairs."

Employee 10
"The employee is leaving because he said he cannot do this type of work."

Employee 11
"Found a better-paying job at the VA Hospital. Nothing could be done to keep her from leaving Deep Valley Center."

Employee 12
"Terminated because she found other employment. Also, she would have been terminated because she had taken leave without proper notification and because the grant she was working on is being discontinued."

Employee 13
"Conflict with supervisor over work schedule. Employee seems to be unable to compromise when the need arises. Employee can be easily replaced since he performs janitorial services."

Employee 14
"Terry Nichols seems to have serious personal family problems and it is affecting her attendance and quality of work. She is a single parent with two very young children and feels a strong responsibility to her family. Unplanned absences and chronic tardiness, however, cause serious work disruptions and have adversely impacted on the services which Deep Valley renders. Her position will be a difficult one to fill."

Exhibit 2. Item 8 of Employee Notification of Separation Form

Question 8. Please provide a brief statement of your reason(s) for termination from Deep Valley Children's Center. Your response will remain anonymous.

Employee 1
"I have been assigned to night duty for the greatest share of my employment at the Center. I have to work alone constantly and need to have regular day-time hours where I can have at least *some* contact with people."

Employee 2
"The suggestions that I made and those which other people made to improve patient care either took too long to be implemented or were never made. The day the center starts paying people and promoting them according to their abilities, then it will be able to retain employees rather than losing them."

Employee 3
"I don't feel that I'm accomplishing anything due to some conflicts of procedures and attitudes among personnel."

Employee 4
"I'm being offered my previous job and I have decided to take it. This way I'll also be able to further my education. I have no complaints toward this facility. It has progressed very much since I was here as a student four years ago. I enjoyed working with the people and the majority of them are definitely interested in their clients."

Employee 5
"Too much bureaucracy. Too many fingers in the pot. Lack of interest for advancement of fellow workers so that they can become better qualified for their positions and provide better care and counseling to the children."

Employee 6
"Poor personnel management procedures and poor training coordination. Overall, poor working conditions and low morale!"

Employee 7
"When I would tell Mr. Morton, the administrator, about the girls and boys sneaking into the lounge at night or being late for activities, he would tell me, 'What can I do about it?' "

Employee 8
"I think the separation questionnaire missed the point. I think the various units of Deep Valley Center need constant assessment of goals and objectives with restatement in clear, concise manner, and leadership responsive to ideas and suggestions of employees. Opportunities for professionals to exercise judgment in completing their job assignment are becoming fewer, thereby resulting in less motivation."

Employee 9
"I want to spend more time in a newly built home, spend more time on outdoor activities and craft work, hobbies, etc. I do think that the salary for this particular position, and similar positions in the center, is too low for the amount of work involved. After working 10 years at this position the salary was very poor in comparison to the counselor positions with the Feds. One woman

left here to work with the Feds for more than I was making after 10 years. That is embarrassing and disgusting.''

Employee 10
"I feel that I couldn't handle this kind of work and of taking care of these kind of people. I guess I over-estimated my own capabilities when taking the position.''

Employee 11
"Direct care nurses have the most responsibility toward patients, yet they receive the lowest pay. Too many bureaucrats who are sitting on their cans, they won't understand this statement. 'Taxation without representation' law should go into effect immediately!''

Employee 12
"I was told that the grant program under which I was working was terminated and that there was no place for me in the center. In effect, I was asked to resign under threat of adverse action. Someone had better recognize the fact the center is about to go quickly down the tube!!!''

Employee 13
"The job itself was misrepresented to me by Mr. Morton. It stated that the job was 8 to 5 Monday through Friday. It did not state that nightwork or weekend duties would be required.''

Employee 14
"Unfair treatment toward me for the thing that I did. A follow-up letter will be sent to the Board of Directors, States Attorney, and the Governor.''

Exhibit 3. Item 7 of the "Employee Notice of Separation" Form

Item 7. Reasons for Termination: Please read through the entire list before you make any mark. Then rate the factors that contributed to your decision to leave Deep Valley Children's Center by ranking the three most important factors in your decision by placing the number (1, 2, and 3) IN FRONT of the reason. Number 1 is the most important reason and number 3 is third most important reason.

_____ My salary was too low
_____ My health is poor
_____ I got married
_____ Unfriendly community
_____ I felt the job was too difficult
_____ I was asked to resign
_____ I am having a baby
_____ I got tired of working
_____ I was laid off
_____ My salary was frozen
_____ Training I desired was not available
_____ I am returning to school
_____ I was discriminated against
_____ I am retiring
_____ Poor working conditions
_____ I felt the job was too dangerous
_____ Poor health facilities in the area
_____ I didn't like the working hours
_____ Poor parking at work
_____ Poor parking in town
_____ My spouse found a better job
_____ Poor recreational facilities
_____ I didn't get along with my supervisor
_____ Job required too much travel
_____ Wanted to reassign me and I didn't agree
_____ I am starting my own business
_____ The job was too physically demanding
_____ I didn't agree with my job classification
_____ I can receive more money elsewhere
_____ I didn't like the working hours
_____ I failed to receive an annual raise
_____ Poor shopping facilities in the area
_____ The center was not using my abilities to best advantage
_____ I didn't agree with my supervisor's way of doing things
_____ I didn't get along with my fellow employees
_____ I didn't like the job
_____ Poor entertainment in the area
_____ Had to care for family member(s)
_____ Poor educational facilities in the area
_____ Poor cultural facilities in the area
_____ No promotional opportunities
_____ My career development was progressing too slowly
Other reasons: (please specify)_____

32

Problems with
Volunteer Workers

Under the New Federalism concept of President Ronald Reagan by which the national government was to reduce or discontinue funds for services considered the responsibility of state governments the State Department of Public Welfare was forced to cut drastically the budget for the agency administering educational programs for handicapped children. This created a crisis for Reginald MacArthur, director of one of the agency's facilities located in a small university town.

MacArthur considered a high staff-client ratio necessary for the proper implementation of his facility's programs. Although no staff positions actually were eliminated, no additional people could be hired and no vacancies created by resignation or retirement could be filled. The crisis was heightened when sixteen handicapped children were transferred to the facility's case load from another state agency. MacArthur applied to the director of the Department of Public Welfare for emergency assistance but did not expect any help for several months if at all.

Because of the facility's location in a university town and the nature of its services, it received many well-meaning offers of volunteer help. These offers often came from students with considerable training in special and adaptive education. In the past MacArthur tended to make only limited use of these volunteers, assigning them to duties as aides and custodians with few chances for carrying out actual instruction and training. Recently, volunteers had received special development training from the department as ombudsmen on behalf of the clients.

In view of the existing financial crisis, MacArthur decided that he would have to place greater reliance on volunteers if he was to provide adequately for the additional children. He reviewed a large number of volunteer applications and selected two persons whose backgrounds seemed the most appropriate.

One was Sharon Bowers, a graduate student in special education who expected to receive her degree within the next six months and said she hoped to work with handicapped children. She was bright and enthusiastic and established immediate rapport with both the children and the professional staff members on her introductory meeting with them. She appeared to be reliable and responsible and was recommended in glowing terms by former employers. Under the circumstances, MacArthur would be inclined to offer Bowers a full-time paid position, but at the moment she was available for only about two hours every afternoon.

The other person chosen was Alice Pearson, a socially prominent local woman with a degree in elementary education. Although she had not taught for several years and her experience had been entirely with normal children, she had excellent local recommendations and several useful political connections. She was able to devote between fifteen and twenty hours a week to the program. After being introduced to the group with which she would be working, however, she seemed overwhelmed with the magnitude of the children's handicaps.

While fitting Bowers and Pearson into the program, MacArthur received a request from Professor Paul Corkin, a faculty member of the university's Department of Education, to include the children in a study that would attempt to measure their educational development and achievement over a twelve-month period. Since the study was designed to evaluate the teaching methods used by agency professionals, MacArthur felt that participation was almost a necessity. Negative results might reveal areas where program content should be improved while positive results would be a useful budgetary negotiating tool. Either way the agency would probably benefit. The study required that some of the children and their assigned staff workers spend several afternoons each week in a controlled experimental environment and that they would be periodically tested.

MacArthur juggled his staff schedules to take best advantage of the volunteer help within the time limits imposed. This required having Bowers and Pearson work together with a group of five children during the period of the experiment. Pearson was also available to supervise during the lunch hour when the agency was particularly short-handed. Since the experiment was scheduled to start immediately, MacArthur was able to provide only a brief orientation session before the volunteers began their duties.

Several weeks passed before Professor Corkin had his first conference with MacArthur. He reported that during the experiment he had noted a great deal of antogonism between the two volunteers, Bowers and Pearson. They were barely civil to each other and competed for the children's attention. The children seemed to sense the conflict, and as a result were nervous, easily upset, and generally uncooperative. The atmosphere was adversely influencing the outcome of the experiment. The professor revealed that Bowers had announced to him her intention of quitting. He was ready to abandon the study unless some change was made.

Further investigation by MacArthur revealed that Bowers was doing an outstanding job. She had developed warm relationships with all the children with whom she worked. Pearson had largely overcome the initial feelings aroused by the contact with the severely handicapped, and was almost always able to be on hand when the agency was in critical need of additional help. She had also proved to be a valuable link with the local community and was engaged in fund-raising activities that would benefit the agency. Although she did not relate to the children as well as Bowers, she could be depended on to keep order.

MacArthur knew that his paid professional staff members were spread as thinly as possible. Altering schedules now would be nearly impossible. He also realized that community volunteers provided valuable services and financial support to the agency that he would hate to lose. He could not afford to offend members of this group yet knew he must do something to resolve this problem.

Questions and Instructions

1. In such a sensitive program dealing with handicapped children, do you think MacArthur is justified in attempting to make greater use of volunteer workers who, despite their best intentions, might harm their young charges?

2. In view of the described situation, what do you think MacArthur can do to save the experimental program?

3. If it came to making a choice between Bowers and Pearson, which do you think MacArthur should keep in the program? Why?

4. What should be MacArthur's overriding concern in resolving the problem?

5. Discuss various choices open to MacArthur as they affect the facility's long-term and short-term well-being.

6. What functions would an ombudsman for handicapped children perform?

7. Should different supervisory approaches be used for volunteer employees in contrast with paid employees? Explain.
8. How can MacArthur make better use of Pearson's and Bowers's skills and talents?

Selected Bibliography

Biddle, William W., *Encouraging Community Development: A Training Guide for Local Workers,* New York: Holt, Rinehart and Winston, 1968.

Carter, Barbara, and Dapper, Gloria, *Organizing School Volunteer Programs,* New York: Citation Press, 1974. See "Training," pp. 85–103, and "Coordination: The Key To An Effective Program," pp. 67–84.

Ilsley, Paul J., and Niemi, John A., *Recruiting and Training Volunteers,* New York: McGraw-Hill, 1981. Ch. 1, "What Is Voluntarism?" pp. 1–9; Ch. 3, "Roles and Responsibilities of a Coordinator of Volunteers," pp. 17–29; Ch. 5, "Recruitment of Volunteers," pp. 44–67; Ch. 6, "Selection, Orientation, Placement, and Training of Volunteers," pp. 58–76; and Ch. 8, "Evaluation of Volunteer-Based Programs," pp. 97–116.

Janowitz, Gayle, *Helping Hands: Volunteer Work in Education,* Chicago: University of Chicago Press, 1965. Ch. 1, "Growth of Volunteer Work," pp. 1–7; Ch. 3, "Children in Need of Help," pp. 24–37; and Ch. 6, "Volunteers," pp. 76–88.

Mainzer, Lewis C., *Political Bureaucracy,* Glenview, Ill.: Scott, Foresman, 1973. See "The Ombudsman," pp. 56–61.

Naylor, Harriet H., *Volunteers Today: Finding, Training, and Working With Them,* New York: Association Press, 1967.

Pollak, Otto, *Human Behavior and the Helping Professions,* New York: Spectrum Publications, 1976. Ch. 4, "The Needs of the Helper and the Client or Patient," pp. 23–31.

Routh, Thomas A., *The Volunteer and Community Agencies,* Springfield, Ill.: Charles C. Thomas, 1972. Ch. 4, "Desirable Qualities in a Volunteer," pp. 35–47.

Scheirer, Ivan, *People Approach,* Boulder, Colo.: National Information Center on Volunteerism, 1977.

Schindler-Rainman, Eva, and Lippitt, Ronald, *The Volunteer Community: Creative Use of Human Resources,* 2nd ed., Fairfax, Va.: NTL Learning Resources, 1975.

Stanton, Esther, *Clients Come Last: Volunteers and Welfare Organizations,* Beverly Hills, Calif.: Sage Publications, 1970.

Stenzel, Anne K., and Fenney, Helen M., *Volunteer Training and Development: A Manual for Community Groups,* New York: Seabury Press, 1968. Ch. 1, "The Voluntary Association, the Volunteer, and the Community." pp. 1–23.

33

A Smoke-Filled Room

Julius Kohn, director of the purchasing division of the State Board of Affairs, grimaced when his secretary told him that C. Robert Burkhard was waiting in the outer office to see him. It was to be Burkhard's customary complaint, Kohn guessed, as a slightly stooped, partly bald man entered the office, pausing a moment to engage in a violent fit of coughing as he approached the desk.

Burkhard was one of four purchasing coordinators who, because of a lack of space, were crowded into a single office. Three of the coordinators were heavy smokers, but Burkhard was a nonsmoker who complained regularly that breathing in fumes emitted from his cigarette-puffing deskmates was not only annoying but harmful to his health.

"Mr. Kohn," Burkhard said, "either I should have a desk where I don't have to breathe in cigarette smoke or else the other coordinators should do their smoking outside our office. It's against the law to smoke in elevators and no-smoking areas are required in restaurants and airplanes. I don't think I should have to put up with smokers all day where I work."

"Bob," Kohn replied, as he usually did to Burkhard's complaint, "you know we just don't have space to move your desk. Anyway, the coordinators have to be close together to confer when problems arise." Then, reminding himself that Burkhard was a malcontent in other matters and not very good at his job, Kohn added: "Maybe you would prefer a transfer to some other department. There's not much I can do because of our lack of office space. I'll speak to the other men about their smoking, but I've done so before without much effect."

Two weeks later Burkhard's wife called in to report that her husband was in the hospital with severe bronchitis and difficulty in breathing. He was in intensive care and it might be two or three weeks before he could return to work.

Two months after Burkhard had been back on the job Kohn was shocked to be notified that he, together with the Board of Affairs and the governor, had been named defendants in a ten-million-dollar damage suit brought by Burkhard in U.S. District Court. Burkhard alleged that his constitutional rights had been violated because officials refused to provide him with a smoke-free place in which to work. Breathing in his fellow workers' cigarette smoke day after day, he contended, had brought on an attack of bronchitis and bronchopneumonia that led to his hospitalization for two weeks and a third week recuperating at home. He had suffered physical damage, he said, from which he would never recover.

Burkhard's petition said further that his repeated complaints and requests to be moved to a clean environment were disregarded and nearly cost him his job because his superiors intimated they wanted him to resign. The suit requested injunctive relief "from a continuing, ongoing, and needless toxic hazard, namely, tobacco smoke in the work environment" as well as monetary damages for the loss of his health and for mental anguish.

Burkhard lost his case in court. The judge ruled that his complaint did not raise a constitutional question and he granted the state's motion to dismiss on the ground the suit failed to "state a claim upon which relief can be granted." He continued: "Providing an employee a smoke-free workplace may be a desirable policy but denial of such a benefit hardly constitutes a violation of constitutional magnitude. Interpreting the constitution to protect nonsmokers from inhaling tobacco smoke would broaden it to limits heretofore unheard of. The Constitution doesn't provide a remedy for every social and economic ill."

Questions and Instructions

1. Do you think employees are entitled to a smoke-free atmosphere in offices and other enclosed workplaces? How might they be guaranteed such an environment if it is not a question of constitutional rights?

2. The Occupational Safety and Health Act of 1970 establishes a commission (OSHA) to "set the standard which most adequately assures to the extent possible . . . that no employees will suffer material impairment of health." Is the problem of cigarette smoke of sufficient gravity to be considered by OSHA?

3. How should Kohn have handled the situation presented by Burkhard's annoying though probably justified complaints in view of reports of the danger of smoke inhalation by the surgeon general of the United States?

Selected Bibliography

Binder, Jim, "The Fulfillment of Perceived Needs: An Assessment of Nursing Environment," *Journal of Health and Human Resources Administration* 2 (November 1979): 221–39.

Bons, Paul M., and Fiedler, Fred E., "Changes in Organizational Leadership and the Behavior of Relationship- and Task-Motivated Leaders," *Administrative Science Quarterly* 21 (September 1976): 454–73.

Dwoskin, Robert P., *Rights of the Public Employee,* Chicago: American Library Association, 1978. Ch. 1, "Historical Background," pp. 1–33.

Foulkes, Fred K., "Learning to Live with OSHA," in Glueck, William F., *Personnel: A Book of Readings,* Dallas: Business Publications, 1979. pp. 310–23.

Hatano, Daryl G., "Employee Rights and Corporate Restrictions: A Balancing of Liberties," *California Management Review* 24 (Winter 1981): 5–31.

Klingner, Donald E., *Public Personnel Management,* Englewood Cliffs, N.J.: 1980. Ch. 18, "Employee Health and Safety," pp. 315–26.

Mathis, Robert L., and Jackson, John H., *Personnel: Contemporary Perspectives and Applications,* 3rd ed., St. Paul: West Publishing Co., 1982. Ch. 14, "Personnel Health and Safety," pp. 383–415.

34

Discord in
Rehabilitation Services

Angela Patterson was elated when, after receiving her bachelor of science degree in social work, she was employed by the State Department of Human Welfare and was assigned to the Division of Rehabilitation Services. Strongly motivated by a desire to help people, she felt that work in this area would be highly rewarding. She was assigned to Lincoln County, the state's most densely populated metropolitan area.

A few days after Patterson had been on the job familiarizing herself with the services of her new organization, the division's director, Melanie Steuben, summoned the staff to a meeting in the conference room and announced that they would hear a presentation on cancer by an insurance salesman. Patterson considered this an unusual proceeding but she settled herself comfortably in her chair prepared to listen. She was mildly shocked to hear the speaker launch not into a general discussion on insurance but instead into a sales talk making use of fear tactics to persuade the state employees to take out personal cancer-insurance policies offering benefits not covered in the government's insurance program.

The following week Patterson received her permanent assignment in Rehabilitation Services—she would work in the Adults and Families Unit as one of ten counselors. Her supervisor was Amy Wagner, who appeared preoccupied when Patterson reported to her glass-inclosed cubicle in the big main office for instructions. Wagner told Patterson that she was late for a meeting on family planning and handed her a manual describing forms and procedures to study until her return.

Patterson went back to her own desk and had been reading the manual for about ten minutes when the insurance salesman she had heard

160

the week before approached, sat down, and began a sales talk and exhibited pamphlets and brochures on the danger of cancer and the need for insurance protection against the high costs of treatment. New in the unit, Patterson was unwilling to ask the man to leave, since she had seen him several times before talking to individual staff members and he appeared to have the run of the office. So she heard him out, but it was hard for her to believe that the department was allowing such a disturbance to go on.

In the days that followed, Patterson learned from fellow employees why the insurance salesman was allowed to interrupt and delay their work and why they submitted to it with only subvocal grumbling: he had been given permission by the division director, Melanie Steuben. It seemed that she had been hard hit emotionally and financially by the death of her mother from cancer, and had become somewhat mono-maniacal on the need for people to have adequate insurance coverage. Staff members felt that her intentions were good and put up with the salesman, though they considered him a nuisance.

Patterson quickly learned the operational procedures in the unit and was satisfied with her growing ability to serve the needs of her clientele. Her client load had increased and she was handling eighty-one cases— almost more than she could manage. She had learned a great deal, she felt, from her fellow counselors, but she did not have much respect for the two supervisors in the Adult and Families Unit. The supervisor to whom she was assigned was Amy Wagner, a big, raw-boned woman who was known as a martinet. She was a stickler for paper work and records, held frequent meetings to harangue the counselors on the need for writing fuller reports, and required that forms and records be redone if they did not meet her perfectionist standards of neatness and thoroughness.

On occasion Patterson felt like revolting against Wagner's devotion to petty detail, which reduced the time the counselors could spend with their clients, but she had been able to suppress her feelings. She thought perhaps the discipline was good for her.

One morning while Patterson was on the telephone discussing the emergency medical problems of a client with Dr. Philip Casement, the head physician assigned to the Adults and Families Unit, she noticed staff members leaving their desks to gather at the end of the office where a number of chairs were grouped to form a meeting place.

Her eye was caught by Amy Wagner, who motioned for her to join the group, but when Patterson saw that the meeting was to be addressed by the insurance salesman she continued her telephone conversation. When she hung up, Wagner again motioned her to come over, but she remained at her desk. The problems facing her client, she felt, were more important than listening again to an insurance salesman whose message she knew almost by heart.

After the salesman had completed his spiel, Wagner rushed up to Patterson's desk and shouted: "Get into my office right now!" Patterson looked up from her papers to see her supervisor red-faced in anger and in the background her fellow workers looking on in curiosity. She said nothing and followed Wagner as she marched angrily into her cubicle and slammed the door after them so hard it almost shattered the glass walls.

"I can't believe the nerve you have," Wagner shouted. "How dare you disobey orders? How do you think I feel to have you ignore me before the eyes of the whole office?" The supervisor continued her tirade for a few minutes and ended: "I assumed you wanted to go somewhere in this unit, but I guess I was wrong. You're never going to get anywhere by willfully disobeying orders."

Humiliated by the confrontation, Patterson returned to her desk and like an automaton continued to work on her client's problem. Later, when she thought the situation over at lunch, she did not know what to do, but she felt she could no longer remain in the Lincoln County office of the Division of Rehabilitation Services.

Questions and Instructions

1. Do you think Angela Patterson can be blamed in any way for the disgraceful scene involving Amy Wagner? If she sought your advice, what course of action would you recommend?

2. Perhaps there's an Amy Wagner in every large organization having some power over employees. What can or should employees do in the face of such tyranny?

3. Do you think that the employees individually or collectively should protest to Melanie Steuben, the division director, about letting the insurance salesman disrupt office work?

4. To what extent do you think employees are justified in acting collectively to protest against an administrator whom they dislike or whom they regard as incompetent or unfair? What about acting collectively to oppose departmental policies or practices?

5. Suppose you are an administrator heading a department or division and you detect a feeling of antagonism among the staff toward you or certain policies and practices? What can you do to improve the situation?

6. Should solicitors, even for charitable projects, be permitted to approach employees during office hours?

Selected Bibliography

Baxter, Leslie A., "Conflict Management: An Episodic Approach," *Small Group Behavior* 13 (February 1982): 23–42.

Drory, Amos, and Gluskinos, Uri M., "Machiavellianism and Leadership," *Journal of Applied Psychology* 65 (February 1980): 81–86.

Lipsky, Michael, *Street-Level Bureaucracy,* New York, Russell Sage Foundation, 1980. See "The Prospects and Problems of Professionalism," pp. 201–04.

Milbourn, Gener, Jr., and Francis, G. James, "All About Job Satisfaction," *Supervisory Management* 26 (August 1981): 35–43.

Neuse, Steven M., "The Public Service Ethic and the Professions in State Government," *Southern Review of Public Administration* 1 (March 1978): 510–28.

Phillips, James S., and Lord, Robert G., "Casual Attributions and Perceptions of Leadership," *Organizational Behavior and Human Performance,* 28 (October 1981): 143–63.

"Special Symposia Issue: Ethics in Government," *Public Personnel Management* 10 (No. 1, 1980): 1–199.

Stahl, O. Glenn, *Public Personnel Administration,* 7th ed., New York: Harper and Row, 1976. Ch. 18, "Discipline, Removal, and Appeals," 307–17.

Stevens, John M., and Webster, Thomas C., "Human Services Integration: Toward Clarification of a Concept," *Journal of Health and Human Resources Administration* 1 (August 1978): 109–26.

Wortman, Camille B., and Linsenmeier, Joan A. W., "Interpersonal Attraction and Techniques of Ingratiation in Organizational Settings," in Straw, Barry M., and Salancik, Gerald R., *New Directions in Organizational Behavior,* Chicago: St. Clair Press, 1977. pp. 133–78.

35

Coproduction for Marrsville?

Reduced grants from national and state administrations bent on cutting their expenditures, a decline in income from a 2 percent city sales tax, and other revenue losses coupled with a high inflation rate that added to the costs of all municipal services had placed Marrsville in a financial bind. City officials took a dim view of proposals for making ends meet—reducing services, increasing the fees for services, and imposing higher taxes. The public, they believed, would accept none of these without protest.

Fresh in their minds was a rate-payers' revolt against the Electric Service Company, which recently obtained a rate hike from the State Public Utilities Commission. Marrsville residents paid an average of $36.50 for 1,000 kilowatt hours—much lower than the average of $50.75 paid elsewhere in the Midwest and of $75.66 paid in the Northeast. Nonetheless, one thousand people attended a protest rally called by LOWER (Lower Our Wild Electric Rates), hundreds turned off their lights for one hour every Wednesday night, and three hundred people carried lighted candles in a march to the local office of the Electric Service Company.

Nevertheless, in addressing the City Council on the financial situation, Mayor Wendell Hollingsworth was adamant about one principle—services rendered that were supported by fees should pay their own way. For example, he said, in no way could the monthly charge for refuse collection of $4 per residence paid a private contractor be justified when the city collected only $3.25. He appointed a task force consisting of two council members, the city manager, the city engineer, and the superintendent of public works to make the refuse

164

system more cost effective without lowering the standards of service. James Caputo, assistant to the city manager, was directed to provide staff assistance to the task force.

At one time Marrsville had its own sanitation department, which gathered and disposed of refuse, but some years ago this task was turned over to a private contractor. Citizens placed their refuse in zinc or plastic containers or polyethylene trash bags in their backyards and twice a week collectors hauled the waste away.

The operation was both costly (the contractor raised his rate each year) and unsatisfactory (residents complained of spilled trash, dogs overturning containers or tearing bags apart, missed pickups, and destructive collectors who seemed purposely to batter the zinc cans or break the lids of plastic containers so that the garbage was exposed, attracting dogs and flies and giving off an offensive smell). The city had introduced a monitoring system with fines levied on the contractor when the service fell below established standards. But this effort had not improved matters and officials concluded that the problems associated with refuse collection were insoluble.

Just out of the university with a degree in public administration and employed by Marrsville only six months, James Caputo saw his assignment on the task force as his first opportunity to demonstrate his more up-to-date approach to administrative problems than that of Winston Marbury, his superior. Marbury had been a city manager for twenty-five years and had become somewhat defeatist, in Caputo's opinion, in his attitude toward innovating civic projects.

Caputo enthusiastically began his research on refuse collection by studying articles describing various city experiences appearing in professional publications and promotional brochures from equipment companies, and by writing cities of a size comparable to Marrsville to find out how they handled the problem. Soon able to speak like an authority on the topic, Caputo could state the advantages and disadvantages of side- or rear-loader truck compactors, the best cubic-yard truck capacity, the optimum size of crews handling a truck, the arguments for and against municipal collection or contract collection of refuse, and comparative costs.

The collection of refuse, Caputo decided, offered an opportunity for implementing a concept he had heard much about in his last semester at the university: coproduction. This was defined by one scholar in typical academic gobbledygook as "an emerging conception of the service-delivery process which envisions direct citizen involvement in the design and delivery of city services with professional service agents." Broaching the subject to the city manager, Caputo said: "We need to get the public involved in city management, and refuse disposal is a good place to begin. Instead of paying men to go to the backyards of people to carry out their garbage cans or trash bags to the street for pickup, the people themselves would take their trash to the curbside."

"The people of Marrsville won't want to carry their trash to the curb," Marbury replied. "For years they've been used to putting their trash in cans or bags in their backyards and forgetting about it. Getting them to go to the trouble of taking out their trash twice a week just won't work."

"But elsewhere coproduction has worked," Caputo argued. "People want to cut down on costs. They will be willing to do things themselves that the city has been doing if they can save money."

"They might if they're forced to do it, but I don't think we've reached that stage yet in Marrsville," Marbury said. "Anyway, there's nothing new in collection systems that require people to take their trash to the curb. Many places have been doing that for years, and it's not very satisfactory. People forget what day the collection is and don't put out their trash. Or they don't have time. Besides it's unsightly having curbs lined with trash bags and cans. They're an open invitation to stray dogs to overturn the cans or tear up the bags and scatter garbage and trash about. Coproduction isn't for Marrsville."

Caputo had a more receptive audience when he talked about his plan to the mayor's refuse committee. The members were impressed by the potential savings in the cost of collection—the recent demonstration against the Electric Service Company showed that the people were opposed to paying more for public services and utilities. The problem was to persuade the people to become partners in applying coproduction to refuse removal. Caputo was asked to present his ideas in a draft program.

Questions and Instructions

1. Describe in detail a publicity and promotional program to persuade the people of Marrsville to carry their trash to the curb.
2. Do you think it advisable to conduct a pilot program before the City Council were to decide to adopt a new program of trash removal?
3. In what other areas of municipal services do you think coproduction might be adopted?
4. Do you think that coproduction would help in holding the line on, or reducing, the costs of providing adequate municipal services?

5. Comment on the following statement made by the mayor of Detroit to the City Council: "It may very well be that for the near future we will have to get used to doing things for our city that we have come to expect our city to do for us."

Selected Bibliography

Bjur, Wesley E., and Siegel, Gilbert B., "Voluntary Citizen Participation in Local Government: Quality, Cost and Commitment," *Midwest Review of Public Administration* 11 (June 1977): 135–49.

Butterfield, Kevin, "The Production and Provision of Public Goods," *American Behavioral Scientist* 24 (March/April 1981): 519–44.

Hanrahan, John D., *Government for Sale: Contracting Out, the New Patronage,* Washington D.C.: American Federation of State, County, and Municipal Employees, 1977.

Heretick, D. A., "Citizens Vote to Cart Their Refuse," *American City and County* 95 (July 1980): 57–58.

Jones, Bryan D., "Party and Bureaucracy: The Influence of Intermediary Groups on Urban Public Service Delivery," *American Political Science Review* 75 (September 1981): 688–700.

Morgan, David R.; Meyer, Michael E.; and England, Robert E., "Alternatives to Municipal Service Delivery: A Four-State Comparison," *Southern Review of Public Administration* 5 (Summer 1981): 184–90.

O'Connor, John, "Refuse Collection Practices 1980: An Exclusive National Survey," *American City and County* 95 (April 1980): 34–38.

Olsen, John B., "Applying Business Management Skills to Local Governmental Operations," *Public Administration Review* 39 (May/June 1979): 282–89.

Rich, Richard C., "Interaction of the Voluntary and Governmental Sectors: Toward an Understanding of the Coproduction of Municipal Services," *Administration and Society* 13 (May 1981): 59–76.

Rosentraub, Mark S., and Sharp, Elaine B., "Consumers as Producers of Social Services: Coproduction and the Level of Social Services," *Southern Review of Public Administration* 4 (March 1981): 502–39.

Savas, E. S., "The Institutional Structure of Local Government Services: A Conceptual Model," *Public Administration Review* 38 (September/October 1978): 412–19.

———, *Privatizing the Public Sector: How to Shrink Government,*

Chatham, N.J.: Chatham House Publishers, 1981. See Ch. 3, "The Nature of Goods and Services," pp. 29–52, and Ch. 4, "Alternative Ways to Provide Services," pp. 53–75.

Sharp, Elaine B., "Toward a New Understanding of Urban Services and Citizen Participation: The Coproduction Concept," *Midwest Review of Public Administration* 14 (June 1980): 105–18.

Whitaker, Gordon, "Coproduction: Citizen Participation in Service Delivery," *Public Administration Review* 40 (May/June 1980): 240–46.

36

A Bounty on Wolves

"The legislative power of the state shall be vested in a legislature" is the opening phrase of Article III of the South Dakota Constitution. Clearly, legislative functions and powers are to be exercised by this body.

The rule-making function is a jealously guarded right of the assembly, though the actual administration and enforcement of legislative policy are carried out by the executive branches at the state and local levels of government. Accompanying the legislative delegation of authority has been the adoption of administrative rules and regulations, for example, those that govern the bounty on wolves.

At the time of South Dakota's statehood, trapping was a major occupation in the Great Plains. Predatory animals were valuable not only for their pelts but also for the bounty, authorized by the state legislature, to be paid to the trapper or hunter for ridding the state of a nuisance. The bounty was administered at the county level of government by the county commissioners under legislative authorization. The original policy regarding the bounty on wolves appeared in the Session Laws of South Dakota in 1890 as follows:

CHAPTER 96.

Providing for a Bounty on Wolves

AN ACT, to Amend Section one, Chapter 63, of the General Laws of 1881, Relating to the Killing of wolves.

Be it Enacted by the Legislature of the State of South Dakota:

1. AMENDMENT. That Section one, of Chapter 63, of the General Laws of 1881, be amended to read as follows:

"The county commissioners of each county in the State of South Dakota shall offer a bounty of three dollars for each and every wolf killed within the limits of their county."
Approved March 7th, 1890.

This system seemed to work well until the trapper brought the same wolf to the county commissioner on several occasions. Such instances brought the need for further legislative guidance to the local government. In order to emphasize legislative intent, Senate Bill 174 of the 1895 legislative session was adopted. As was frequently the case, the following bill was approved as an emergency measure:

CHAPTER 33.
Bounty for Killing Wolves

AN ACT to Amend Section 2287 of the Compiled Laws of 1887, being Section 3 of Chapter 63 of the Session Laws of 1881, Relating to Bounties for the Killing of Wolves.

Be it Enacted by the Legislature of the State of South Dakota:

1. AMENDMENT—DUTY OF AUDITOR. That Section 2287 of the Compiled Laws of 1887, being Section 3 of Chapter 63 of the Session Laws of 1881, relating to bounties for the killing of wolves be amended so as to read as follows:

Section 2287. The county auditor shall retain said affidavit [one made by a hunter or trapper] until the next regular meeting of the board of county commissioners, and the board shall audit the claim and order a warrant drawn upon the county treasurer for the bounty in favor of the party killing said wolf, the county auditor is further required to mutilate said scalp by punching at least two holes in each of the ears thereof, each hole to be at least one-fourth of an inch in diameter. No bounty shall be paid where the scalp is presented mutilated in the manner provided in this section.

2. EMERGENCY. An emergency is hereby declared to exist, and this act shall be in force and effect from and after its passage and approval.
Approved March 1, 1895.

By 1895 administrative policy had been clearly established. The county auditor filed an affidavit with the county commissioner and policed the bounty policy for the Legislature. To insure that a bounty was paid only once for each wolf killed, the auditor punched two holes, one-quarter inch in diameter, in each ear of the animal. The trapper received the bounty and was subsequently free to market the pelt.

Two years elapsed between legislative sessions, and the bounty system seemed to function well. During the 1895–97 period, however, events started working against the established bounty system. The county auditor inspected the dead animals, punched the holes in the animals' ears, and instructed the treasurer to pay the trappers. The county auditors probably did not enjoy this function of their job and recognized that many trappers were getting around the system. The Legislature once again returned to the problem and passed the following bill in 1897:

CHAPTER 136.

Relating to the Destruction of Coyotes, Wolves and Mountain Lions

AN ACT to Encourage the Destruction of Coyotes, Wolves, and Mountain Lions Within the State of South Dakota, to Provide a Bounty for the Killing of the Same; to Prevent Fraud in Obtaining Such Bounty and to Repeal Acts and Parts of Acts in Conflict Therewith and to Provide Penalty for the Violation Thereof.

Be it Enacted by the Legislature of the State of South Dakota:

1. BOUNTY. There shall be paid, as hereinafter provided, for the killing within the boundaries of this State, of the animals hereinafter mentioned, the following bounties, to wit: For each coyote so killed $1.00, for each wolf so killed $3.00, and for each mountain lion so killed $3.00.

2. HOW OBTAINED. Any person killing in this State, after the passage of this Act, one or more of the above named animals, and who shall desire to claim the bounty therefor, shall, within sixty days from the killing thereof, exhibit the scalp with the ears entire and tail connected of such animal to the county treasurer of that county in this State in which said animal shall have been killed, and shall at the same time file with the treasurer his affidavit in writing, taken before him as such treasurer, which affidavit shall be substantially in the form following, to wit:

I do solemnly swear that the skin . . , or the scalp . . with the ears entire and the tail . . connected, by . . . . . . now exhibited to the treasurer of the county of . . . . State of South Dakota, w . . . . taken from . . . . animal . . by . . . . . . killed within said county and State since the passage of the Act of the legislature of the State of South Dakota, approved the . . . . day of . . . . , 1899.

3. DUTY OF TREASURER. It shall be the duty of each treasurer of each county in which the scalp with the ears entire and tail connected of any of the above animals is exhibited to him, to examine such scalp with the ears entire and tail connected so exhibited, and if he find the scalp with the ears and tail connected have not been patched, covered, punched or cut, he shall then mark each ear by punching therein a hole not less than one-half inch in diameter, and shall then return each scalp, ears and tail to the one exhibiting the same.

4. TREASURER TO MAKE CERTIFICATE TO STATE AUDITOR. If, upon the filing of the affidavit required in Section 2 and upon the examination required in Section 3 of this Act, it shall appear to the satisfaction of such treasurer that such animal was killed in said county and State and that the scalp with the ears entire and tail connected has not been covered, patched, punched or cut, he shall issue and deliver to the person exhibiting the same a certificate addressed to the auditor of the State of South Dakota, substantially in the form following, to wit:

State of South Dakota,
County of . . . .
    I, ... , county treasurer of . . . . county, South Dakota, do hereby certify that . . . . has exhibited to me this . . . . day of . . . . , 189 . . , the skin or scalp with the ears entire and the tail connected of . . . . and has filed his affidavit with me that he killed such animal from which the skin or scalp with the ears entire and tail connected w . . . . . killed in the above county.
    And I further certify that I have examined and punched the ears of the above mentioned skin . . or scalp . . with the ears entire and tail . . connected, according to law, this . . . . day of . . . . , 189 . .
    And I further certify that there is due to the within named . . . . the sum of . . . . ($) dollars.
        [SEAL]

        . . . .
        County treasurer of . . . . county, South Dakota.

    Said certificate shall show the number and species of skin or skins or parts of skin so examined or punched and shall be signed by the county treasurer in his official capacity, attested by his seal. The treasurer shall receive from the party to whom the certificate is issued, the sum of ten cents for each and every skin so punched, which shall be in full compensation for all the services rendered.

    It became the responsibility of the county treasurer to insure that bounty practice was in compliance with legislative intent. To make sure that county officials received sufficient evidence, the trapper had to deliver the scalp, the entire ears, and tail—all connected. To further insure that double payment was prevented, the holes were increased to one-half inch in diameter.
    The legislation passed in 1897 was quite complete and one would think that the Legislature had covered every conceivable angle of fraud or deception. The trappers were ingenious individuals, though, and perhaps the county treasurers were too lax. Another two-year legislative cycle passed, and the 1899 Legislature returned to pass House Bill 97. Section 3 of that bill directed the following:

Sec. 3. DUTY OF COUNTY COMMISSIONERS. It shall be the duty of the county commissioners of each county in which the scalp with the ears entire and tail connected of any of the above animals is exhibited, to examine such scalp with the ears entire and tail connected, so exhibited, and if they find the scalp with the ears and tail connected has not been patched, covered, punched or cut, they shall then and there destroy the scalp together with the ears by burning the same to ashes and shall then return the balance of the hide to the one exhibiting the same.

House Bill 97 took the county auditor and the county treasurer out of the hide-inspection business and the reins were firmly placed in the hands of the county commissioners. Also, no trapper would collect twice because the past practice of punching holes in the ears of the animal was replaced by burning the scalp and the ears.

The practice appeared to have worked. The Legislature did not address the bounty issue for several sessions. Forty-five years later, the county commissioners decided to get out of the business of policing bounties. The economy of the state had changed considerably and few trappers made a living from killing wolves and collecting the bounty.

In 1943, the Legislature passed House Bill 162, which said:

CHAPTER 98

Amending Law Relating to Payment of Bounties

AN ACT Entitled, An Act to Amend Chapter 25.1002 of the South Dakota Code of 1939, Relating to Bounties Paid from State Funds.

Be It Enacted by the Legislature of the State of South Dakota:

Section 1. That Chapter 25.1002 of the South Dakota Code of 1939 be, and the same is hereby amended to read as follows:

25.1002. HOW OBTAINED. Any person killing in this state one or more of the animals named in the preceding section, shall make an affidavit of the fact of the killing of such animal or animals, the date of killing, the place where such animal or animals were captured or killed, and a brief statement of the method of capture or killing, and a statement of the amount of bounty claimed. The person claiming such bounty shall present such affidavit to the auditor of the county within which such animal or animals were captured or killed, together with the skin or skins of such animal or animals, showing the entire head of skins as to each animal including the ears thereon and including the upper and lower jaws together with the lips of the animal attached to such skin, and such auditor shall carefully examine such skin and if it appears that such skin has not been patched, covered, punched, or cut, the auditor shall cut from such skin the skin of the lower jaw and preserve it in an envelope attached to such affidavit, and such auditor shall indorse upon such affidavit a certificate of the date when the same was presented and the name and address of the person presenting the same. The same shall be presented to the board of county commissioners at its next meeting for approval. Such board shall carefully examine such affidavit and if satisfied that there is no fraud connected with the claim, shall approve the same by an approval signed by the chairman of such board and attested by the county auditor, under the seal of the county, and shall thereupon destroy the lips of such animal presented with such claim. The approved claim shall thereupon be forwarded to the Director, and upon approval by the Commission shall be presented to the State Auditor who shall issue his warrant therefor and mail the same to the person entitled thereto at his address to be shown upon the said affidavit.

Such bounty shall be paid to the person killing the animals for which the bounty is claimed, or his estate only, and to no other person; Provided, that such approved claim may be assigned by the person killing such animals as collateral security for an indebtedness incurred in good faith by such person, such warrant to be made payable to the assignee and assignor of such claim.

The auditor was back in control. The holes were not going to be punched because the Legislature instructed the official to cut the skin from the lip and the lower jaw bone. The county commissioners would merely approve the payment of the bounty.

As state government grew, various departments were created to handle the day-to-day administrative operations of the state. In 1961, the Legislature delegated the authority for marking skins to the Department of Game, Fish and Parks:

25.1002 Procedure on payment of bounties;

1. Any resident of this State in order to claim such bounty, shall within ten (10) days after killing any such animal mentioned in the preceding section, present and deliver only the complete skin of such animal to the auditor of the county of this state in which the animal was killed. Such auditor shall examine such skin and all parts thereof to determine whether such skin has been previously bountied in this or some other state and to determine whether there is any fraud or irregularity connected with the same. If the auditor has any doubt or question as to any skin he shall refer such skin to the game warden for investigation. After the warden's investigation, such warden shall return the skin to the auditor with the recommendation that such skin be accepted or rejected. The Commission shall, by regulation, provide the method of marking the skin accepted for bounty payment for the purpose of identification.

This act of the Legislature was codified as South Dakota Compiled Laws (SDCL) 40-36-19:

40-36-19. Marking of skin accepted for bounty. The game, fish and parks commission shall, by regulation, provide the method of marking the skin accepted for bounty payment for the purpose of identification.

This action brought to a close the legislative involvement in deciding who would inspect and mark skins for the collection of bounties. The many statutes were replaced by ARSD 41:08:03:01:

41:08:03:01. Affidavit and requirements for bounty collection. No person shall collect any bounty for any of the animals named in SDCL 41-36-15, unless the claim is completed on an affidavit described as follows:

STATE OF SOUTH DAKOTA
COUNTY OF _____
I, _____ of _____ , holder of the valid resident general hunting license number _____ , (if land-owner or occupant circle one) do solemnly swear that the following described animal(s), of which the complete skin(s) now are exhibited by me to the county auditor, have been killed by me in _____ county, and that true and correct information is given below as to the facts relating to the killing of such animal(s).

No.	Species	Age— Adult or Pup	Kill Location Sec. Twp.	Method of Kill	Date of Kill	Bounty Due
___	___	___	___	___	___	___
___	___	___	___	___	___	___
___	___	___	___	___	___	___
___	___	___	___	___	___	___

And I do further swear that no allowance or bounty has been received or paid for the killing of such animal(s), that there is due me for killing such animal(s) the sum of $_____.

_____ , Claimant

Subscribed and sworn to before me this _____ day of _____ , 19____ , and I hereby certify that the above named claimant presented the complete skin(s) to me on this date and that I have caused the complete skin of the lower lip to be removed.

_____ , County Auditor

The courts have agreed with the practice of legislative delegation of authority as long as there is a presence of legislative policy. This sentiment is summarized in *Utah Idaho Sugar Co.* v. *Temmey* (1942):

> There is no constitutional objection to delegation of an administrative agency of quasi-legislative duties, so long as the applicable statute promulgates a legislative policy and outlines the standard to be followed in its execution.

This policy is further stated in *Boe* v. *Foss* (1956):

> Although the legislature cannot abdicate or delegate its essential power to enact basic policies into law, it can, having written broad policy into law, delegate quasi-legislative power or functions, in the execution of that policy, to executive or administrative officers or agencies, provided it adopts understandable standards to guide the exercise of such powers;

The reason for the Legislature's delegating certain bounty details to the Game, Fish and Parks Department is also summarized in case law. The case of *Affiliated Distillers Brands Corp.* v. *Gillis* (1964) explained the reasoning for the existence of administrative rules. The case further provides a basic framework for a legislative review of the statutes that provide for the delegation of authority:

> [The] theory of administrative rulemaking is that certain fields and in some respects the public interest is better served by delegating a large part of detailed lawmaking to expert administrators, controlled by policies, objects and standards laid down by the Legislature, rather than having all the details spelled out through the traditional legislative process; the two prerequisites to administrative rulemaking are (1) an expressed legislative will and (2) legislative imposition of limitations on administrative agencies' powers to adopt rules and regulations; . . . . it is an unlawful delegation of legislative powers to repose absolute, unregulated and undefined discretion in an administrative agency even if it is presumed that the agency will not act arbitrarily but will exercise sound judgment and good faith.

The case of marking skins for the purpose of bounty payment illustrates the use of the legislative delegation of authority. Through proper guidance from the Legislature, administrative agencies supplied the technical framework for the implementation of law.

Questions and Instructions

1. How does this case depict the delegation of authority by the State Legislature? Why do you think it took so many legislative enactments to deal with, ostensibly, such a relatively simple matter—payment of a bounty to the killer of an animal that was declared a nuisance? Explain.
2. If you were a county auditor in 1895, what suggestions would you have made for the system of policing the bounty on wolves in South Dakota?
3. Do you feel that the procedures for marking skins used by the Department of Game, Fish and Parks since 1961 could be improved upon? What changes would you recommend and why?
4. If you were a county auditor, would you have personally punched or marked the skins or delegated this responsibility? Why? What are the potential reactions that subordinates might have in performing this marking duty?
5. Do you know of any other set of administrative regulations that systematically and comprehensively deal with a matter of such seeming unimportance? Why is it that to an outside observer some matters may appear trivial or insignificant, but to an insider they can be very important? How is this notion of selective perception related to administrative or organizational behavior in general? Explain.
6. Recently, there has been a generalized concern by state legislatures that they have "delegated" too much authority to administrative agencies. What are the major techniques that are being employed to address this concern?
7. Do you believe too much authority has been delegated to administrative agencies? If so, in what areas, and can you provide any specific examples?

Selected Bibliography

Asimow, Michael, "Interpretative Rules and Agency Statements," *Michigan Law Review* 75 (January 1977): 520–84.

Berkley, George E., *The Craft of Public Administration,* 3rd ed., Boston: Allyn and Bacon, 1981. Ch. 11, "Administrative Law and Control," pp. 383–423.

Breyer, Stephen G., and Stewart, Richard B., *Administrative Law and Regulatory Policy,* Boston: Little, Brown, 1979.

Christenson, James A., and Sachs, Carolyn E., "The Impact of Government Size and Numbers of Administrative Units on the Quality of Public Services," *Administrative Science Quarterly* 25 (March 1980): 89–101.

Davis, Kenneth Culp, *Administrative Law and Government,* St. Paul: West Publishing Co., 1975. See Ch. 1, "The Administrative Process," pp. 6–38, and Ch. 2, "Delegation," pp. 39–52.

Dimock, Marshall E., *Law and Dynamic Administration,* New York: Praeger, 1980.

Freedman, James O., *Crisis and Legitimacy,* Cambridge: Cambridge University Press, 1978. See Part I, "Sources of Crisis in the Administrative Process," pp. 13–122.

Gellhorn, Ernest, *Administrative Law and Process in a Nutshell,* St. Paul: West Publishing Co., 1972. See Ch. 2, "Nonjudicial Controls: The Political Process," pp. 29–41, and Ch. 4, "Agency Jurisdiction," pp. 50–75.

Gellhorn, Walter, and Byse, Clark, *Administrative Law,* Mineola, N.Y.: Foundation Press, 1974. See "Reasons for Establishment of Administrative Agencies," pp. 2–22, and "Characteristics of Administrative Agencies," pp. 23–53. Also, see Ch. 2, "Legislative and Executive Control of Administrative Action," pp. 54–142.

Gifford, Daniel J., "Rulemaking and Rulemaking Review: Struggling Toward a New Paradigm," *Administrative Law Review* 32 (Fall 1980): 577–620.

Jowell, Jeffrey L., *Law and Bureaucracy: Administrative Discretion and the Limits of Legal Action,* Port Washington, N.Y.: Dunellen Publishing, 1975. Ch. 6, "Legal Control of Bureaucracy," pp. 11–38.

Kaufman, Herbert, *Red Tape: Its Origins, Uses, and Abuses,* Washington, D.C.: Brookings Institution, 1977.

Lowi, Theodore J., *The End of Liberalism,* 2nd ed., New York: W. W. Norton, 1979. Ch. 5, "Liberal Jurisprudence: Policy without Law," pp. 92–126, and "Rule of Law by Administrative Formality," pp. 302–5.

Mainzer, Lewis C., *Political Bureaucracy,* Glenview, Ill.: Scott, Foresman, 1973. Ch. 2, "Public Administration Under Law," pp. 27–67.

Peters, John G., and Welch, Susan, "Political Corruption in America: A

Search for Definitions and a Theory," *American Political Science Review,* 72 (September 1978): 974–84.

Tucker, Thomas H., "Sunshine—The Dubious New God," *Administrative Law Review* 32 (Summer 1980): 537–53.

Turi, Andrew S., "The Legal Environment of Public Administration," *Administration Law Review* 33 (Winter 1981): 133–49.

37

An Alcoholic Problem

Oak Grove, a town of about fifteen thousand people, is the home of Central State University, whose students make up about one-half its population. Before 1947 package liquor sales in Oak Grove were made by private retail businesses, eight firms being so engaged that year. The increase in students after World War II, owing largely to the benefits of the GI Bill, led to a substantial increase in liquor sales. Some liquor was sold out of private dwellings near the university. University and town officials became concerned about the lack of control over liquor sales and the resulting problems: an increase in alcohol-related arrests and an unfavorable image for Oak Grove and the university.

Because of this situation, efforts to establish a municipal liquor store began. Although additional revenue was an obvious benefit of such an enterprise, control of liquor sales was the primary objective. On April 15, 1947, the people of Oak Grove voted 749 to 475 to establish a city liquor store. Originally situated on East 5th Street, the store was moved to a more central downtown location in 1962.

Many people, however, became dissatisfied with the municipal operation of a liquor store. Some believed that the city should not have a monopoly of the liquor business and urged that it be turned over to private enterprise. Others felt that it was morally wrong for the city to be in the liquor business. As one citizen put it: "The city is profiting from people's weaknesses."

Recently a liquor store employee was charged with selling an intoxicating substance to a minor. The arrest resulted from an unusual set of circumstances. Harry Stone, a police officer, and Jack Arnold, accompanied by Keith, his sixteen-year-old son, were visiting on the sidewalk in front of the liquor store. Arnold bet Stone that Keith could buy liquor in the store. Keith entered the store and bought liquor from a clerk who had noted the three talking outside and was aware that the police officer was still present. Upon completion of the sale, Stone entered the liquor store and arrested the clerk for selling liquor to a minor. Because of the circumstances, the City Council requested that the city of Oak Grove rather than the clerk be charged with the offense. This request was granted, and the city was fined for having violated a state law. The fine was later suspended on condition that the city be guilty of no similar violations within a year.

A few months later, the city was again charged with selling liquor to a minor. The violations were discovered during attempts to collect personal checks made out by a minor to the Municipal Liquor Store that were returned to the city stamped "insufficient funds." This new charge resulted in a thousand-dollar fine, the closing of the store for three days, and a one-year probation.

Faced with the prospect of losing the liquor license, the City Council decided to formulate a strict policy concerning liquor sales. After conferring with the manager of the liquor store, the council developed the following policy:

1. All patrons, regardless of age or personal acquaintance with the clerk, must present identification including proof of age before their purchase will be completed.

2. Any clerk who reports a minor attempting to buy liquor to the police will receive a $25 "bounty" if the report results in an arrest.

3. Any clerk found selling liquor to a minor will be discharged immediately.

A hand-printed sign stating "Proof of age must accompany *all* purchases" was posted. The policy was successful in preventing further sales to minors but it also resulted in some complaints. It slowed down the flow of customers through the check-out area and adults were annoyed by the requirement to present identification.

Because of the complaints, the City Council reviewed its policy on blanket identifications and adopted a new policy requiring clerks to ask for identification from anyone who appeared to be under forty-two— twice the legal age of twenty-one. A sign to this effect was posted in the store.

Questions and Instructions

1. Is the age-forty-two identification-limit policy an improvement over the blanket-identification policy? Explain.

2. Comment on the propriety of the clerk's arrest for selling liquor to Arnold's son.
3. What are the advantages or disadvantages of cities owning and operating facilities such as liquor stores, hospitals, cable television, and electric power plants?
4. Explain why you agree or disagree with the statement that "the city should not be in the liquor business."

Selected Bibliography

Adrian, Charles R., and Press, Charles, *Governing Urban America,* 5th ed., New York: McGraw-Hill, 1977. See "The City Manager," pp. 195–203, for a discussion of the qualifications, selection, duties, and special administrative and political relations of the manager, and "City Managers and City Councilmen," pp. 226–47.

Brudney, Jeffrey L., and England, Robert E., "Public Attitudes Toward Community Services: Implications for Policy," *Midwest Review of Public Administration* 14 (September 1980): 200–04.

Caraley, Demetrios, *City Governments and Urban Problems,* Englewood Cliffs, N.J.: Prentice-Hall, 1977. Ch. 10, "City Managers and City Councilmen," pp. 226–47, and Ch. 11, "City Administrators and Career Bureaucrats," pp. 248–71.

Harmon, Michael M., "Administrative Policy Formulation and the Public Interest," *Public Administration Review* 29 (September/October 1969): 483–91.

Jerome, William Travers, III, "Organization—The Framework," in Golembiewski, Robert T.; Gibson, Frank; Cornog, Geoffrey Y., *Public Administration: Readings in Institutions, Processes, Behavior, Policy,* 3rd ed., Chicago: Rand McNally, 1976. pp. 380–95.

Morgan, David R., *Managing Urban America,* North Scituate, Mass.: Duxbury Press, 1979. See "City Managers," pp. 77–79; "The Council-Manager Policy-Making Relationship," pp. 83–85; and "The Dynamics of Policy Making," pp. 88–90.

Starling, Grover, *Managing the Public Sector,* Homewood, Ill.: Dorsey, 1977. See "Discipline and Grievances," pp. 389–92.

38

Personnel Dilemma:
Terminate or Retain

In a reorganization of the State Department of Education a planning commission was established to coordinate activities and programs of its more than fifty sections and divisions and to institute and carry out comprehensive programs for the public schools and institutions of higher learning. Commission members were the superintendent of public instruction, the secretary of the State Board of Education, and the directors of the Federal Programs, Finance, and Instruction divisions of the department. Staffing of the commission was provided by the State Board of Education, headed by Dr. Frank Jordan.

In July, Dr. Jordan received funds to hire an additional secretary to perform secretarial and clerical services for the planning commission. The board at one time had only one secretary for six professional staff persons, and she could not handle that work load and take on additional duties for the commission.

Jordan's administrative assistant, Barbara White, who served as personnel officer and supervisor of the clerical staff, began working with the Department of Personnel to classify the new position and announce the opening. She consulted with the board's office planner, Pamela Goldsmith, and the facilities coordinator, John Rodriguez, to determine the classification for the new position. No one was sure what duties would be assigned to the person hired other than that he or she act as secretary to the planning commission. The job would include making arrangements for meetings, preparing agendas, recording and transcribing minutes, and providing data and materials requested by commission members. It was thought that the person would also serve as secretary to Goldsmith and perhaps do some work for Rodriguez.

183

After reviewing the anticipated duties with Dr. Jordan, White submitted a job summary to the Department of Personnel requesting a Secretary Grade I classification. The qualifications for this position were graduation from high school, one year of secretarial experience, and the ability to type 45 wmp and take dictation at 80 wpm. The classification was approved and the opening was announced.

The Department of Personnel submitted to the board a list of four eligible applicants and after interviewing them Dr. Jordan and White decided to employ Edith Reichel. Her experience was not entirely what was wanted—she had held only one secretarial position and had worked the past three years as a clerk in the state auditor's office—but she was enthusiastic about getting the job and expressed a willingness to improve her skills and take on new responsibilities. In addition, she won Dr. Jordan's sympathy because she was divorced and had two small children to support.

After Reichel began working, it soon became apparent to Barbara White that employing her had been a mistake. Reichel was a heavy smoker and cigarette ash covered her desk and papers, she was restless and disrupted office work by visiting with other staff members, and she was inattentive when receiving instructions, thus often making mistakes that resulted in her work having to be redone. Moreover, the position required abilities Reichel did not have. Goldsmith was working on a comprehensive plan for reorganizing the filing system of the department and needed assistance in her studies that she could not entrust to Reichel.

Antagonism also quickly arose between the board's regular secretary, Hazel Holmberg, and Reichel. Instead of lightening Holmberg's too-heavy work load, Reichel added to the burden. Because of Reichel's inefficiency, Holmberg had to assist her in collecting material for the commission meetings and, since Reichel's shorthand was poor, she had to take the minutes as well. In consequence, Holmberg complained to White and threatened to seek a transfer unless something was done.

White consulted Pamela Goldsmith about Reichel's performance and found that she too considered it unsatisfactory. They held a counseling session with Reichel, who, apologetic, blamed her deficiencies on problems with her two children and promised to improve. For some weeks her work was almost satisfactory, and it looked as though the problem was resolved. But Reichel soon slipped back into her old habits, and those most concerned with her work—White, Goldsmith, and Rodriguez—discussed getting rid of her while she was still on probation. None of the three, however, was willing to assume the responsibility for taking action.

Thus the question of whether to start proceedings to release or retain Reichel remained in limbo until near the end of the fifth month of her employment she failed to report for work one morning. The planning commission was to meet at ten o'clock, and telephone calls to Reichel at her home to find out where she had placed the data and papers required for the members went unanswered. Fortunately, these items were discovered by Holmberg just before the meeting began. Reichel called the office at eleven o'clock to say that she had taken a bus to visit friends in a neighboring town the night before and missed the bus back. She did not return to work until the next morning.

White reported to Dr. Jordan the difficulties encountered with Reichel, informing him that only a few more weeks remained in her probationary period. If no action were taken, she would become a permanent employee and it would be hard to remove her even if her work continued unsatisfactory. Although Jordan was busy trying to meet a deadline for completing the department budget, he promised to talk the situation over with Reichel. When she appeared in his office, he was so preoccupied with budgetary matters that he merely told her there had been some compliants about her work and urged her to try to improve it, which he felt sure she could.

After leaving Dr. Jordan's office, Reichel related to White what had occurred, saying that he had been "very nice" and reassuring about the quality of her work and her future in the department. Later, discussing the matter with Goldsmith, White said that apparently Jordan, rushed in getting the budget together, would not take the time to deal with such a minor matter as a Grade I secretary's deficiencies. They would have to make every effort to help her improve. To this end, White arranged for Reichel to attend a week-long secretarial training workshop to brush up on her typing and shorthand. At the end of the probationary period, Reichel became a permanent employee.

Reichel's good intentions did not last long and she lapsed again into her old ways. Other staff members, believing her poor performance placed an extra burden on them, complained of her slipshod work to employees in other offices at the capitol. Through friends, word of this got back to Reichel. She became very upset and in an emotional confrontation with White exclaimed that she wished she had never taken the job in the first place and that there had never been any fault found with her work in the state auditor's office. Dr. Jordan and White, she said, had not been honest with her.

Repeated complaints of staff members to Jordan finally persuaded him that to restore staff morale he would have to get rid of her and arrange for someone else to do the secretarial work for the planning commission. Since there was no really strong basis for firing Reichel, he decided to reclassify her position to a Secretary Grade II and reassign her to work in one of the auxiliary programs attached to the department.

Questions and Instructions

1. How would you allocate the blame in permitting Reichel to complete her probation and become a permanent staff member?
2. Would an orientation and training program and closer supervision have prevented the situation involving Reichel from developing?
3. What do you think of the manner in which the problem was finally resolved?
4. Do you think that Reichel was correct in her belief that her superiors had not dealt honestly with her?
5. Is it fair to the state for administrators to keep an employee who performs poorly out of sympathy for her or his personal problems or because they find reprimanding or firing a person too painful an experience? How tough must administrators be?

Selected Bibliography

Brim-Donohoe, Lue Rachelle, "A Case for Human Resources Development," *Public Personnel Management* 10 (No. 4, 1981): 365–70.

Brooks, Ronald A., "Don't Fire Your Executives—Trade Them," *Personnel Journal* 58 (May 1979): 308–10.

Dwoskin, Robert P., *Rights of the Public Employee,* Chicago: American Library Association, 1978. Ch. 2, "Exclusion and Dismissal from Public Service," pp. 34–79, and Ch. 6, "Procedural Due Process Rights," pp. 214–38.

Freedman, James O., *Crisis and Legitimacy,* Cambridge: Cambridge University Press, 1978. Ch. 8, "The Significance of Public Attitudes Toward Agency Goals: The EEOC," pp. 105–15.

Filley, Alan C., *Interpersonal Conflict Resolution,* Glenview, Ill.: Scott, Foresman, 1975.

Flynn, W. Randolph, and Stratton, William E., "Managing Problem Employees," *Human Resource Management* 20 (Summer 1981): 28–32.

Greiner, John M.; Hatry, Harry P.; Koss, Margo P.; Millar, Annie P.; and Woodward, Jane P., *Productivity and Motivation,* Washington,

D.C.: Urban Institute Press, 1981. See "Four Important Motivational Techniques," pp. 7–9, and "Some Recommendations for Improving Employee Motivation Over the Long Run," pp. 417–23.

Huseman, Richard C.; Lahiff, James M.; and Hatfield, John D., *Interpersonal Communications in Organizations,* Boston: Holbrook Press, 1976. Ch. 6, "Communication and Conflict," pp. 89–103.

Maslow, Abraham H., "A Theory of Motivation," *Psychological Review* 50 (July 1943): 370–96.

McGregor, Douglas, *Leadership and Motivation,* Cambridge, Mass.: Massachusetts Institute of Technology Press, 1968.

Meyers, Deborah, and Abrahamson, Lee M., "Firing with Finesse: A Rationale for Outplacement," *Personnel Journal* 54 (August 1975): 432–34, 437.

Stanton, Ervin S., "The Discharged Employee and the EEO Laws," *Personnel Journal* 55 (March 1976): 128–29, 133.

Tracey, William R., "Put-Down Techniques: Are You Guilty of Them?" *Personnel Journal* 58 (May 1979): 311–13.

Truskie, Stanley D., "In-House Supervisory Training Programs: High Caliber, High Impact," *Personnel Journal* 58 (June 1979): 371–73.

39

In Whose Best Interest?

Edward Holbrook was approaching the end of his six-month probationary period as a counselor in a regional office of the Vocational Rehabilitation Service, an agency of the State Department of Human Welfare, and the time had come for his supervisor, Thomas Fuentes, to assess his work.

Holbrook held bachelor-of-arts and master-of-arts degrees with a major in history and a minor in political science. The Vocational Rehabilitation Service required a master's degree in liberal arts or science but did not specify courses in social work or sociology, though this background was considered desirable in employing people. Holbrook had impressed his job interviewers with his apparent energy and eagerness to work in vocational rehabilitation.

New counselors were employed at the Counselor I level. Their duty was to meet with the clients, assess their needs, provide information to guide them in planning their careers, and help them find suitable work. Many of the clients were just out of high school and had disabilities that would require assistance. Others needed monetary assistance while they were learning a trade or profession.

A major consideration in the evaluation of counselors at the end of their probationary period was whether they were meeting their quotas of case closures, the target being sixty case closures a year. Other considerations in the evaluation were the length of the clients' employment, their satisfaction with their jobs, and the value of the assistance given them by Vocational Rehabilitation.

Fuentes regarded Holbrook as competent enough because he had surpassed the minimum performance standards required of new counselors. He had observed that Holbrook displayed eagerness in quickly attaining case closures. The surest way to quick closure was with clients who seemed uninterested in higher education and who were willing to enter vo-tech programs that did not take long to complete and that enabled them to get jobs in a comparatively short period of time. Fuentes had noted that many of Holbrook's referrals had been for vo-tech training, but these did not seem out of line with the referrals of other counselors and he had endorsed them.

After Fuentes had drafted his assessment of Holbrook's work, a highly complimentary one, he learned from one of the service employees that Holbrook's brother owned a trade school in which Holbrook had an interest in the form of some stock given him as a wedding present. Disturbed at hearing this, Fuentes reviewed the file on Holbrook's clients and noted that a suspiciously high number were enrolled in his brother's school.

Fuentes's initial feeling was that of being trapped. He had frequently praised Holbrook for his productivity and felt that such productivity would enable him to be a competent supervisor in the years to come. Now Fuentes appeared to be faced with the problem of productivity gains at the expense of questionable activities. He decided to attend to the problem at once and wrote Holbrook a note asking him to report to his office at ten o'clock the next morning.

At the meeting, Fuentes quickly got down to the matter at issue. "Ed," he said, "I received word yesterday that you have part interest in a trade school with your brother. Is that correct?"

"Yes, sir, my brother gave me a few shares as a present."

"Well, I reviewed your case load, and I found that many of your clients are enrolled in your brother's school."

"Sir, if you think I'm being dishonest, I can assure you that I'm not. I have been concerned only about the placement of my clients and I know my brother's school is reputable and will teach a trade as well as, and often better than, some of the other training schools in town."

At this point, Fuentes remembered Holbrook's competency in all other aspects and became concerned about maintaining a compatible relationship and not making a hasty judgment. He decided the best solution would be to resolve the legal ramifications of the problem.

"Ed, I know your brother runs a quality school," he said. "However, if you remember, the rule book presented to you at the time you were employed contains a section pertaining to conflicts of interest. With you owning a part of your brother's business, it looks as if you may be guilty of a conflict of interest."

Holbrook said that this might appear to be so to an outsider and that he could see the problem. He went on to assure Fuentes that the referrals had not been made out of any monetary interest—his brother's school had a large enrollment and his referrals to it would not make or break it. "My only concern," Holbrook said, "was to help out my clients."

In a brief lecture, Fuentes stressed the need for impartiality in all counselors. Holbrook's job, he said, consisted of assessing the educational needs of a person and determining what kind of school—vo-tech or college—would be best for him depending on his or her interests or abilities. Holbrook should explain to clients, Fuentes said, the amount of money they could or could not receive from the state. When a client asked questions about a certain school, Fuentes said, the counselor should not be overly opinionated, since the ultimate decision was left to the client.

To remove any suspicion of a conflict of interest, Holbrook offered to return his gift shares in the school to his brother, and Fuentes accepted this as an adequate solution to the problem. He felt convinced that Holbrook had been sincere in his belief that he had always acted in the best interests of his clients and that in the future he would be particularly careful in helping them choose a school. He decided to submit his favorable report on Holbrook as a probationer.

Holbrook, for his part, was satisfied with the conclusion of the conference, but in the weeks to come he occasionally had moments of unease. He had never been called on the carpet before by supervisors, and he felt that he and Fuentes did not have the same rapport they had had before the incident. Sometimes at conferences with clients he had the feeling that Fuentes was looking over his shoulder. However, with time these feelings disappeared completely.

Questions and Instructions

1. What were some of the positive and negative aspects of Fuentes's handling of the situation?
2. How would you handle the situation as a personnel manager and what are some of the remedial actions open?
3. How does the private sector differ from the public sector regarding conflict of interest?
4. Are case closures a good indication of vocational-rehabilitation-counselor productivity? Explain.

Selected Bibliography

Committee for Economic Development, *Improving Management of the Public Work Force,* New York: Committee for Economic

Development, 1978. Ch. 6, "Employee Performance and Satisfaction," pp. 103–25.

Bozeman, Barry, *Public Management and Policy Analysis,* New York: St. Martin's Press, 1979. Ch. 3, "Policy Philosophies, Public Management, and the Public Interest," pp. 60–82.

Dewey, John, *The Public and Its Problems,* New York: Holt, 1927.

Drucker, Peter F., "The Sickness of Government," *Public Interest* 14 (Winter 1969): 3–23.

Dvorin, Eugene P., and Simmons, Robert H., *From Amoral to Humane Bureaucracy,* San Francisco, Calif.: Canfield Press, 1972. Ch. 5, "Toward a Theory of the Public Interest," pp. 36–46.

Gordon, George J., *Public Administration in America,* 2nd ed., New York: St. Martin's Press, 1982. See "Ethics, Morality, and Corruption," pp. 546–50.

Halatin, T. J., and Flannery, William T., "Keeping Your Employees Turned On—Professionally," *Supervisory Management* 26 (October 1981): 10–14.

Hersey, Paul, and Blanchard, Kenneth H., "So You Want to Know Your Leadership Style," *Training and Development Journal* 35 (June 1981): 34–54.

Jacob, Charles E., *Policy and Bureaucracy,* Princeton, N.J.: D. Van Nostrand, 1966. Ch. 8, "Public Policy and the Public Interest," pp. 192–202.

Janka, Katherine; Luke, Robert A.; and Morrison, Charles A., *People, Performance . . . Results!* Washington, D.C.: National Training and Development Service Press, 1977. Ch. 1, "What Makes Employees More Effective?" pp. 11–22.

Lipsky, Michael, *Street-Level Bureaucracy,* New York: Russell Sage Foundation, 1980. See Ch. 5, "Relations with Clients," pp. 54–70, and "Keeping New Professionals New," pp. 204–11.

Maslow, Abraham H., "The Superior Person," in Bennis, Warren G., ed., *American Bureaucracy,* Chicago: Aldine, 1970. pp. 27–37.

Morrow, Allyn A., and Thayer, Frederick C., "Materialism and Humanism: Organizational Theory's Odd Couple," *Administration and Society* 10 (May 1978): 86–106.

Murray, R. Stuart, "Managerial Perceptions of Two Appraisal Systems," *California Management Review* 23 (Spring 1981): 92–96.

Poston, Ersa, and Broadnax, Walter D., eds., "Ethics and Morality in Government: A Public Policy Forum," *Bureaucrat* 4 (April 1975): 3–65.

See Case No. 4, "A Moral Dilemma," for additional references dealing with conflicts of interest.

40

Police Crime in Fullerton

Fullerton was a quiet Midwestern community with a population of fifteen thousand where major crimes were rare. Its Police Department had forty-five employees, forty of whom were police officers.

On Tuesday at 1:15 A.M. police officers Bill Ness and Fred Roberts answered an alarm call at Tom's Super Valu. When they arrived they noticed that the door had been jimmied open. They conducted a search and found no one inside the store. Fred then called Jimmy Kotter, the store's owner, and asked him to come down to the store to make a list of any missing items.

After making the call, Roberts noticed that Ness had grabbed two large smoked hams on display in the window cooler and was walking out the door. Roberts asked him what he was doing.

"I'm taking these home as evidence," Ness laughingly said. "Old man Kotter will never notice that two hams are missing. What he doesn't know won't hurt him."

"I don't know if you should be doing this," replied Roberts.

"Wise up, kid," said Ness. "Half the members of the force are supplementing their income like this."

Though the neighborhood was well lighted, Ness, as he was putting the hams inside the police car, did not spot Kotter walking down the street. Kotter ran over to Ness and asked him what he was doing with the hams. Ness tried bluffing his way out of this sticky situation. Realizing that Kotter did not believe his story, Ness defended himself by saying, "You're really making a big deal out of this. It's just a couple of lousy hams!" He returned the hams to the store. After completing their report of the break-in, both officers left, but Kotter was furious that a

192

police officer would try to steal two hams from him. The next morning, Kotter filed a written complaint against both officers.

When Tom Davis, chief of police, read Kotter's complaint, he immediately called Ness and Roberts into his office. Both officers admitted that Kotter's charges were true. As punishment, Davis suspended both men from duty without pay for two weeks. Davis could have fired them and perhaps even pressed criminal charges against them. But morale in the department had been low recently and he felt that imposing such a harsh punishment would do nothing to improve it.

Arnold Dillon, Fullerton's city manager, was very angry when he heard about the incident. There was no doubt in his mind that both officers should not only have been dismissed but charged with theft as well. He knew that he should take some action to rectify what he perceived as a double standard of justice, but was not sure what to do.

Questions and Instructions

1. Is Fred Roberts equally as guilty as Bill Ness?
2. Do you feel that Chief Davis's punishment of Ness and Roberts was adequate?
3. What, if anything, should the city manager, Arnold Dillon, do?
4. What should Roberts have done or said when Ness was attempting to take the hams?
5. Has a crime been committed by the officers that should have resulted in the action taken? Is more severe action required?
6. In such a situation should the city manager fire someone before that person is found guilty in a court or through an administrative hearing?
7. What policies should be instituted by both the manager and the police chief to insure there are adequate procedures to take care of such problems in the future?
8. Should a general investigation into the Police Department be instituted? Should the investigation also include a study of the administration of the department including its salary and job structure and hiring and promotion practices?

Selected Bibliography

Bittner, Egon, "Esprit de Corps and the Code of Secrecy," in Goldsmith, Jack, and Goldsmith, Sharon S., eds. *The Police Commu-*

nity: Dimensions of an Occupational Subculture, Pacific Palisades, Calif.: Palisades Publishers, 1974. pp. 237–46.

Burnham, David, "How Police Corruption Is Built into the System— and a Few Ideas for What to Do About It," in Sherman, Lawrence W., *Police Corruption,* Garden City, N.Y.: 1974. pp. 305–14.

Chruden, Herbert J., and Sherman, Arthur W., Jr., *Personnel Management: The Utilization of Human Resources,* 6th ed., Cincinnati: South-Western Publishing Co., 1980. See "Employee Discipline," pp. 411–19.

Hale, Charles D., *Police Patrol, Operations and Management,* New York: John Wiley and Sons, 1981. Ch. 4, "Occupational Hazards of Police Patrol," pp. 58–84.

Klockars, Carl B., "The Dirty Harry Problem," *Annals of the American Academy of Political and Social Science* 452 (November 1980): 33–47.

MacNamara, Donal E. J., and Schultz, Donald O., *"Discipline in American Policing,"* in MacNamara, Donal E. J., ed., *Criminal Justice 81/82,* Guilford, Conn.: Dushkin Publishing Group, 1981. pp. 110–16.

Sacks, Harvey, "Notes on Police Assessment of Moral Character," in Manning, Peter K., and Van Maanen, John, eds., *Policing: A View from the Street,* Santa Monica, Calif.: Goodyear Publishing Co., 1978. pp. 187–202.

Sheley, Joseph F., *Understanding Crime,* Belmont, Calif.: Wadsworth, 1979. See "The Police," pp. 170–77.

Souryal, Sam S., *Police Administration and Management,* St. Paul: West Publishing Co., 1977. Ch. 12, "Police Professionalism," pp. 394–415, and Ch. 13, "Suppression of Police Corruption," pp. 416–34.

Whisenand, Paul M., and Ferguson, Fred R., *The Managing of Police Organizations,* 2nd ed., Englewood Cliffs, N.J.: Prentice-Hall, 1978. Ch. 10, "Monitoring Integrity," pp. 345–74.

White, Susan O., "A Perspective on Police Professionalization," in Goldsmith, Jack, and Goldsmith, Sharon S., eds. *The Police Community: Dimensions of an Occupational Subculture,* Pacific Palisades, Calif.: Palisades Publishers, 1974. pp. 39–62.

Wilson, James Q., *Varieties of Police Behavior,* Cambridge, Mass.: Harvard University Press, 1968.

41

Restoring Peace at Maysville

Robert Haworth was the manager of operations for the State Department of Natural Resources, an agency that dealt with wildlife conservation, stream pollution, soil erosion, and other environmental problems. His responsibilities included supervision of more than a hundred people assigned to fifteen districts. Thirty of the employees reported directly to him. The district field offices were responsible for working with individuals, groups, municipalities, and counties in implementing programs designed to improve and preserve natural resources. The state provided funds and technical assistance for these programs.

The typical field office had a professional person as the supervisor and several para-professionals. The professional was required to have a four-year college degree and was the manager of the operation. The para-professionals were technicians receiving supervision and guidance from the professional.

Late one Friday afternoon in October, Haworth received a call from Jefferson Parsons, supervisor of the Maysville field office. Obviously upset, Parsons told him that Gary Foraker, technician at Maysville, had just stormed out of the office, declaring that he was resigning. Questioning revealed that the two men had become involved in a quarrel that had started over a minor "beef" of Foraker that he had received a citation from the state office for exceeding unit goals for which Parsons had not given him any recognition. Parsons closed the conversation by saying he thought Foraker would call Haworth that night at home and resign. "That's all right with me," Parsons said. "I don't feel I could work with him after this."

Before leaving the office that evening Haworth quickly reviewed the personnel files of Parsons and Foraker. Parsons was four years out of college and twenty-six years old. He had trained in three different locations in the state, spending only a few months in each, and had quickly risen from a trainee to his present supervisory position that he had held for fourteen months. He was manager of the Maysville office and also supervised a subunit at Hilton twenty miles away.

Haworth recalled that an experienced technician at Hilton, James Harold, had died of a heart attack in July and a new, inexperienced technician, Ernest Bart, had been hired in September. Parsons had been spending one day of each week in the Hilton office before Harold's death but was now spending three days a week there. Parsons had two other technicians besides Foraker and a woman professional trainee, Martha Sessions, twenty-three years old, who was one year out of college and had been in the Maysville office six months. Haworth had previously noted a weakness in Parsons's supervisory abilities—he seemed to have a one-track mind and disliked tackling more than one problem at a time. Haworth had discussed this with him and documented it in the file.

Foraker, Haworth noted, was forty-seven years old and had lived in the Maysville area all his life. He had worked for the agency seven years and had risen two pay grades during this time. He had only a high-school education but despite this had expressed a wish to further his education. To this end he had enrolled in two engineering courses by correspondence but had finished neither. He had two letters of commendation in his file for excellence in performance of work on special projects.

With the background of the two men in mind, Haworth went home feeling that he was prepared to deal at least temporarily with the situation should Foraker call.

[Note: Before reading the complete case history, consider the questions and instructions below.]

Questions and Instructions

1. What attitude do you think Haworth should take toward Foraker should he receive a call from him that night?
2. How involved should Haworth get in the situation not knowing any more details than he now has?
3. Do you think the differences between Parsons and Foraker are so deep-seated that they cannot be resolved and the two men cannot work together again?

4.   With the information you have, how would you deal with Foraker when he calls?

Haworth was preparing to watch a movie on television that evening when the telephone rang and he heard Foraker's voice when he picked up the receiver. Foraker apologized for calling Haworth at home and then got down to the purpose of the call. "Mr. Haworth," he said, "Jeff Parsons and I had a row this afternoon. I don't think I want to work under him any longer and I want to resign."

"I'm sorry to hear that," Haworth replied. "I think the office at Maysville has been doing a great job. I thought we had a good team there. What seems to be the matter?"

"It's Parsons," Foraker said. "He doesn't think enough of me to keep me informed about what's happening, or the other technicians either. Also, he's not providing direction for our trainee Martha Sessions. He spends most of his time over at Hilton and doesn't give enough time to more important programs here at Maysville."

"Well, hold your horses about this," Haworth replied. "Let's not do anything hasty. Why don't I drive up to Maysville the first of the week and get together with you and Parsons and talk the situation over. I think if we let matters rest over the weekend and then sit down and talk things over we can straighten them out."

Foraker agreed to this and Haworth, to make the forthcoming conference appear less official, suggested that they meet Monday morning in Foraker's home. The next day Haworth told Parsons of the telephone call and the meeting with Foraker at his home. "I'll pick you up about ten o'clock," Haworth said, "and we'll go and see Foraker."

When Haworth and Parsons arrived at Foraker's home on Monday morning he met them at the door and invited them into the kitchen for coffee. The meeting was more like two friends visiting a third friend than a formal session to iron out an official problem. They talked about fishing, the weather, and the quail season before getting down to business.

"I think if we talk things over and get each other's viewpoint we should be able to settle matters satisfactorily," Haworth said. "I know you've been doing good work," he continued addressing Foraker, "and the Maysville office will miss you. And I'm sure Jeff won't easily find someone who knows the area as well and can step right in to do your work."

Foraker, asked by Haworth to give his view, repeated what he had said in his telephone call to Haworth. He and Martha Sessions were not receiving any guidance or direction from Parsons and they never knew what was going on at the office. The office exceeded yearly goals, he continued, and received a performance award, but Parsons had never bothered to commend the staff for the work that earned the award. "We feel we should be treated like human beings, not robots," he said.

"I'm sorry about this," Parsons said. "I just didn't know. I guess I just don't do a good job of communicating with people. I've been so busy over at Hilton trying to get things straightened out, I've just not had the time to attend to matters as I should here in Maysville."

Parsons added that he supposed he should have proposed Foraker for an award but it hadn't occurred to him. He had never been in one place long enough to learn how much such commendation meant to staff members. "This is my first supervisory position," Parsons said, "and I guess I've had too many things on my mind to take care of them all."

"Well, I can see you have a lot on your mind," Foraker said to Parsons. "I guess I went off half-cocked. I really don't want to quit the agency. I've always liked the work, helping the region I grew up in and know best."

"There's enough blame for all of us to share," Haworth interjected. "The important thing is to try to see each other's point of view and do our job."

The three shook hands and Haworth and Parsons left to return to the office followed by Foraker in his own car. Haworth had disliked spending most of the day settling a small dispute but felt the trip had been worthwhile if peace had been restored at Maysville.

Questions and Instructions

1. How do you evaluate Haworth's handling of the situation?
2. Do you think Haworth shares any blame for letting the situation develop in the first place? What can he do to prevent such situations from developing in the future?
3. What follow-up measures might it be desirable for Haworth to take in regard to Maysville?
4. Merit awards and citations are designed to reward employees for tasks well done, to build up self-esteem, to provide recognition, and to raise morale. In the situation at Maysville this purpose clearly was not fulfilled. Discuss the value of such recognition devices in management.

Selected Bibliography

Anthony, Peter David, "Work and the Loss of Meaning," *Social Science Journal* 32 (No. 3, 1980): 416–26.

Austin, Terence W., "What Can Managers Learn from Leadership Theories," *Supervisory Management* 26 (July 1981): 22–31.

Bozeman, Barry, *Public Management and Policy Analysis,* New York: St. Martin's Press, 1979. Ch. 5, "Organization Structure and Design," pp. 112–36.

Browne, Philip, and Golembiewski, Robert, "The Line-Staff Concept Revisited," *Academy of Management Journal* 17 (September 1974): 406–17.

Gibson, Frank K., and Teasley, Clyde E., "The Humanistic Model of Organizational Motivation: A Review of Research Support," *Public Administration Review* 33 (January/February 1973): 89–96.

Greiner, John M.; Hatry, Harry P.; Koss, Margo P.; Millar, Annie P.; and Woodward, Jane P., *Productivity and Motivation,* Washington, D.C.: Urban Institute Press, 1981. Ch. 6, "Special Concerns Associated with Implementing Monetary Incentive Plans," pp. 95–105.

Hall, Richard H., *Organizations: Structure and Process,* 2nd ed. Englewood Cliffs, N.J.: Prentice-Hall, Inc., 1977. Ch. 10, "Communications and Organizational Change," pp. 266–300.

Janka, Katherine; Luke, Robert; and Morrison, Charles, *People, Performance . . . Results!* Washington, D.C.: National Training and Development Press, 1977. Ch. 6, "Implementing an Effectiveness Program," pp. 73–84.

Klingner, Donald E., *Public Personnel Management,* Palo Alto, Calif.: Mayfield Publishing Company, 1981. Ch. 5, "Rewarding and Public Personnel Management," pp. 215–93.

Lee, Robert D., Jr., *Public Personnel Systems,* Baltimore: University Park Press, 1979. Ch. 11, "Motivation Theory," pp. 303–23, and Ch. 12, "Motivation in Daily Operations," pp. 325–63.

Leidecker, Joel K., and Hall, James J., "Motivation: Good Theory— Poor Application," *Training and Development Journal* 35 (June 1981): 152–55.

Nigro, Felix A., and Nigro, Lloyd G., *Modern Public Administration,* 5th ed., New York: Harper and Row, 1980. Ch. 8, "The Geography of Organization," pp. 169–89.

Palmer, Walter W., and Dean, Charles C., "Increasing Employee Productivity and Reducing Turnover," *Training and Development Journal* 27 (March 1973): 53–55.

Porter, Lyman W., and Steers, Richard M., "Organization, Work, and Personal Factors in Employee Turnover and Absenteeism," in Hammer, W. Clay, and Schmidt, Frank L., *Contemporary Problems in Personnel,* Rev. ed., Chicago: St. Clair Press, 1977. pp. 362–76.

42

Equalizing Overtime Assignments

Kent Lemons had worked in the maintenance shops of the Air Force Air Logistics Center eleven years and held the rank of WG-10 journeyman mechanic when, angered at what he considered favoritism in the assignment of overtime work, he filed a grievance against his employer. A good family man and a church-goer, Lemons was usually even-tempered, but if he felt he had been treated unjustly he could be aroused to action.

Lemons's immediate supervisor, Oscar Putnam, was an easygoing fellow who was a pal to all the employees in the shop. Lax in his authority, Putnam was easily manipulated by workers who wanted soft jobs or special privileges.

Lemons was a steady worker with a good record and not prone to ask favors. Some months after being assigned to Putnam's unit, he became resentful because the supervisor did not always use the overtime roster in distributing overtime among the employees. Lemons, as well as others, had been skipped on a number of occasions.

The situation that finally aroused his ire occurred in March when four four-hour blocks of overtime were approved—two for the evening of March 17 and two for March 18—to repair four fuel-control units for jet engines on aircraft grounded as inoperable.

On the evening of March 17, two mechanics, Lane Deerfield and Adam Merryman, were working on the control units and the task was not completed when their regular shift ended—two units still were to be repaired. They were directed to continue their work and completed the repairs on the two units by the end of their four-hour overtime on March 18. According to the overtime roster, Lemons would have been next in line for overtime assignment. Five other employees also had prior rights to overtime before Deerfield and Merryman.

Two days later Lemons filed a grievance reporting what had happened and said in conclusion: "It is requested that I be paid eight hours' overtime missed because I was bypassed on the overtime roster."

Lemons received an answer to his grievance on March 30 that stated in part: "An emergency existed to get these jet engines out; thus, a violation of the union contract was not committed. Your overtime request is denied."

With the support of his union, Lemons appealed to arbitration and a hearing was conducted on May 10. The union's position was that Article XX (see Exhibit 1 at the end of this case) of the Labor-Management Agreement was violated when the employer failed to give Lemons an opportunity to work overtime and that no emergency situation existed that justified bypassing prescribed procedures.

The union presented several witnesses who testified that the employer failed to use the overtime roster, thereby denying Lemons his rightful turn to work overtime. In addition, the union steward argued that the employer was aware of the situation sufficiently in advance to consult and use the overtime roster and inform Lemons, who was working on the swing shift from 4 P.M. to midnight. The employees who received the overtime assignment, the steward said, were on the graveyard shift from midnight to 8 A.M.

The employer's position was that under Article XIV of the contract (see Exhibit 2 at the end of this case) management had clearly retained the right to take whatever action might be necessary to carry out the mission of the Air Force in emergencies. Article XX of the contract, it was contended, was not violated in assigning overtime work on the evenings of March 17 and 18 to employees who had been previously assigned critical work of an emergency nature. It was also held that even in nonemergency situations the practice in the shop was not to switch workers during the assembly of a specific unit. Finally, management contended that Lemons would not have been entitled to overtime work even if the roster had been used: on March 17 five other employees were higher on the roster.

The arbitrator reversed the decision of the grievance board and found in favor of Lemons. His findings were that the employer had the right to take whatever actions were necessary to carry out the mission of the Air Force in emergencies but had not properly raised this contention as a defense and had not adequately supported it with evidence. Therefore, he agreed with the union's contention that an emergency had not existed and this defense was not valid. Moreover, he did not subscribe to the employer's contention that Lemons was not entitled to be called for overtime and would not have been called if the overtime roster had been used, because this contention assumed a statement of facts not in evidence.

Questions and Instructions

1. What options other than filing a grievance did Lemons have? What might be the consequences to him of the actions taken?
2. What practices should management follow to avoid situations like the one that led to Lemons's filing his grievance?
3. Which verdict in the Lemons case do you think right and proper— that of the grievance board or that of the arbitrator? Justify your conclusion by analyzing all alleged facts in the case, noting any that are inconsistent or dubious, the contentions of Lemons, the union, and the employer, and Articles XIV and XX of the Labor-Management Agreement.

Selected Bibliography

Adams, J. Stacy, "Toward an Understanding of Inequity," *Journal of Abnormal Psychology* 67 (November 1963): 422–36.

Bloom, David E., "Is Arbitration *Really* Compatible with Bargaining?" *Industrial Relations* 20 (Fall 1981): 233–44.

Committee for Economic Development, *Improving Management of the Public Work Force,* New York: Committee for Economic Development, 1978. Ch. 4, "Collective Bargaining," pp. 62–90.

Garman, Phillips L., "Grievance Procedures in Health Care Establishments," *Journal of Health and Human Resources Administration* 2 (August 1979): 73–87.

Golembiewski, Robert T., "Civil Service and Managing Work," in Golembiewski, Robert T.; Gibson, Frank; and Cornog, Geoffrey Y., *Public Administration: Readings in Institutions, Processes, Behavior, Policy,* 3rd ed., Chicago: Rand McNally, 1976. pp. 265–92.

Lester, Richard I., "Leadership: Some Principles and Concepts," *Personnel Journal* 60 (November 1981): 868–70.

Klingner, Donald E., "Federal Labor Relations After the Civil Service Reform Act," *Public Personnel Management* 9 (No. 3, 1980): 172–83.

Miller, George, "Management Guidelines: Being a Good Communicator," *Supervisory Management* 26 (April 1981): 20–26.

Podsakoff, Philip M., "Determinants of a Supervisor's Use of Rewards and Punishments: A Literature Review and Suggestions for Further Research," *Organizational Behavior and Human Performance* 29 (February 1982): 58–83.

United States Office of Personnel Management, *Manager's Handbook,* Washington, D.C.: United States Office of Personnel Management, 1980. Ch. 8, "Appeals and Grievances," pp. 98–105.

Zagovia, Sam, Ed., *Public Works and Public Unions,* Englewood Cliffs, N.J.: Prentice-Hall, 1972.

Exhibit 1. Article XX of the Labor-Management Agreement

Overtime

Section A: The opportunity for overtime assignments will be rotated equitably among employees within the lowest organizational segment, in accordance with the particular skills determined to be necessary to accomplish the work to be performed on overtime.

Section B: In designating employees to work overtime the employer agrees to provide affected employees with advance notice when it is shown sufficiently in advance that employees may be required to work overtime on their usual days off. Employees will be notified of the overtime assignments no later than the start of their scheduled lunch periods on the day prior to the last day before their days off. The union recognizes that situations beyond the control of the employer may preclude advance notice. In these situations, the designated stewards, upon request, will be informed of the reason for the late notice of overtime assignments.

Section C: Rotational systems based on rosters established by seniority shall be utilized. Records of overtime worked and refused shall be maintained by supervisors to assure that each employee receives equitable consideration. These records may be reviewed by the designated steward upon request.

Exhibit 2. Article XIV of the Labor-Management Agreement

Management Rights

Section A: The employer retains the right in accordance with applicable laws, regulations, and the Executive Order to do the following:

1. Direct employees of the activity.

2. Hire, promote, transfer, assign, and retain employees in positions of the activity; and to suspend, demote, discharge, or take other disciplinary action against employees.

3. Relieve employees from duties because of lack of work or for other legitimate reasons.

4. Maintain the efficiency of the government operations entrusted to the employer.

5. Determine the methods, means, and personnel by which such operations are to be conducted.

6. Take whatever actions may be necessary to carry out the mission of the Air Force in situations of emergency.

43

Union Contract Negotiations in Springfield

The city of Springfield began negotiations in June 1982 with the American Federation of State, County, and Municipal Employees local for a three-year contract. The city's negotiations were conducted by City Manager Adam Arbuthnot under guidelines recommended by the labor negotiations committee of the City Council and approved by the full council. The union demanded an across-the-board wage hike of 10 percent and increased fringe benefits.

Progress in the negotiations and the positions of the local were reported regularly to the committee and council over the next several months, and the council held three special meetings each lasting more than two hours to hear from department heads and to discuss wages and benefits. The council reviewed data on wage increases for the past five years and compared these to rises in the cost-of-living index. The data revealed that nearly all employees had received pay hikes equal to, and in many instances exceeding, the rise in the cost of living during the period. Springfield's employees, according to the statistics, had fared better than workers nationally, and the council considered that its past wage actions had been reasonable.

In determining the wage increase for employees to keep up with the cost of living the council decided that increases in benefits during the year mandated by the federal government should be considered. These included the city's share in the Social Security tax increase and unemployment-compensation insurance premiums. The council also decided to take into consideration the employer's share of insurance premiums. It concluded that a wage increase for the next year should not exceed 4.59 percent for all employees.

The council was largely composed of small businessmen who hired only a few employees. They believed they were familiar with pay and working conditions in the community and felt that city employees were adequately compensated in comparison with employees in the private sector. They were bolstered in this belief in that there was a small turnover in nontechnical and semitechnical positions in city employment.

The city, however, was forced to modify its 4.59 percent limit on wage increases because of the union's firmness in its demands and continued rises in the monthly cost-of-living index. It increased the rate to 5.95 percent in August, to 6.3 percent in September, and finally to 6.5 percent in October. Council members believed 6.5 percent was a very reasonable offer in that fringe benefits (retirement, Social Security, workers' compensation, and unemployment compensation) would raise the de facto pay and benefits increases to 7.2 percent.

Council members acknowledged that the average cost-of-living index would exceed 7.5 percent but maintained that their offer was fair because in 1981 the city had given a cost-of-living increase that exceeded the actual cost-of-living rise by .5 percent. In further justification, they maintained that the increases in the federally mandated Social Security tax and unemployment-compensation tax plus health-insurance cost increases raised benefits another 1 percent. The overall increase offered by the city, taking into consideration the proposed wage and benefits increase of 7.2 percent, the previous year's increase of .5 percent, and benefits increase of 1 percent, amounted to 8.7 percent.

By late October all issues between the city and union were tentatively resolved except for the union's insistence on a 7.5-percent, rather than the city's 6.5-percent, wage increase. An impasse having been reached, the union filed a request for conciliation and fact-finding with the state labor commissioner. Upon his recommendation, a three-year agreement calling for a 7.0 percent increase for 1983 and additional increases the next two years at the rate of increase in the cost of living was accepted by both parties and signed on December 19.

Meanwhile, developments began over what seemed to be a minor matter—filling a vacancy in the Municipal Light Department—that were to upset the agreement. Two electric linemen (one the union steward and the other the secretary of the local) approached Mayor Thomas Wentwaller and asked to appear before the council to express employee concerns about employing an additional lineman. The linemen suggested that money could be made available for hiring better-qualified linemen by charging for services that the city had been previously providing at no cost to electricity users. The council approved their suggestion and imposed a new service charge that permitted a pay increase for linemen.

The council believed that the increase was made with the full knowledge of the union, since the two linemen were members and officers and the president was also a lineman. Also, in the past the union had left decisions on merit increases and individual wage adjustments to the city. The council thought this situation was no different from others in which adjustments had been made and no complaints had been filed.

Although there was some grumbling about this action among the rank and file of the union, it took no formal action until April 1983, when it filed a complaint with the state labor commissioner. It accused the city of violating collective-bargaining procedures and interfering with the union's affairs. The union contended that the city was required to hold to the 7-percent salary increase, that it had improperly given raises above that figure to a selected occupational classification (electric linemen), and that it had made special provisions for rates of pay and wages for specific individuals in the bargaining unit without inclusion of the union representative.

The union recognized the need for the city to award the pay increase to the linemen in order to compete with the private sector, especially the Southern Public Utility Corporation, but felt that competitive salary and wage problems existed in every department and that the same considerations and adjustments should be given to all employees. The union further believed that the city's unfair labor practice was creating a serious morale problem among employees that could have an adverse effect on the amount and the quality of work performed. The union asked that the city be ordered to return to the bargaining table and renegotiate rates of pay and wages for all employees covered by the bargaining unit.

The city itself saw the need for a higher percentage across-the-board increase than the 7.0 percent in the contract because of continued rises in the cost of living but decided to hold to it because of the complaint of engaging in improper practices filed with the labor commissioner. The city's defense filed with the commissioner made the following points:

1. The city's wage scales were competitive overall but a salary raise was necessary to fill the vacant lineman position.

2. The city had used benefits paid its employees as part of the percentage raise offered the union.

3. Union members had by-passed their official representatives in asking the increase for the linemen.

4. Merit raises had never before been the subject of grievances against the city.

5. The unlawful labor-practice suit was not filed until five months after the contract was signed.

Questions and Instructions

1. If you were the labor commissioner, how would you rule in the case? Why?
2. As a student learning about public personnel administration, how would you react to the following observations?
   a. The lineman should not have been recognized for purposes of salary and wage negotiation by the City Council.
   b. The basis for the wage increase should have been that it was a merit increase rather than an adjustment to the salary schedule.
   c. The city manager was the official negotiator for the city and therefore should have been the party who conducted negotiations with the union.
   d. Street Department employees are not so skilled as linemen and therefore should not expect the same salary schedule.
   e. Regional competition for obtaining linemen is greater than for obtaining help in such departments as Street Repair, Sanitation, Water, and Police; the latter jobs are competitive only locally.
3. Do you think that public employees should have the right to form unions for the purpose of collective bargaining? Why?
4. Do you think public employees have the right to strike? Discuss.
5. In the area of labor-management relations, what functions should the mayor perform? the city manager? the City Council?

Selected Bibliography

Aaron, Benjamin; Grodin, Joseph R.; and Stern, James L., eds., *Public Sector Bargaining,* Washington, D.C.: Bureau of National Affairs, 1979.

Bluestone, Irving, "Emerging Trends in Collective Bargaining," in Kerr, Clark, and Rosow, Jerome M., eds., *Work in America: The Decade Ahead,* New York: Van Nostrand Reinhold, 1979. pp. 231–52.

Charles, Henry T., "Urban Manager Roles in the '70's," *Public Administration Review* 31 (January/February 1971): 20–27.

Gottlieb, Bernard, "Steadying the See-Saw of Public Sector Pay," *Personnel Management* 13 (March 1981): 32–35.

Greiner, John M.; Hatry, Harry P.; Koss, Margo P.; Millar, Annie P.; and Woodward, Jane P., *Productivity and Motivation,* Washington, D.C.: Urban Institute Press, 1981. Ch. 2, "The Nature of Monetary Incentives," pp. 17–26; Ch. 3, "Types of Monetary Incentives

Used in the Public Sector," pp. 27–32; Ch. 4, "Incentives Involving Bonuses and Other One-Time Monetary Rewards," pp. 33–66; and Ch. 6, "Special Concerns Associated with Implementing Monetary Incentive Plans," pp. 95–105.

International City Management Association, *Employment Agreements Between Managers and Governing Bodies,* Washington, D.C.: International City Management Association, 1981.

Kalleberg, Arne L., "Work Values and Job Rewards: A Theory of Job Satisfaction," *American Sociological Review* 42 (February 1977): 124–43.

Lewin, David, and Horton, Raymond D., "The Impact of Collective Bargaining on the Merit System in Government," *Arbitration Journal* 30 (September 1975): 199–211.

Mosher, Lanning S., "Facing the Realities of Public Employee Bargaining," in Klingner, Donald E., *Public Personnel Management,* Palo Alto, Calif.: Mayfield Publishing Co., 1981. pp. 339–44.

Schick, Richard P., and Couturier, Jean J., *The Public Interest in Government Labor Relations,* Cambridge, Mass.: Ballinger Publishing, 1977.

Stahl, O. Glenn, *Public Personnel Administration,* 7th ed., New York: Harper and Row, 1976. Ch. 20, "Collective Negotiation and Bargaining," pp. 338–56.

Stanley, David T., *Managing Local Government Under Union Pressure,* Washington, D.C.: Brookings Institution, 1972. Ch. 4, "Effect on Classification, Pay, and Benefits," pp. 60–88.

Torrence, William D., "Collective Bargaining and Labor Relations Training of State-Level Management," *Public Personnel Management* 11 (July/August 1973): 156–60.

Wellington, Harry, and Winter, Ralph K., Jr., *The Unions and the Cities,* Washington, D.C.: Brookings Institution, 1971.

44

Pariah in the Public Library

The Dale City Public Library was governed by a six-member board appointed by the mayor for two-year terms. It met standards for accreditation by the State Library Association by employing a director with a master's degree in library science, by having a minimum of fifty thousand volumes for circulation and five thousand volumes for reference, and by maintaining other requirements in staffing and facilities specified for a Class B city like Dale City. In addition to the director, the staff comprised three full-time assistant librarians, two part-time employees used chiefly at the check-out desk, and a janitor. From ten to fifteen volunteers served regularly in the library, and an association, Friends of the Library, carried on various activities for the benefit of the institution.

The previous year, the director of the library had resigned to take a similar position in a library in a larger city, and one of the assistant librarians, Suzanne Bickley, had been named acting director. Bickley was a member of a prominent family in the community and also popular with the library's clientele. While a search for a new director was under way, Bickley did outstanding work in supervising the moving of the library to a new building. Although Bickley lacked a master's degree in library science—she had a bachelor-of-arts degree with a major in English and had accumulated only six credits in library science in postgraduate work—she applied for the position of director.

Bickley's application created a dilemma for the library board in choosing a new director. It appreciated her efficiency in directing the library during the months following the director's resignation—especially her handling of the problems in the removal to a new building—and most members considered her capable of filling the position. She also had the backing of the officers and most of the members of Friends of the Library as well as her associates in the library. But if the library board were to name her director, it would mean losing state accreditation. Though a municipal library did not necessarily have to be accredited by the state, loss of accreditation would cause it to be dropped from membership in the State Association of Public Libraries and make it ineligible for state grants-in-aid and very likely for federal grants as well.

At a meeting at which board members heard from Bickley supporters, the board voted 5 to 1 to appoint an outside candidate to the directorship mainly in order to keep the library eligible for governmental grants-in-aid. The successful candidate was Juanita Smithers, who had earned a master's degree in library science at the state university and who had two years' experience as an assistant librarian in a neighboring city. Smithers was not a complete stranger to Dale City, however, since she had attended Dale City Junior College two years before going on to the university.

Smithers's appointment caused an immediate uproar among Bickley's many supporters, who filled the letters column of the Dale City *Daily News* with protests for a week. Bickley contributed to the agitation by filing a suit in District Court against the library board alleging improprieties in the procedures followed in appointing the new director.

Smithers met with great hostility when she assumed the directorship. Bickley was openly rude, other staff members were uncooperative, the number of volunteer workers dropped, and the Friends of the Library discontinued some of its supportive activities. The situation had not improved very much after three months and Smithers was on the verge of resigning.

Questions and Instructions

1. Do you think Smithers should complain to the library board about the rudeness of Bickley and the lack of cooperation from other library employees?
2. What suggestions do you have for courses of action Smithers might institute to win acceptance in the community? to win acceptance from her staff?
3. Should the library board intervene in the situation?
4. What are some of the advantages and disadvantages of promoting from within an organization? from outside an organization?

Selected Bibliography

Alderfer, Clayton P., and Brown, L. Dave, *Learning from Changing: Organizational Diagnosis and Development*, Beverly Hills, Calif.: Sage Publications, 1975.

Caraley, Demetrios, *City Governments and Urban Problems*, Englewood Cliffs, N.J.: Prentice-Hall, 1977. Ch. 13, "City Private Elites," 288–316.

Huntley, Robert J., and MacDonald, Robert J., "Urban Managers: Organizational Preferences, Managerial Styles, and Social Policy Roles," in *Municipal Yearbook 1975*, Washington, D.C.: International City Management Association, 1975. pp. 149–59.

Klingner, Donald E., *Public Personnel Management*, Englewood Cliffs, N.J.: Prentice-Hall, 1980. Ch. 7, "Job Analysis, Classification, and Evaluation," pp. 106–32, and Part 4, "Staffing," pp. 135–204.

Luthans, Fred, and Chapman, J. Brad, "The Female Leadership Dilemma," *Public Personnel Management* 4 (May/June 1975): 173–79.

Nirenberg, John, "Constraints to Effective Motivation," *Supervisory Management* 26 (November 1981): 24–29.

Provan, Keith G., "Board Power and Organizational Effectiveness Among Human Services Agencies," *Academy of Management Journal* 23 (June 1980): 221–36.

Radin, Beryl A., "Leadership Training for Women in State and Local Government," *Public Personnel Management* 9 (March/April 1980): 52–60.

Rice, Robert W., "Leader LPC and Follower Satisfaction: A Review," *Organizational Behavior and Human Performance* 28 (August 1981): 1–25.

Roos, Leslie L., Jr., and Hall, Roger I., "Influence Diagrams and Organizational Power," *Administrative Science Quarterly* 25 (March 1980): 57–71.

Schmitt, David R., "Performance Under Cooperation or Competition," *American Behavioral Scientist* 24 (May/June 1981): 649–79.

Shafritz, Jay M.; Balk, Walter L.; Hyde, Albert C.; and Rosenbloom, David H., *Personnel Management in Government: Politics and Process*, New York: Marcel Dekker, 1978. Ch. 7. "Recruitment, Selection, and Placement," pp. 117–39.

Stahl, O. Glenn, *Public Personnel Administration*, 7th ed., New York: Harper and Row, 1976. Ch. 5, "Classification of Positions," pp. 74–92.

Trounstine, Philip J., and Christensen, Terry, *Movers and Shakers: The Study of Community Power*, New York: St. Martin's, 1982. Ch. 2,

"Social Science and the Study of Community Power," pp. 17–53, and Ch. 3, "A Primer in Power Structure Study," pp. 54–77.

Van Wagner, Karen, and Swanson, Cheryl, "From Machiavelli to Ms.: Differences in Male-Female Power Styles," *Public Administration Review,* 39 (January/February 1979): 66–72.

Weaver, Charles N., "What Women Want in a Job," *Personnel Administrator* 22 (June 1977): 66–71.

45

From Showplace to Eyesore

Built in downtown Zenith in 1912, the fourteen-story Wilson Hotel dominated the skyline. At that time Zenith was a railroad and meat-packing center, and the hotel was a showplace of the prosperous city, the preferred stopping place for traveling businessmen, the scene of conventions, and the setting for balls and other social events. It had been purchased in the 1920s by a hotel chain, which had operated it successfully until the late 1950s when it began to deteriorate as patronage fell off.

By this time Zenith was experiencing problems common to many cities of its size. Its two main industries were declining as meatpacking became decentralized and railroads lost passengers to private automobiles and airlines and freight to trucking. As these businesses declined, so did the center city. Population shifted to the suburbs and developers of new office buildings and shopping centers avoided the declining central city. Motels rather than hotels attracted travelers and conventions.

By 1964 the Wilson needed extensive renovation, and the hotel chain, finding it a money-losing operation, sold it to a property-management company based in New York that was buying similar properties in other Midwestern cities. As the downtown grew seedier in the following years, the new owners of the Wilson found it could not be profitably operated even as a second-class hotel. To cut costs, they reduced services and deferred maintenance, and as the hotel got shabbier it became chiefly a residence for people on welfare and elder citizens living on Social Security.

In the late 1960s the Chamber of Commerce and civic leaders became increasingly concerned over the condition of the downtown business district, and urban-renewal plans of varying scope were drawn up and debated. At last, in 1970, a renewal program was begun with the aid of matching funds from the federal government. Several blocks of old buildings were razed, and new municipal buildings, a convention center, and a civic auditorium were constructed. But the grandiose renewal project was still incomplete when the source of money dried up, hurried by a tax revolt resulting in a state property-tax "lid" bill.

Not included among the structures scheduled for demolition in the first phase of the urban-renewal project, the Wilson Hotel had continued to decline. Its income was low and it had become so much a center for "undesirables" that the owners at last decided to close it. In the late 1970s the elaborate sandstone cornices on the upper three stories were badly deteriorated and pieces were falling to the pavement. The hazard was so great that the city was forced to build a covered walkway around the structure on two sides, extending into the parking lane of the busy streets. The management firm had given up any attempt to maintain the hotel building and property taxes were $250,000 in arrears.

In 1980 hope for the Wilson Hotel was revived when it was purchased by a local syndicate, headed by a former mayor and one of Zenith's largest real estate developers. They planned to pay the back taxes and convert the hotel into an office building. A year later work was proceeding on the renovation project when a fire damaged the structure so badly that the financial backers were forced to abandon the project. The unpaid taxes continued to mount.

At the same time the hotel continued to deteriorate. It became the haunt of vagrants, drug addicts, and alcoholic derelicts, who in bad weather often started fires to keep themselves warm. Calls to the fire department to extinguish these blazes were frequent. Newspaper, television, and radio editorials criticized the city for failure to do something about the structure, and civic-improvement groups agitated that the eyesore be either renovated or demolished.

But though the Wilson Hotel was frequently brought up at meetings of the City Planning Commission and the City Council, no one could conceive of a practicable plan to resolve the problem the hotel created. The owners suggested obtaining a federal grant and converting the hotel into a subsidized housing project for senior citizens, but this plan failed. The owners were willing to sell if they could get back their original investment, but there were no buyers. The hotel was valued on the property-tax lists at $400,000 but its real value was probably much less. Back taxes now had reached $350,000, which any new owner would have to pay. The city considered condemning the property for tax default, but even at a tax auction it probably would not sell. Moreover, under state law, when a property was sold for taxes, the previous owner had two years in which to pay the taxes and reclaim the property. If the city took over the property, it would forfeit the taxes and also bear the estimated $200,000 cost of demolition before the land could be offered for sale. The City Council was reluctant to incur this expense.

Another year passed and the hotel still stood, slowly disintegrating. Although it was certified by the city Building Department as structurally sound, renovation of the solid old structure would cost more than razing it and erecting a new structure. It became an issue in the city election of 1982, and the winning mayoralty candidate promised, among other reforms, to do something about the hotel. One avenue of help had come from the state legislature, which had established a body called the Urban Renovation Authority with power to act on behalf of a city or county government to condemn and sell such properties as the Wilson. This could not be done immediately, however, because any nongovernmental purchaser would still have to contend with the two-year rule that allowed the old owner to pay off taxes and reclaim the property.

Upon taking office, the new mayor told the city planning director to find a solution to the long-festering Wilson Hotel problem. The city could not afford to renovate the building out of its own resources, and because no purchaser with any credible prospect of restoring it appeared, demolition seemed to be more realistic. This would raise an outcry from historical-preservation groups, but the city attorney advised that, although they might take their suit to court, the city would win its case. Extensive renovation could not be undertaken without urban-renewal grants, which in the 1980s seemed unlikely. Having tossed the hot potato of the Wilson Hotel to the planning director, the mayor went on to devote himself to fulfilling other campaign promises.

Questions and Instructions

1. You are the planning director. Consider the assumptions below, and come up with recommendations to make to the mayor.
   a. The hotel cannot be allowed to stand any longer. Can you suggest any economical way in which it could be renovated, or should the city abandon this idea?
   b. The hotel possibly can be incorporated into the city's long-range urban-renewal and development plans. Bear in mind that the city would like to avoid any more drain on its finances than necessary.
2. How much criticism should the city receive for allowing this problem to go on for so long? In what ways might the problem have been resolved in the past?

Selected Bibliography

Adrian, Charles R., and Press, Charles, *Governing Urban America*, 5th ed., New York: McGraw-Hill, 1977. Ch. 14, "The Physical Design of Cities," pp. 335–59.

Brewer, Garry, *Politicians, Bureaucrats and the Consultants: A Critique of Urban Problem Solving*, New York: Basic Books, 1973.

DeGrove, John M., "State-Local Relations: The Challenge of New Federalism," *National Civic Review* 71 (February 1982): 75–83.

Fox, Douglas M., *The Politics of City and State Bureaucracy*, Pacific Palisades, Calif.: Goodyear Publishers, 1974.

Gruen, Victor, *The Heart of Our Cities*, New York, Simon and Schuster, 1964. Ch. 6, "Flight and Blight," pp. 73–82, and Ch. 8, "The False Friends of the City," pp. 98–113.

Kleber, Thomas P., "Forty Common Goal-Setting Errors," *Human Resources Management* 11 (Fall 1972): 10–13.

Lindley, Christopher, "Changing Policy Management Responsibilities of Local Legislative Bodies," *Public Administration Review* 35 (December 1975): 794–97.

Lowenstein, Louis K., and McGrath, Dorn C., Jr., "The Planning Imperative in America's Future," in Dentler, Robert A., ed., *Urban Problems: Perspectives and Solutions*, Chicago: Rand McNally, 1977. pp. 28–34.

Mikulecky, Thomas J., "Intergovernmental Relations Strategies for the Local Manager," *Public Administration Review* 40 (July/August 1980): 379–81.

Molotch, Harvey, "The City as a Growth Machine," *American Journal of Sociology* 82 (September 1976): 309–32.

Morgan, David, *Managing Urban America: The Politics and Administration of America's Cities*, North Scituate, Mass.: Duxbury Press, 1979. Ch. 3, "Urban Policy Making," pp. 68–95.

Reagan, Michael D., and Sanzone, John G., *The New Federalism*, New York: Oxford University Press, 1981.

Rosenbaum, Nelson M., *Citizen Involvement in Land Use Governance: Issues and Methods*, Washington, D.C.: Urban Institute, 1975.

Scott, David C., "Making Decisions," in Powers, Stanley; Brown, F. Gerald; and Arnold, David S., eds., *Developing the Municipal Organization*, Washington, D.C.: International City Management Association, 1974. pp. 102–12.

Stephens, G. Ross, "State Centralization and the Erosion of Local Autonomy," *Journal of Politics* 36 (February 1974): 44–76.

Stinchomb, Jean L., "The Failure of Community Leadership: Urban Renewal in Toledo," in Stinchcomb, Jean L., *Reform and Reac-*

tion: City Politics in Toledo, Belmont, Calif.: Wadsworth Publishing, 1968. pp. 129–50.

White, Louise G., "Improving the Goal-Setting Process in Local Government," *Public Administration Review* 42 (January/February 1982): 77–83.

Wilson, James Q., "Planning and Politics: Citizen Participation in Urban Renewal," in Wilson, James Q., ed., *Urban Renewal: The Record and the Controversy,* Cambridge, Mass.: Massachusetts Institute of Technology Press, 1966. pp. 407–21.

Wright, Deil S., *Understanding Intergovernmental Relations,* 2nd ed., North Scituate, Mass.: Duxbury Press, 1978.

Yates, Douglas, *The Ungovernable City: The Politics of Urban Problems and Policy Making,* Cambridge, Mass.: Massachusetts Institute of Technology Press, 1978.

Yates, Douglas, "Urban Government as a Policy-Making System," in Masotti, Louis, and Lineberry, Robert, *The New Urban Politics,* Cambridge, Mass.: Ballinger, 1976. pp. 235–64.

46

The Ordeal of Change

Alex Stone was an aggressive and determined young man with a drive to get things done quickly and efficiently. He had received a bachelor's and then a master's degree in public administration with a major in city management from a large Midwestern university. Upon receiving his second degree at the age of twenty-three, he turned to the network of earlier graduates known as the "True Connection" for assistance in getting a job. The alumni helped him obtain his first position as assistant city manager in Plainview, a city of about 100,000 population.

The city manager of Plainview was Frank Bartels, a member of the True Connection, who demanded much of his assistant but who took pains to teach him his job. In Plainview, Stone displayed his managerial talents best in municipal finance, job classification, and organization. He was respected rather than liked by employees, and he realized this. He never pretended to be a good politician, he would say, and preferred to leave the politicking and public relations to Bartels.

After five years as assistant city manager, Stone realized he had come to a dead end insofar as his own advancement in Plainview was concerned. He discussed his prospects with Bartels, who advised him to "strike out for his own city." Taking stock of his own assets and liabilities, Stone decided that Bartels was right. He realized that he had made some mistakes but he thought these were canceled by the recognition he had received for tasks expeditiously performed in Plainview.

Stone, as one would expect from his character, began his job search in a practical way. He prepared a comprehensive resume, passed the word among the True Connection and notified the job-placement office of his alma mater that he was looking for a new position and answered advertisements in the city-management and public-administration publications. But jobs were scarce in the central part of the state, where he hoped to locate. He did not, however, rule out going further afield. Finally, after several disappointments, he learned of an ideal opening in Sparta, a city in the state with a population of 175,000, that offered a salary of $38,500. With strong references from Bartels and Professor John McGee, the chairman of his graduate committee, and the support of the True Connection, Stone was invited to Sparta for interviews with the mayor, City Council members, and the city manager. These interviews went well, and an offer was quickly extended. Stone was elated and told Bartels on his departure from Plainview that he looked forward "to calling the shots from City Hall."

Stone found his first weeks on the job exciting. City officials, elective and appointive, were friendly and informative about municipal affairs and they welcomed a dynamic young administrator whom they thought likely to solve long-standing problems, some of which, Stone discovered, were acute. These did not worry him. He accepted the challenge of solving them, convinced that he would register his personal imprint on the city with a more efficiently operated government.

Singling out the personnel system for his first close examination, Stone asked for a summary profile of all employees and for a copy of all personnel policies, rules, and regulations. He was initially most interested in the system of job classification and pay, an area that he felt his knowledge and experience especially had prepared him to tackle.

After spending hours studying the reports, Stone discovered many disparities in job classification and many inequities in pay. The problem, he decided, was that the system, in operation for twenty-five years, had not been basically overhauled to meet the needs of a government that had assumed new services and responsibilities in recent years of rapid growth. Instead of being incorporated into the basic scheme, new classifications were added so that there was a multiplicity of them. In effect, Stone concluded, the generalizations and flexibility necessary for an adequate position classification had led to abuses within each "job family" or those jobs that were alike in the work performed and the skills needed for the required tasks. He decided, also, that misuse of seniority in making job assignments had played a part in the disparities he found in the system.

Because of the complexity of the problem, Stone felt that an outside evaluation of the personnel system by a management firm should be conducted. He submitted a request for proposal (RFP) to Public Management Consultants, a privately owned and locally based firm. It proposed that the position-classification system be examined through desk audits so that jobs could be properly grouped on the basis of job-related characteristics that pertained to satisfactory work performance.

The evaluation required two months. The report stated that "confusion is the only standard operating in the present classification system." It suggested a new hierarchical arrangement of positions based on the knowledge required, supervision given and received, complexity of the work performed, scope and effort of the tasks, physical demands of the work, and personal contacts and their purposes. Stone sent copies of the report to council members and recommended its adoption. After a brief discussion of the report at a regular meeting, the council approved it by a vote of 4 to 1.

The next day Stone sent copies of the report to the director of personnel and the heads of line departments with a memo ordering them to implement the new classification system as quickly as possible. He stated that the new plan would bring about major changes in office arrangements, power and pay hierarchies, and office accountability.

City employees had been aware of the study being conducted of the classification system, but they had no idea of its extent until now. They reacted with fear and resentment. Those who held positions that would be reclassified were upset because generally they had become accustomed to doing things in certain ways and dreaded the uncertainty of new conditions. Some complained that the reclassification scheme would produce new inequities. In brief, they preferred following familiar paths to embarking on new ones.

At a meeting the department heads told Stone that implementation of the new system was encountering difficulties. Some of the more outspoken declared it would cause more problems than it would solve. Stone was shocked. He could not understand why a system worked out so carefully to introduce efficiency and economy into city operations and to correct inequities in work assignments and pay could meet with such opposition. Reform, he discovered, was easier to propose than to effect.

Questions and Instructions

1. If you were Stone, would you seek advice from Bartels? If you would not, why not? If you would, why? If you were Bartels, what advice would you offer Stone?
2. Is it fair to change job classifications for people who have tenure?
3. Would it have been desirable for Stone to have consulted with the heads of line departments before hiring Public Management Consultants? before bringing the reclassification plan before the City Council? before issuing the implementing order? Why?
4. What might happen to Stone's career in Sparta if he insists upon immediate implementation of the classification plan? If he backs

down now, is it likely departmental heads and employees will see him as immature, inexperienced, and indecisive?

5. How is job classification related to human-resource planning?
6. What lessons should Stone have learned from this experience that might be helpful to him in making administrative and policy decisions? Discuss.
7. What appear to be Stone's basic faults as an administrator?
8. What criteria would you use in selecting an outside consultant? Should the consultant only be study oriented—that is, concerned with a personnel study—or should he or she also be process oriented—concerned with change implementation?

Selected Bibliography

Bowen, Don L., and Collett, Merrill J., "When and How to Use a Consultant: Guidelines for Public Managers," *Public Administration Review* 38 (September/October 1978): 476–81.

Boynton, Robert Paul, and Wright, Deil S., "Mayor-Manager Relationships in Large Council-Manager Cities: A Reinterpretation," *Public Administration Review* 31 (January/February 1971): 28–36.

Carrell, Jeptha J., "The City Manager and His Council: Sources of Conflict," *Public Administration Review* 22 (December 1962): 203–8.

Caruth, Don; Middlebrook, Bill; and Davis, Debra, "How to Communicate to Be Understood," *Supervisory Management* 27 (February 1982): 30–37.

Eddy, William B., "The Management of Change," in Powers, Stanley; Brown, F. Gerald; and Arnold, Davis S., eds., *Developing the Municipal Organization,* Washington, D.C.: International City Management Association, 1974. pp. 147–59.

Fletcher, Thomas W., "What Is the Future of Our Cities and the City Manager?" *Public Administration Review* 31 (January/February 1971): 14–20.

Frankenhuis, Jean Pierre, "How to Get a Good Consultant," *Harvard Business Review* 55 (November/December 1977): 133–39.

Ghropade, Jai, and Atchison, Thomas J., "The Concept of Job Analysis: A Review and Some Suggestions," *Public Personnel Management* 9 (No. 3, 1980): 134–44.

Jones, Pamela R.; Kaye, Beverly; and Taylor, Hugh R., "You Want Me to Do What?" *Training and Development Journal* 35 (July 1981): 56–62.

Kantor, Rosabeth Moss, "Power, Leadership, and Participatory Management," *Theory into Practice* 20 (Autumn 1981): 219–24.

Korda, Michael, *Power: How to Get It, How to Use It,* New York: Random House, 1975.

Kotter, John P., and Schlesinger, Leonard A., "Choosing Strategies for Change," *Harvard Business Review* 57 (March/April 1979): 106–14.

Lawton, Esther C., and Suskin, Harold, *Elements of Position Classification in Local Government,* Chicago: International Personnel Management Association, 1976.

Patti, Rino J., "Organizational Resistance and Change: The View From Below," *Social Science Review* 48 (September 1974): 367–83.

Rehfuss, John, "Managing the Consultantship Process," *Public Administration Review* 39 (May/June 1979): 211–14.

Shafritz, Jay M.; Balk, Walter L.; Hyde, Albert C.; and Rosenbloom, David H., *Personnel Management in Government: Politics and Process,* New York: Marcel Dekker, 1978. Ch. 6, "Position Classification and Pay," pp. 93–116.

Solomon, Robert J., "Determining the Fairness of Salary in Public Employment," *Public Personnel Management* 9 (No. 3, 1980): 154–59.

Stromberg, Charles H., and Wilcox, Robert F., *The Urban Manager As an Agent of Planned Change,* Denver: The Graduate School of Public Affairs, University of Colorado-Denver, 1977.

Thayer, Paul W., "Personnel Challenges in the Eighties," *Public Personnel Management* 9 (No. 4, 1980): 327–35.

Thompson, John T., "Helping Line Managers to Be Change Agents," *Training and Development Journal* 35 (April 1981): 52–56.

U.S. Office of Personnel Management, *Position Classification: A Guide for City and County Managers,* Washington, D.C.: Government Printing Office, 1979.

———, *Goals and Techniques for a Merit Pay System,* Washington, D.C.: Government Printing Office, 1981.

West, Jonathan P., and David, Charles, "City and County Supervisors' Perceptions of Local Government Merit Systems," *International Journal of Public Administration* 1 (No. 1, 1979): 31–42.

47

Sick Leave or AWOL

Paul Kahoe had been employed five years by the Federal Aviation Administration (FAA). He joined as an Air Traffic Control Specialist (Station) GS-7 upon receiving an honorable discharge from the United States Air Force, where he had been an air traffic controller. His first assignment with the FAA was with a Flight Service Station (FSS) in Arkansas. After three years he was transferred to another station in Nebraska. His performance was satisfactory and he was advanced to the grade of GS-11.

The previous year on August 21 Kahoe submitted a request to his team supervisor, George Wiesener, for annual leave plus an additional period of leave without pay from September 15 to November 1. In an accompanying letter he explained that he wished to "join a select expeditionary force in the capacity of production consultant" for a journey to the Marshall Islands to locate the wreckage of the airplane flown by the famous aviator Amelia Earhart, lost in the Pacific in 1937. He himself had contributed $20,000 to the project.

His supervisor, Wiesener, was also the watch-scheduling officer responsible for coordinating annual leaves for station personnel. Normal procedures called for all controllers to submit their leave schedules between January and March. Based on the requests, the watch schedule was made out for the year. Any requests submitted after March 1 were approved only if the watch schedule could be covered.

After checking the schedule for the period, Wiesener informed Arthur Lightner, the station supervisor, of Kahoe's request. He explained that it could not be accommodated without creating an overtime situation. He added that fourteen days of the six-week period pre-

224

sented especially difficult operational problems. Lightner called the regional office to determine if overtime would be allowed in this instance. He was advised that it could not be authorized—that overtime could be given only to cover previously authorized annual leave, sick leave, and training.

Informed by Wiesener that his request was denied, Kahoe became upset and said he might resign to go on the expedition and hope to be reinstated on his return. Following the conversation, Wiesener documented it on a Memorandum for Record (MFR).

Wiesener heard nothing more about the leave until September 12 when, talking with Fred Summers, a friend and co-worker of Kahoe, Summers asked, "Have you gotten Kahoe's watch covered?" Wiesener asked him to elaborate and Summers replied that Kahoe was taking sick leave and would go on the Marshall Islands expedition. Disturbed by this information, Wiesener telephoned Dr. Edward Perth, the flight surgeon for the station, to ask for advice on how to handle the situation if Kahoe were to request extended sick leave. He was advised, if this should happen, to make no decision until receiving supporting medical information from Kahoe's physician. A release would have to be requested from Kahoe for Dr. Perth to review his medical records. As before, Wiesener prepared a memorandum of the conversation. He gave the information on Kahoe to Lightner and received an outline on how to handle the situation should Kahoe ask for sick leave. Kahoe was to be told that a detailed medical statement was required, and it might be necessary for an FAA medical examiner to confirm the stated health condition.

Early on the morning of September 17 Kahoe called in sick. That afternoon he came into the station and handed Wiesener a letter signed by Dr. Fleming Peterson. The letter itself was not dated but bore a notarization dated September 17. The letter stated: "Paul Kahoe is a patient of mine. I have examined him and consulted Dr. Charles Atkinson in Omaha. It is my opinion that he should be placed on sick leave until further notice." Wiesener asked Kahoe how much sick leave he would need and was told "a couple of months." Wiesener informed Kahoe of the procedure that had to be followed for the leave request to be approved or disapproved, explaining that this would take a few days.

Wiesener again consulted Lightner, who advised him to inform Kahoe that his sick leave was disapproved until his medical records could be reviewed. Kahoe was to be assigned to administrative duties at the station pending review of the request. Seeking to get in touch with Kahoe to inform him of the decision, Wiesener called his home three times, leaving word on a message recorder for him to return the calls.

On the third call, he stated that the sick leave was disapproved until the medical condition could be verified. Next day both Wiesener and Lightner went to Kahoe's home to acquaint him with the decision about the request for sick leave and found no one there. On returning to his office Lightner wrote Kahoe a letter explaining the situation and the attempts to reach him by telephone and a personal visit. Kahoe was told to return to work or he would be considered AWOL until he justified his sick-leave request. Later in the day the mail brought a letter from Kahoe releasing his medical records, but Lightner's letter to him was returned the next week stamped "unclaimed."

Kahoe's medical history as reported by his physician, Dr. Peterson, related that on August 24 Kahoe on an office visit had complained of symptoms of heart problems and of feelings of anxiety and depression. Dr. Peterson had examined him but found nothing physically wrong. On a second visit by Kahoe on September 7, Peterson found him still nervous and depressed and was told he was unable to sleep or concentrate. The doctor prescribed a mild medication for sleep and suggested that he obtain a sick leave.

Kahoe returned to Dr. Peterson's office on September 14 and reported that the medication did not seem to be doing any good. He was placed on stronger medication and advised to return if there were adverse side effects. Kahoe saw Peterson again on September 17 and since no undue symptoms had developed was told to check back in about two weeks. The doctor stated that he could find no obvious cause for depression and that the amount of leave time Kahoe might need was indeterminable. He planned to reevaluate Kahoe's condition when he returned in two weeks. His diagnosis was that Kahoe suffered from anxiety, neurosis, and depression. On October 4 Dr. Perth wrote Dr. Peterson requesting information on the reevaluation and received the reply that Kahoe had not kept the appointment and that attempts to reach him at his home had been unsuccessful.

Kahoe finally got in touch with the station on October 22 when he reported for duty. Asked when he had returned to the area, he stated that it was on October 19 but he had not reported then because he knew he needed a release from Dr. Peterson, which he had obtained on October 22. Dr. Peterson had completed a form covering the leave from August 22 through October 22 and wrote Dr. Perth on October 22 that Kahoe was released to full active duty on that date, seemed to be recovered, had taken no medication for ten days, and had probably suffered an anxiety spell with mild depression which had abated. No future problems were foreseen.

On returning to work, Kahoe was assigned administrative duties. He declined to inform Wiesener and Lightner of his whereabouts during his absence, asserting that it was not relevant. During an investigative discussion on November 1, however, he admitted that he had taken the trip to the Marshall Islands.

Questions and Instructions

1. As regional personnel consultant for the FAA, you are assigned to review the case involving Kahoe and to make recommendations to Lightner on what action to take. You find there are four courses open to the station supervisor:
    a. He can take no action at all, returning Kahoe to full duty under the assumption that the sick leave was approved and therefore the matter is closed.
    b. He can consider Kahoe as having been AWOL and suspend him without pay, perhaps for the same number of days he had been AWOL.
    c. He can find that Kahoe is guilty of infractions of rules but that his offense is not so serious that he should lose his job; he can be retained in the FSS but at a reduced GS grade.
    d. He can decide that Kahoe's offense is so serious that action should be instituted to terminate his employment.
2. Write a summary of the case analyzing the factors that should be taken into consideration in arriving at a conclusion as to what should be done about Kahoe. Analyze the four choices listed above and give reasons why you would accept or reject each of them.

Selected Bibliography

Cherns, Albert, "Work and Values: Shifting Patterns in Industrial Society," *International Social Science Journal* 32 (No. 3, 1980): 427–41.

Denhardt, Robert B., and Perkins, Jan, "The Coming Death of Administration Man," *Public Administration Review* (July/August 1976): 379–84.

Dobel, J. Patrick, "The Corruption of a State," *American Political Science Review* 72 (September 1978): 958–73.

Fiedler, Fred E., "Leadership Effectiveness," *American Behavioral Scientist* 24 (May/June 1981): 619–32.

Golembiewski, Robert T., and Proehl, Carl W., Jr., "Public Sector Applications of Flexible Work Hours: A Review of Available Experiences," in Klingner, Donald E., *Public Personnel Management: Readings in Contexts and Strategies,* Palo Alto, Calif.: Mayfield Publishing, 1981. pp. 251–75.

Greiner, John M.; Hatry, Harry P.; Koss, Margo P.; Millar, Annie P.; and Woodward, Jane P., *Productivity and Motivation,* Washington, D.C.: Urban Institute Press, 1981. Ch. 27, "The Potential Effect of Contract Stipulations on Motivational Programs," pp. 359–80.

Hart, David K., "Social Equity, Justice and the Equitable Administrator," *Public Administration Review* (January/February 1974): 3–11.

Lindo, David K., *Supervision Can Be Easy!* New York: AMACON, 1979. Part 1, "Be More Than You Are," pp. 2–33; Part 3, "Evaluation Techniques," pp. 85–167; and Part 4, "Remember to Supervise Yourself," pp. 169–223.

Mosher, Frederick C., "The Public Service in the Temporary Society," *Public Administration Review* 31 (January/February 1971): 47–62.

Muchinsky, Paul M., "Employee Absenteeism: A Review of the Literature," in Glueck, William F., *Personnel: A Book of Readings,* Dallas: Business Publications, 1979. pp. 474–94.

Nirenberg, John, "Motivation as If People Matter," *Supervisory Management* 26 (October 1981): 22–25.

Rabin, Jack, "The Profession of Public Administration," *Bureaucrat* 10 (Winter 1981–82); 10–12.

Shafritz, Jay M.; Balk, Walter L.; Hyde, Albert C.; and Rosenbloom, David H., *Personnel Management in Government: Politics and Process,* New York: Marcel Dekker, 1978. Part 4, "Employee Rights," pp. 143–87.

Sharff, Lee E., and Gordon, Sol, eds., *Federal Personnel Guide 1979,* Washington, D.C.: Federal Personnel Publications, 1979. See "Leave," pp. 46–48.

Stahl, O. Glenn, *Public Personnel Administration,* 7th ed., New York: Harper and Row, 1976. Ch. 18, "Discipline, Removal, and Appeals," pp. 307–37.

Thompson, Dennis F., "Moral Responsibility of Public Officials: The Problem of Many Hands," *American Political Science Review* 74 (December 1980): 905–16.

United States Office of Personnel Management, *Manager's Handbook,* Washington, D.C.: U.S. Office of Personnel Management, 1980. Ch. 8, "Appeals and Grievances," pp. 98–105; Ch. 9, "Attendance and Leave," pp. 106–17; and Ch. 12, "A Healthy Workforce," pp. 142–51.

48

Reverse Discrimination in the Commission on Human Relations

The State Commission on Human Relations had a position open on the retirement of George Landing, the present supervisor. Landing had held the post since the establishment of the commission in 1971, and was partly responsible for whatever success and acceptance it had gained. In choosing a replacement James Nelson, commission director, wished to appoint a person with Landing's skill of firmness joined with tact in handling problems arising in human relations.

Three commission employees were eligible for promotion to the position. They were Frank Ladd, Betty Paulson, and Bradley Jenkins. Nelson reviewed their qualifications.

Frank Ladd, age sixty-one, the oldest employee on the commission, had been a member of the staff for six years. He was a university graduate with a bachelor's degree in business administration. He had been a dependable employee but had never done outstanding work.

Betty Paulson, age forty-two, held a master's degree in public administration. She had been on the commission staff five years and earlier had worked several years in other state offices. She had shown a capacity for making sound decisions, for carrying out her duties effectively, and for getting along well with other staff members.

Bradley Jenkins, age twenty-nine, had joined the commission staff six years before upon receiving his master's degree in business administration. From the beginning of his employment, Jenkins had been energetic, innovative, and ambitious, and clearly destined for a top job in the government.

In weighing the qualifications of these three persons Nelson decided to eliminate Ladd because of his undistinguished service and because in a few years' time he would be eligible for retirement. That left either Paulson or Jenkins to be appointed.

Nelson considered both about equally qualified and believed either would do well. Because of Jenkins's seniority with the commission, Nelson would be justified in promoting him. But since the state had been accused of sex discrimination by women's-rights groups for placing so few women in executive positions, he thought it would look good for the commission to be supervised by a woman. He therefore announced that Betty Paulson would be the new supervisor.

Three days later Nelson was shocked when he was called to the governor's office and informed that Jenkins had protested his failure to receive the appointment, declaring it was a case of sex discrimination, which the commission was charged by law to prevent. Jenkins asserted that he had been denied promotion because he was a man and Paulson had received it because she was a woman. In response to Jenkins, the governor told him that he had appointed Nelson manager of the commission with the authority to fill all positions within the commission. The governor had then suggested, he told Nelson, that Jenkins talk with Nelson and that if afterward he still felt he had been unfairly treated to follow the prescribed procedure in discrimination cases by presenting his case to the state grievance board.

Questions and Instructions

1. If you were Nelson who would you have named as supervisor? Discuss the pros and cons of the reasoning followed by Nelson in making his choice.
2. If you were Jenkins would you have gone to the governor to protest your failure to receive the promotion?
3. Do you think Jenkins has a valid grievance to bring before the state board?
4. As Nelson, what would you tell Jenkins if he came to you for an explanation of why you chose Paulson over him? How much of an explanation is owed to an employee for dismissing him or her from a job or for failing to promote him or her?
5. Is reverse discrimination ever justified in pursuing an affirmative-action policy?

Selected Bibliography

Bellone, Carl J., and Darling, Douglas H., "Implementing Affirmative

Action Programs: Problems and Strategies," *Public Personnel Management* 9 (No. 3, 1980): 184–91.

Burton, Gene E., and Pathak, Dev S., "101 Ways to Discriminate Against Equal Employment Opportunity," *Personnel Administrator* 22 (August 1977): 42–46, 48–49.

Cascio, Wayne F., *Applied Psychology in Personnel Management,* Reston, Va.: Reston Publishing Co., 1978. Ch. 2, "The Law and Personnel Management," pp. 11–35; Ch. 12, "Managerial Selection," pp. 233–57; and Appendix A, "Legal Guidelines on Employee Selection—Explanation and Commentary," pp. 368–73.

Choi, Yearn H., "Economy and Equity in Public Personnel Management: A Liberalism/Conservatism Synthesis," *Public Personnel Management* 8 (January/February 1979): 223–28.

Holley, William H., and Feild, Hubert S., "Equal Employment Opportunity and Its Implications for Personnel Practices," in Glueck, William F., *Personnel: A Book of Readings,* Dallas: Business Publications, 1979. pp. 349–58.

Holt, Thaddeus, "Personnel Selection and the Supreme Court," in Hammer, W. Clay, and Schmidt, Frank L., *Contemporary Problems in Personnel,* rev. ed., Chicago: St. Clair Press, 1977. pp. 147–59.

Horstman, Dee Ann S., "New Judicial Standards Check for Adverse Impact: Their Meaning for Personnel Practices," *Public Personnel Management* 7 (November/December 1978): 347–53.

Klingner, Donald E., *Public Personnel Management: Contexts and Strategies,* Englewood Cliffs, N.J.: Prentice-Hall, 1980. Ch. 20, "Affirmative Action," 354–80.

Lee, Robert D., Jr., *Public Personnel Systems,* Baltimore: University Park Press, 1979. Ch. 8, "Equal Rights and Affirmative Action," pp. 241–80.

Livingston, John C., *Fair Game? Inequality and Affirmative Action,* San Francisco: W. H. Freeman, 1979. Ch. 3, "The Case Against Affirmative Action," pp. 28–35, and Ch. 5, "Reverse Discrimination," pp. 48–63.

Mark, Jerome A., "Measuring Productivity in Government," *Public Productivity Review* 5 (March 1981): 21–44.

Muchmore, Lynn, "Governor as Manager," *State Government* 54 (No. 3, 1981): 71–75.

Sauser, William I., Jr., "Evaluating Employee Performance: Needs, Problems and Possible Solutions, *Public Personnel Management* 9 (January/February 1980): 11–18.

Sherman, Mitchell, "Equal Employment Opportunity: Legal Issues and Societal Consequences," *Public Personnel Management* 7 (January/February 1978): 127–34.

Shire, Donald, "Age Discrimination in Employment," *Personnel Administrator* 20 (June 1975): 28–30.

Short, Ronald R., "Managing Unlearning," *Training and Development Journal* 35 (July 1981): 37–44.

49

Check-out for the Old Library

Stromberg, a Northwestern city of about ten thousand people, had completed the construction of a new public library, financed in part by a federal grant. The City Council was faced now with a decision on what to do with the old library building, which had been appraised at $50,000. It had been built in 1903 with a $10,000 donation from the Carnegie Library Fund. The granite-faced, two-story structure containing 4,262 square feet needed structural reinforcement and extensive repairs as well as new heating, air-conditioning, and electrical systems. The cost of rehabilitating the building had been set at a minimum of $25,000.

Discussion of what to do at a City Council meeting was so indecisive that members approved a motion that the city manager, Archibald Manders, be instructed to solicit the public's opinion by placing the following notice in the local newspaper:

> The city is considering the disposition of the old library building and land at the corner of Main Street and Elm Avenue and is seeking proposals for its use or sale.
>
> Any individual or group desiring to use or purchase it or with a good idea for its use by the community please contact Mayor Oscar Meacham at the City Hall.

At the next council meeting Mayor Meacham read three letters from among a number he had received regarding the old library building that he said represented, in his view, a significant body of public opinion.

The Stromberg chapter of the American Association of University

Women (AAUW) wrote that it had gone on record in support of the preservation of the Carnegie Public Library building. "We are strongly opposed to any sale of the building," the letter said. "We feel it is a building that should be preserved as both a landmark and historic structure of Stromberg." The association suggested leasing of the building at a minimum sum to the Stromberg Area Arts Council and the Stromberg Area Teen Center.

The suggestion made by the American Association of University Women was endorsed by the Teen Center and Arts Council in a letter from Porter A. Olmstead, director of the Teen Center. "As far as we have heard, the Teen Center and Arts Council are the only service organizations that are seriously attempting to obtain the Carnegie Library, maintain it, and keep it for the community to use and enjoy," Olmstead wrote.

Mrs. Anthony A. Parrott, long a leader in social and cultural affairs, wrote strongly condemning any thought of demolition of the building. "Not only is it a landmark and eligible for registration as a historic site, but it is a major part of the cultural history of Stromberg," she pointed out. She described the structure as one of the few buildings in Stromberg of "real architectural charm and distinction." She declared that the "quartzite of the exterior and the oak of the interior could not be duplicated at any price."

Mayor Meacham also informed the council that one person had shown an interest in purchasing the old building and renovating it for office space. A representative of the library board, Mrs. Allen Bartleby, spoke in favor of selling the building and using the proceeds to purchase furniture and books for the new library. Further consideration of the building's disposition was postponed until the next council meeting.

At this meeting City Manager Manders presented a proposal at the request of a local law firm that desired to lease the library building. It offered to lease it from the city for a five-year period with rental payments of $800 a month. The firm would receive a credit of up to $300 a month for repairs and improvements it might make. The city would pay for electrical, heating, and plumbing improvements at an estimated cost of $12,000. At the expiration of the lease, the firm would retain first rights to renew the arrangement for another five-year term.

A motion approving the lease agreement between the city and the law firm was passed by a vote of 6 to 1. Those in favor held that it was the most economically sound proposal for what one council member called "a white elephant." The old structure, it was argued, was in such disrepair that an extra mill levy would have to be added to the property tax to pay for renovation, and upkeep of the structure would be a continuing burden. By leasing the building it would be preserved and satisfy those who valued it as an architectural asset and historic landmark. Marshall Alberts, Ward 1 council member, who cast the one dissenting vote, expressed his belief that public funds should not be used for private benefit and that the city should not be in "the landlord business."

The council's decision was attacked in an editorial in the next day's issue of the Stromberg *News,* and in the following week letters to the editor appeared vehemently condemning the "sell out" to the law firm and the council's failure to use the historic landmark for the benefit of the entire community. The agitation against the council's decision was climaxed by a public meeting at which council members individually and collectively were denounced.

Two weeks later the city received a summons to answer in District Court a suit brought by a taxpayer, Theodore Andrews, to annul the lease on the following grounds:

1. It was beyond the defendant city's power and authority to lease its property to a private person for a private purpose.
2. The purported lease was in effect a contract for a public improvement that the city entered into contrary to the bidding procedures prescribed under municipal ordinances.
3. The lease restricted the city in the use of its property and its power to alienate the same for a period of more than one year.

Questions and Instructions

1. Should the City Council have sought the public's opinion on what to do with the old library building and then ignore what seemed to be that opinion?
2. Was it ethically proper for the city manager to present a persuasive offer for use of the building by the law firm?
3. To what extent should city officials, elective or appointive, follow public opinion in making decisions about municipal affairs? Can the public ever be sufficiently informed to pass upon certain matters? What should be the role of public opinion in governmental matters?
4. If public opinion is to be sought on a question, is an open hearing by a civic body adequate or should the question be submitted to the people in a referendum vote?
5. Besides a newspaper notice requesting ideas, a civic hearing, or a referendum, what other mechanisms for soliciting public opinion might have been useful in this situation and how would you proceed to use them? Would such mechanisms be feasible?

6. What commitment does a city owe to the past and to the future as far as historical sites and land use are concerned?
7. Should a search for outside financial or other assistance have been conducted?

Selected Bibliography

Anderson, Desmond, L., ed., *Municipal Public Relations,* Chicago: International City Management Association, 1966.

Arnold, David S., "Public Relations," in Banovetz, James M., ed., *Managing the Modern City,* Washington, D.C.: International City Management Association, 1971. pp. 377–401.

Broadnax, Walter D., "Making Public Agencies Accountable," in Vocino, Thomas, and Rabin, Jack, eds., *Contemporary Public Administration,* New York: Harcourt Brace Jovanovich, 1981. pp. 397–415.

Frederickson, H. George, ed., "Symposium of Social Equity and Public Administration," *Public Administration Review* 34 (January/February 1974): 1–51.

Huffcut, W. Harwood, ed., *Basic Techniques of Public Contracts Practice,* Berkeley, Calif.: California Continuing Education of the Bar, 1977.

Kiebola, Leo, "Government and Business: Adversaries or Partners for the Public Good," *Personnel Administrator* 20 (May 1975): 34–39.

Kline, Robert L., and Blanchard, Paul D., "Professionalism and the City Manager: An Examination of Unanswered Questions," *Midwest Review of Public Administration* 7 (July 1973): 163–74.

Lippmann, Walter, *Essays in the Public Philosophy,* Boston: Little Brown, 1955.

———, *Public Opinion,* New York: Macmillan, 1947. See Part IV, "Interests," pp. 159–90, and Part VII, "Newspapers," pp. 317–65.

McTighe, John J., "Management Strategies to Deal with Shrinking Resources," *Public Administration Review* 39 (January/February 1979): 86–90.

Schubert, Glendon, *The Public Interest, A Critique of the Theory of a Political Concept,* Glencoe, Ill.: Free Press, 1960.

Staats, Elmer B., "An Era of Enduring Scarcity: Challenges and Opportunities," *National Civic Review* 69 (January 1980): 13–21.

Stillman, Richard J., *The Rise of the City Manager: A Public Professional in Local Government,* Albuquerque, N.M.: University of New Mexico Press, 1974.

Taebel, Delbert A., "Strategies to Make Bureaucrats Responsive," *Social Work* 17 (November 1972): 38–43.

Thomas, John Clayton, "Governmental Overload in the United States," *Administration and Society* 11 (February 1980): 371–91.

Tullock, Gordon, *Private Wants, Public Means: An Economic Analysis of the Desirable Scope of Government,* New York: Basic Books, 1970.

White, Louise G., "Improving the Goal-Setting Process in Local Government," *Public Administration Review* 42 (January/February 1982): 77–83.

Whitesett, David A., "Making Sense of Management Theories," *Personnel* 52 (May/June 1975): 44–52.

50

Meeting the Press

Readers of the *Capital Record* were shocked one morning to see under the byline of Gordon Redfield, the newspaper's chief investigative reporter, an account of the abuse of mentally retarded children in the three institutions operated by the State Department of Public Welfare. The story was announced as the first of a series.

In all three schools, the story alleged, mentally and physically handicapped residents had been subjected to repeated assaults by adult attendants who whipped, kicked, gagged, and battered them. Children unable to take care of themselves were frequently left unattended, the article continued, some to sit or lie in soiled diapers for hours.

The article quoted a former employee, a professional health-care worker, who told Redfield of one incident at the Meadowland School. After an eight-year-old girl with Down's syndrome refused to drink a glass of water, an attendant first slapped her repeatedly and then threw the water in her face.

In another incident, the former employee said, an attendant was treated for a hand injury he suffered when he struck a child at the school. "He hit the child with such force that he fractured his hand," she said.

At Hopeville School, Redfield reported, homosexuality among students was widespread and younger children were permitted to be mistreated by older residents. According to the story, residents were encouraged to assault a misbehaving child when an attendant wanted to punish a student but was worried about getting into trouble for striking him. An attendant would say, "Hey, Jimmy, go over there and show him you mean business," the story said.

The story related that at the third school, Greenbriar Center, two female attendants had submerged a retarded girl's head in a toilet bowl and flushed it while teaching her personal hygiene. Among the incidents taking place at the center were beating, "stretching," in which children were held down while their arms and legs were pulled up behind them, and controlling children by squeezing and twisting their genitals, sticking girls in the breasts with pins, and burning residents with cigarettes.

"The month-long investigation of the three schools," Redfield wrote, "paints a picture of a system that condones violence while offering no support to those who attempt to report abusive, sometimes sadistic, treatment."

Television and radio news reporters, correspondents for the Associated Press and United Press International, and capitol correspondents for other newspapers eager to obtain the reaction to the allegations by officials in the Department of Welfare crowded the entranceway to the departmental offices when they opened at nine o'clock on the morning Redfield's first article appeared.

The director of the department, Jacob Christopher, arrived red-faced in anger and forced his way through the noisy crowd. "They're all lies," he shouted when asked about the Redfield charges, and he refused to answer other questions. "I've got more important things to do than concern myself with such slanders."

Later in the morning Karl Munster, Christopher's executive secretary, appeared before the reporters and fielded questions about the accuracy of the allegations and what the Department of Welfare intended to do in the way of verifying them. "The reports are replete with gross distortions and are wholly inaccurate and unjust," Munster said. "Redfield has taken bits and pieces out of context to give a completely false picture." He announced that beginning tomorrow there would be a series of press conferences at which staff members of the Welfare Department would present evidence to refute the charges in Redfield's story. "The so-called exposé," Munster said, "is doing a great injustice to staff and children in the state schools."

Because of the refusal of the Welfare Department to supply information, radio and television newscasts during the day, the afternoon newspapers, and dispatches of the wire services repeated the charges originally published in the *Capital Record*. Governor Winfield James at his noon press conference said he had "complete confidence" in the welfare director. "Only one side of the story has been given as yet," the governor said. "When the Welfare Department is able to gather information to present to the media, a different picture of conditions in the state schools will emerge."

Helen Osterman, superintendent of Meadowland School, questioned by one wire-service reporter, said that Redfield never tried to discuss conditions in the school with her. "He was here and asked a lot of questions about the school and town," Osterman said, "but he never brought up any allegations about the abuse of children. The allegations are not based on facts. We have one of the best schools for retarded children in the country." The superintendents at Greenbriar and Hopeville refused to talk to reporters, saying that they had been instructed to refer all inquiries to the Welfare Department.

At the scheduled press conference the next day reporters reacted angrily when they were told by Christopher's executive secretary, Karl Munster, that the welfare director was unable to attend. "The decision to have Mr. Christopher forgo a confrontation with the press," Munster said, "was based on the recommendation of counsel and staff." However, the director had prepared a statement about the allegations of abuse.

Christopher's statement was a blistering attack against sensationalism in the press. "It is impossible, and frankly undesirable, to answer every single slanderous and outrageous claim made by what, in my judgment, is irresponsible journalism," Christopher said. "The allegations so far made constitute a one-sided presentation of circumstances which have been thoroughly investigated by the department and remedies instituted when wrongs were found."

After Munster had read Christopher's statement, he introduced to the reporters Roswell McIntosh, Welfare Department attorney, and said that insofar as possible they would answer all questions from reporters. As the press conference continued, it soon became clear that not much information would be available. The reporters were told that many details had to be held confidential because they concerned medical matters. Munster and McIntosh sparred with reporters over whether welfare officials were going back on promises to release information, and whether they were trying to control the media through the format of an announced series of news conferences on the allegations.

"I'd give anything if we could open the complete files," Munster said. "It would make our case so much stronger. But it would be a violation of medical ethics for us to reveal information that should be held in confidence." He disclosed that he had a list of abuse reports made in the past year that had been checked by child-welfare units working with local district attorneys and not the department. Of a dozen alleged incidents, Munster said, only one was confirmed—that of the toilet-bowl incident—and the two employees involved had been fired.

The press conference ended with a promise by Munster to be prepared to give more information the next day when staff members would have had more time to obtain details. Reporters departed complaining of a cover-up by the Welfare Department. Later in the day they were further irked when they learned that the department had employed a public-relations specialist, Clyde Manfred, to help in its campaign to counter allegations surrounding the state schools for the retarded.

That the Welfare Department was more intent in protecting itself than in discovering the facts about the *Capital Record*'s charges was indicated next day when Munster opened the press conference by introducing Lester Schlegel, president of the Parent and Guardian Association at the Greenbriar Center. "We are receiving solid support from the associations of parents and guardians for the centers," he said.

Schlegel said he had visited Greenbriar unannounced several times and never saw a state employee abusing a retarded inmate. "As a parent of a child, I am appalled at the news coverage," Schlegel said. "If there was abuse going on, I would be the first person to come down on their necks." He disclosed that he was sending letters to all parents of children at Greenbriar asking them "to share my feelings of protest." "I want them to write their legislators, the newspapers, the governor—whoever it takes," he declared.

The second press conference was about as frustrating for reporters as that of the first day. Some instances of abuse cited in the *Capital Record*'s reports, it seemed, could not be clarified because of the confidentiality of medical reports, others were explained away by improbable excuses, and the stories of former employees of conditions could not be trusted. Reporters roared with laughter when Munster explained that the story of an employee who had injured a hand by striking a retarded student too hard was false. The employee apparently was so frustrated when he himself was hit by a student he was trying to control that he struck a wall and bruised his hand. However, because of the allegations made by the newspaper, the department would look further into the matter.

Munster renewed his criticism of former employees from whom reporters obtained information about abuse at the schools. Of the employee who said she saw a young girl stuck in the breasts with pins, Munster said she had been urged to provide more detailed information, including names and dates, but she had failed to do so. "If she had knowledge of a crime, she ought to be calling the police or the district attorney and not the press," Munster said. "Child abuse is a criminal offense and anyone with knowledge of such an offense should report it to the district attorney or other appropriate authorities."

Later in the day it was revealed that support of the Welfare Department was not quite so strong among parent-guardian groups as Munster had indicated at his morning press conference. Mrs. Rosa Gonzalez, president of the group at Hopeville, said she had been asked to attend the conference but had declined. "My child is receiving good treatment at the school," she said, "but I am concerned about the charges. I think the news accounts might spur more interest in the welfare of the retarded, and if it does that will be a good thing. I'm not sure that putting the retarded away in schools far from their families is a good thing. There should be a better way."

Criticism of the care of the retarded in large institutions was also expressed by Mildred Carnahan, chairman of the Council for the Mentally Retarded. "There are always going to be problems in institutional settings," she said. "That's one of the reasons why we are trying to get money to fund some sheltered workshops in the state for these people. We are trying to get two million dollars from the legislature for thirty-five such workshops."

Apparently bowing to the widespread publicity about conditions in the schools for the retarded and media charges of a cover-up, Governor James announced four days after the *Capital Record* series began that he had asked the State Bureau of Investigation to conduct a probe of the charges. The governor said that he had asked the newspaper for a complete set of its series as well as any data documenting the allegations but that his request had been denied.

James said he would not ask the welfare director or any department officials to leave their positions while the investigation was under way. It would interfere with the operations of the department, James said. "I don't think it's fair," he added, "to say you need new leadership until the investigation is completed."

Once the investigation was completed, James said, the bureau's report would be turned over to the appropriate district attorneys to determine if laws were violated and criminal charges were warranted. By law, he explained, the bureau's report could be divulged only to prosecutors and not the public, any wrongdoing to be revealed only if charges were filed.

The allegations of abuse of the retarded were also discussed in the legislature, but a resolution in the house to conduct an investigation was voted down on the ground that the Bureau of Investigation was the proper body to probe into possibly criminal matters.

Questions and Instructions

1. In general, how would you describe the Department of Welfare's relations with the press?
2. Do you think the department was attempting to conceal from the

public conditions in the school or was it merely reacting naturally to adverse publicity?

3. Did the welfare director's legal counsel and staff make the right decision when they advised him not to confront reporters at the press conference?

4. Do you think the Welfare Department representatives were sincere in calling a series of press conferences to provide information or, as reporters charged, was it an attempt to manipulate the press?

5. Was it a wise move for the department to employ a public-relations specialist to advise it in dealing with the press in respect to the allegations of child abuse?

6. If you were a public-information or press-relations employee of the Welfare Department, how would you have handled the situation created by the newspaper's exposé?

7. Do you think it desirable for a government agency to employ a press-relations or public-information specialist? If so, how would you specify his or her duties?

8. When administrators are confronted by scandals or wrongdoing in their agencies, would it be wiser for them to be frank and open with the press or to seek to conceal the facts? Discuss.

9. From the information in this case history, how would you rate the Welfare Department as to goals and practices?

Selected Bibliography

Anderson, Desmond L., ed., *Municipal Public Relations,* Chicago: International City Management Association, 1966.

Belk, Judy V., "What to Do When the News Is Bad," *Public Management* 62 (September 1980): 8–10.

Berkley, George E., *The Craft of Public Administration,* 3rd ed., Boston: Allyn and Bacon, 1981. See "The Questions of Secrecy," pp. 257–64, and "Public Relations," pp. 436–46.

Cutlip, Scott M., and Center, Allen H., *Effective Public Relations,* 4th ed., Englewood Cliffs, N.J.: Prentice-Hall, 1971. Ch. 17, "Working with the Media," pp. 406–28; Ch. 22, "The Practice: Welfare Agencies, Hospitals and Churches," pp. 501–27; and Ch. 23, "The Practice: Governments and Citizens," pp. 528–57.

Gilbert, William H., ed., *Public Relations in Local Government,* Washington, D.C.: International City Management Association, 1975.

Kelly, Stanley, Jr., *Professional Public Relations and Political Power,*

Baltimore: Johns Hopkins Press, 1956. Ch. 7, "The Political Role of the Public Relations Man," pp. 202–35.

Scheffer, Walter F., "The Clienteles of Executive Branch Agencies," in Vocino, Thomas, and Rabin, Jack, eds., *Contemporary Public Administration,* New York: Harcourt Brace Jovanovich, 1981. See "Public Relations," pp. 136–37.

Schmidt, Frances, and Weiner, Harold N., ed., *Public Relations in Health and Welfare,* New York: Columbia University Press, 1966.

Starling, Grover, *Managing the Public Sector,* rev. ed., Homewood, Ill.: Dorsey Press, 1982. See "Distortion," pp. 145–49.

51

Treated Like Dogs

Margaret McChesney, personnel director for the city of Oakdale, was greatly disturbed after Cranston Hume, investigative reporter for the *Daily Tribune,* left her office after telling her that the 250 employees in the Street Maintenance Division were disgruntled and talked among themselves of a violent confrontation with officials if working conditions did not improve.

She herself had heard rumors to this effect but had not realized how extensive the dissatisfaction was until Hume told her of interviews he had conducted at the maintenance yard on three evenings. It was another instance, she felt, of the poor communication between her office, the city manager, the street-maintenance director, and the business agent of the American Federation of State, County, and Municipal Employees local: it took a reporter to let one know what was going on. The situation was bad, she thought, and publicity could only make it worse.

Her fears were confirmed two days later when the *Daily Tribune* carried Hume's story under an eight-column headline on page one, "Angry Street Workers Predicting Confrontation with City," and continued for almost a full page on the inside.

"The maintenance workers are angry," Hume had written. "They're looking for respect. They want someone—either the city administration or the union to which they pay dues—to listen to their grievances and do something. More than a score of workers interviewed at quitting time at the maintenance yard complained that their supervisors treat them as if they are inmates in a prison or slaves on a southern plantation."

As she read quotation after quotation from workers, McChesney's consternation grew, and nothing that other city officials and the union business agent were reported to have said indicated that they were prepared to handle the situation with understanding or effectiveness.

Some of the more telling complaints of workers appeared early in the story. "They treat us like we was in prison or something," Wayne North, an eleven-year veteran of the Street Division was quoted as saying. "A lot of people, when they get up in the morning, they just hate to go to work."

Another worker, Vincent Esposito, said: "They treat all the men—black or white—like dogs. It's just like hell. I just hate to walk through that gate in the morning. It's the same for all of the boys."

Minority workers were equally vehement. Joseph Washington, a truck driver, said: "When a black guy gets old, they say either quit or be fired. When a white guy gets old, they keep him on. You go in the yard and look. We've got old white guys all over this place."

A crew worker, Bobby Anderson, agreed, interjecting, "You won't see no old black men around here."

Hester Adams, who said she was fired because she overslept one morning, was incensed over the treatment of women maintenance workers. "I do believe my job was in jeopardy from the very day I started," she said. "From the very beginning they told me I didn't want this job. They said I wouldn't be able to stand the heat. Generally, everybody fears for their job. I knew for a fact women would not advance. I was told not to even try."

But if women saw little opportunity for advancement while working in Street Maintenance, the same was true of many of the men. "If you're hired as a laborer, you stay a laborer," Ernie Devers, an employee of ten years' standing said. "You know, you want to try to better yourself. You don't want to be a laborer all your life. But you have to sneak behind your foreman's back to get a transfer."

"You want to know how you make foreman?" interposed Ben Costello. "Snitching. That's how."

Others complained, in respect to advancement, that the director of the Street Division, Luther Schultz, played favorites. "If you're in the clique, everything is rosy," Matthew McNeil said. "If you're not, you don't stand no more chance of getting ahead than a snowball in hell."

Some complained that promotions were based on oral examinations rather than seniority or demonstrated job skills. "They give an oral test," said Terry O'Hara. "They don't give no other test. How can you prove if you passed or flunked?"

Workers considered many of the rules governing the maintenance division as petty and criticized enforcement as inconsistent and unfair.

"If you want to go to the bathroom, you have to ask your foreman," said Martin Steinberg, a crew worker. "If he's not there, you ask the crew chief. If he's not there, you get wrote up."

The news story said that written reprimands and other forms of punishment were doled out with no apparent adherence to an established policy. Martha Dolfuss, for example, was quoted as saying: "There are no rules on reprimands. One person might be late once and get a reprimand. I might be late five times and I might not get one."

A rule forbade all maintenance workers from entering stores to buy food or drink at lunchtime or during their twice-daily, fifteen-minute break periods. Nevertheless, workers complained, foremen ignored this and other rules for themselves while they imposed them on the men they supervised. "The bosses can do anything they want, can go anywhere they want any time," complained George Alfredo. "You've got to get permission to go to the bathroom. If you get a Coke while you're there, you get a reprimand."

"The rule book says 'city employees,'" said Dolfuss. "If foremen aren't city employees, then who is?"

As she read the complaints, McChesney came to realize what most of the workers seemed to feel but seldom were able to express: they wanted to be treated like human beings. One worker, Art Matthews, put it very well: "There's a different set of rules for us than other city employees. We're treated like a bunch of machines. There's no consideration for your personal feelings whatsoever. It's like a war—it's management on one side and us on the other."

Hume's story summed up the situation: "What the Street Division is facing," the reporter wrote, "is a near-total breakdown in the established system of resolving disputes. No one in management, the workers believe, apparently wants to listen."

McChesney decided this conclusion was borne out in part by comments made by City Manager Edward Mayes, Street Division Director Luther Schultz, and even the union agent Karl Moscowitz. They did not say anything strongly adverse about the street-maintenance workers, but they were not particularly favorable either.

Mayes said that frequent complaints by citizens of lazy municipal employees and poor maintenance made it difficult to relax stringent work rules that were adopted to insure efficiency. "You may be inclined to believe the complaints you hear every day about how incompetent and dilatory the people who work for the city are," he said. "In most cases, the complaints are unfounded, but taxpayers have a right to expect people who work for them to put in a day's work for a day's pay."

Schultz belittled the notion that there was a serious labor-management problem in his division. "Any employer that has about 250 people working for him," Schultz said, "is bound to have some personnel problems. Things right now aren't any worse than in the past."

Schultz defended the use of oral examinations in deciding on promotions. He explained that these were used in order not to discriminate against employees who could not read or write well. "We do not mistreat anybody," he continued. "We treat everybody fair and equal. We expect no more than a day's work for a day's pay. If we didn't have strict work rules, there would be chaos."

The union agent, Moscowitz, shrugged off most of the complaints made by maintenance employees. "You should check the work records of some of those employees," he said. "They've got such good benefits they abuse them."

Moskowitz spoke in favor of the work rules, saying that conditions in the past had become so slack that regulations had to be adopted. "I don't necessarily agree with all the things that the city does," he said. "I try to see the employees' side—that's what they pay me for. But I also understand management's problems. I learned a long time ago that if you don't tell workers when they're wrong, you can get into deep trouble."

Reading a comment by the city manager, McChesney had to agree with him that the union had not been especially active in the workers' defense, because it informed her, as Moscowitz had not, that dissatisfaction in the Street Division had reached the stage of almost open revolt. The city manager was reported as saying: "The union is there to assure people they have some place to go with their complaints. If they can't talk to their supervisors, they should talk to their union steward. If they can't work with that person, they ought to get a new one."

McChesney had told the *Daily Tribune* reporter of her efforts to improve the labor-management communications, which received a paragraph buried deep in the news article. She had not mentioned that in her efforts she had received little cooperation from other city officials. One of the plans she had proposed was the establishment of "quality circles" in which employees would be given an opportunity to bring up their problems and suggest how they might be resolved. Her fellow managers did not think much of the idea.

She had explained to the reporter that quality circles (QCs) are small groups of people, ideally seven or eight members of an organization, who perform similar tasks in the same area and who voluntarily participate in regular meetings to identify, analyze, and solve quality, productivity, and organizational problems. Although conceived in Japan, QCs have been one of the fastest-growing concepts in the United States in terms of behavioral and managerial applications. She had explained that QCs are used in government, the armed forces, hospitals, and insurance, banking, manufacturing, and public-utility firms. They are designed to reduce errors and enhance the quality of the finished goods or services, promote cooperation and teamwork, increase job involvement and employee motivation, facilitate organizational communication, and develop the leadership capabilities of managers and workers.

McChesney had urged that the city experiment in the use of QCs, but Mayes, the city manager, had objected that the plan seemed to him too time-consuming and theoretical and Schultz, the Street Division director, had said the idea would not work with street-maintenance workers—they would not want to be bothered.

That evening McChesney noted that television news reporters had followed up on the *Daily Tribune*'s article with their own interviews with workers at the street-maintenance yard. The workers seemed to be enjoying their moment in the spotlight. She went to bed with some foreboding of how the situation might develop; she did not think it would just go away.

Questions and Instructions

1. What actions might be taken by officials to ward off an immediate confrontation between the city and the street-maintenance workers?
2. What are the responsibilities of the personnel manager in maintaining labor peace? the mayor and City Council? the division directors?
3. Do you think that the newspaper and television publicity about the dissatisfactions of the maintenance workers will make a strike or confrontation more or less likely?
4. There does not seem to be rapport between the Oakdale city manager, personnel director, and division directors. Should they work together more closely to detect and prevent such situations as that arising in the Street Maintenance Division?
5. Do you think the quality-circle idea would be successful in solving the problems of worker dissatisfaction? How would you implement such a program? What city office should be in charge of such a program? Should the labor union be brought into the program?
6. What other programs—an employee publication, social affairs, sports programs, recreation clubs—might be introduced to develop better relations between the city and its employees? Discuss and evaluate.

7. What behavioral assumptions underpin participative management techniques and approaches? How do they differ from
   authoritarian approaches? Explain.
8. Is there any way of improving the image of unskilled-labor jobs in
   the eyes of the workers and the public?

Selected Bibliography

Argyris, Chris, and Cyert, Richard M., *Leadership in the 80's,* Cambridge,
    Mass.: Institute for Educational Management, Harvard University,
    1980.

Bryant, Stephen, and Kearns, Joseph, "Workers' Brains as Well as Their
    Bodies: Quality Circles in a Federal Facility," *Public Administration
    Review* 42 (March/April 1982): 144–150.

Contino, Ronald, and Lorusso, Robert M., "The Theory Z Turnaround of a
    Public Agency," *Public Administration Review* 42 (January/February
    1982): 66–72.

Dewar, Donald L., *Quality Circles: Answers to 100 Frequently Asked
    Questions,* Red Bluff, Calif.: Quality Circle Institute, 1979.

Fisher, John E., "Dealing with Office Politics in Authoritarian-Dominated
    Staff Organizations," *Public Personnel Management* 8 (January/
    February 1979): 56–63.

Fisher, John E., "The Authoritarian As Anti-Manager," *Public Personnel
    Management* 7 (January/February 1978): 33–41.

King, Albert S., "Expectation Effects in Organization Change," *Administra-
    tive Science Quarterly* 19 (June 1974): 221–30.

Klein, Gerald D., "Implementing Quality Circles: A Hard Look at Some of
    the Realities," *Personnel* 58 (November/December 1981): 11–20.

Landau, Martin, and Stout, Russell, Jr., "To Manage Is Not to Control: Or
    the Folly of Type II Errors," *Public Administration Review* 39 (March/
    April 1979): 148–56.

Lyden, Fremont J., "Power Driven Managers Make the Best Bosses," *Pub-
    lic Administration Review* 36 (March/April 1976): 201–2.

Monte, Rudeen, "The Productivity Environment of Trust, Autonomy, and
    Initiative," *Quality Circles Journal* 4 (August 1981): 13–15.

Neugarten, Dail Ann, "Themes and Issues in Public Sector Productivity,"
    Public Personnel Management 9 (No. 4, 1980): 229–34.

Rendall, Elaine, "Quality Circles—A 'Third Wave' Intervention," *Training
    and Development Journal* 35 (March 1981): 28–31.

Rosow, Jerome M., "Quality of Work Life Issues for the 1980's," *Training
    and Development Journal* (March 1981): 33–52.

Walker, Donald E., "When the Tough Get Going, the Going Gets Tough:
    The Myth of Muscle Administration," *Public Administration Review*
    36 (July/August 1976): 439–45.

APPENDIX

Case Studies Keyed to Topics

The text gives major emphasis to topics marked by asterisks.

1. The Good/Bad Administrator
   Communication Problems, Discipline, Employee Rights, Fairness, *Interpersonal Relations, Job Satisfaction, *Managerial Style, Morale, Performance Evaluation, Protests Organized by Employees, *Teamwork and Cooperation
2. Special Privileges for Officials?
   Ethical Questions, Fairness, Flexitime, Morale, Professionalism, *Rules and Regulations, Whistle Blowing
3. A $5,000 Anonymous Phone Call?
   *Complaints of Public, Conduct Codes, Discipline, Employee Rights, *Field–Central Office Relations, Professionalism, Public and Community Relations, Resignations
4. A Moral Dilemma
   Conduct Codes, Conflict of Interest, *Ethical Questions, Fairness, Legal Requirements, Managerial Style, Political Relations, Professionalism
5. A Plethora of Problems
   Communication Problems, Compensation and Fringe Benefits, Grievances, *Interpersonal Relations, *Job Classification and Placement, Job Satisfaction, Managerial Style, Morale, Motivation, *Power and Authority, Stress Management
6. Blocking the Super Block
   Communication Problems, Legislative Relations, *Planning and Goal Setting, Policy Making and Implementation, *Public and Community Relations
7. Sick Leave in Spring Valley
   *Compensation and Fringe Benefits, Fiscal-Budgetary Matters,

Motivation, Retrenchment, Rules and Regulations, *Union-Management Relations

Intra-agency Relations, *Job Enrichment, Job Satisfaction, Managerial Style, Morale, Motivation, News-Media Relations, *Quality of Work Life, *Quality Circles, Union-Management Relations